PRAISE FOR *DYING WELL*

"*Dying Well*'s account is a mix of love, sorrow, and practicality that is at the heart of what we, as a society, need to do to more normalize a process that modern medicine has tried so hard to shield us from."
Adam R. Silverman MD, FACP
Vice President, Population Health, Saint Francis
Health Care Partners
Co-Chair, Care Decisions Connecticut

"*Dying Well* is not about illness, but about embracing reality at the end of life and making the necessary decisions that honor a life well lived. Sue Hoben takes us along with her and her husband, Bruce, on this last journey together as a couple after he has a terminal diagnosis. They approach this transition the same way they approached all of life's challenges—with heart and humor shaped by their deep love and respect."
Judy L. Mandel
New York Times best-selling author of *Replacement Child: A Memoir*

"In Sue Hoben's clear-eyed, incisive memoir, the reader will find much more than an emotional experience. This is a love story, but it is also an account of successful navigation of a complex medical system. Take a box of tissues and prepare to be touched and to learn many lessons that will serve you well when you or a member of your family is seriously ill, or fatally ill and dying. Our society pushes death under the rug. The courage of Sue and Bruce Hoben includes a refusal to do so, an open approach to this tough situation that eventuated in the greatest of gifts to those who loved Bruce, and a major fulfillment of the arc and nature of Bruce's remarkable embrace of the last part of his life, that harvested what he had planted for all the decades before."

Henry Schneiderman MD, MACP
Section Chief, Geriatrics and Palliative Care, Saint Francis Hospital and Medical Center/Trinity Health of New England
Professor of Medicine, UConn Health Center
Professor of Medicine, Quinnipiac University School of Medicine
Clinical Professor, Nursing, Yale University

DYING WELL
Our Journey of Love and Loss

Susan Ducharme Hoben

Canton Press

COLLINSVILLE, CT

Canton Press/Susan Ducharme Hoben
info@susanducharmehoben.com
www.susanducharmehoben.com

Book Layout © 2018 Book Design Templates
Copy editing and production by Stephanie Gunning
Cover design by Gus Yoo
Author photograph by Marion Berlanger

Dying Well/ Susan Ducharme Hoben. —1st ed.
ISBN 978-0-9997498-0-7

Library of Congress Control Number 2018936961

There is a strength that comes from knowing you will die and still refusing to love with anything less than your whole self.

—BRIAN ANDREAS

CONTENTS

"You should write a book," my friend told me. "It's a love story." Through tears, I thanked her, but informed her I was not a writer. "A writer is simply someone with a story to tell," she responded.

It was only months later, after experiencing my first bereavement group meeting, that I knew with certainty I did have a story that needed to be told. One after another, grieving spouses recounted heart-wrenching tales full of tears, anger, regret, and loneliness. There were many common threads.

- Though their spouses had been diagnosed with incurable diseases, they were struggling with acceptance.
- Perhaps fearful of the inevitable outcome, the couples had not talked about what was on the horizon.
- Their spouses died in hospitals, with medical personnel trying to work miracles right up to the bitter end. They had not even been in the room with their loved ones at the moment of death.
- They did not feel good about their spouses' medical care or their hospital experiences.
- They felt friends and family, likely not knowing what to do or say, had abandoned them.

When it was my turn to share, I was reluctant to speak, feeling almost guilty that my experience had been so different. Was my experience not the norm? Had we done something different? Was there more than one way to face impending death? It was at that moment I decided my friend was right; I did have a story to tell. I would become a writer.

When the time had come for my husband, Bruce, to make hard decisions, he chose quality of life over quantity, having formed his end-of-life wishes over a lifetime of watching people die, and just as importantly, watching people live. When Bruce decided to stop treatment, it was not because we were giving up hope, as some might have said. Rather, we were redirecting our hope to focus on attaining the best life possible for the time that was left. It was strangely calming to have a more certain future. Our time would be spent doing what he loved to do, with the people he loved most, being present and savoring every moment.

At the end of Bruce's physical and spiritual journey, he was calm and peaceful, without fear or regrets. From the beginning, he had set a tone that inspired all who knew him to mourn his passing but celebrate his life. My transition to being a widow was immeasurably eased by his compassion for others in the face of his own death. He died in character, celebrating life, with boundless compassion and no regrets, his sense of humor intact. We had been saying goodbye and easing his path for months, knowing what was coming. These last months were some of the most celebratory, peaceful, and intimate we had shared during our forty-six years together.

For most people, death comes only after a long medical struggle with an incurable condition. Far too many people die in hospitals, in pain, isolated from loved ones. Although 90 percent of those on Medicare say they want end-of-life care at home, only one-third receive it. Bruce was able to die at home surrounded by his loving family, having fully lived his life right up until the end.

There is a growing interest in exploring how we die, and many books, including several best sellers, address this. Most memoirs, books often written by a surviving spouse or child, recount the grief and pain of their loss. While we all face different circumstances, I hope my story will help you, the reader, to find ways to make this last stage of life as peaceful and dignified as possible for you and those you love.

CHAPTER ONE

A BROKEN HEART

Saturday morning, December 23, 2000

"Come with me, please."

It was clear to whom the request was directed. The room was empty except for us, the magazines neatly stacked in piles, the trash cans clean, our voices the only sound.

I turned to Bruce, next to me. *What's up?*

We wordlessly complied, following the sonographer down a sterile and eerily quiet hallway framed by closed doors, each with a plaque identifying the name and medical specialty of its absent occupant. She had told us I was her only patient, and she was the only one in the office, so I wondered who we were headed to see. As she directed us to the only open door, I read the office nameplate: Steven Horowitz, M.D., Cardiology.

Dr. Horowitz, in his mid-fifties, introduced himself as he motioned us to take a seat. His short hair was parted low on the left side though not quite a comb over. Rimless glasses rested on a somewhat wide and prominent nose. He seemed uncomfortable and dispensed with the small talk. "Your echocardiogram shows you have a tumor in your heart."

The room became silent except for the roar in my ears. This can't be happening. I'm only three weeks away from a clean bill of health! I had been feeling physically better every day, even with the daily radiation. The red scar on my breast was softening. The strong effects of chemotherapy were wearing off and the side effects of radiation did not come close to those of chemo. With a few days off for holidays I was on target to finish treatments on January 13. I had been focusing on that date for weeks, confident that I was cured. A fuzz of hair was growing back, the poison would end, I would survive and return to being my normal strong, confident self. Bruce and I had both watched the echocardiogram screen, chatting and joking with the sonographer, with no inkling as to what we were seeing.

"Has the cancer spread?" My eyes pleaded for the right answer.

"No. It's a benign tumor called a myxoma." He paused to let that sink in. "You're having trouble breathing because the tumor is the size of a jumbo egg and has started to block the flow of blood from the upper chamber of your heart to the lower chamber."

I must be having a nightmare. Not the one when I can't find the room where my final exam is being held, or the one when I'm in the right place but I haven't done any of the course work. No, this was different. This was like the ones that start benignly and then spiral through less familiar and ever more frightening places, leading eventually to stark terror that something very bad is about to happen.

"They're not cancerous, but they can be life threatening."

This nightmare was becoming harder to process with each new element. Is this me he's talking about? I couldn't hear anything. I could only see a fuzzy image, blurred around the periphery. I sat mute, unable to talk or even think rationally. My trance seemed to last for hours but I'm sure it was only a few minutes. When I fought my way back, I was quietly crying. Bruce had my hand and was talking.

"What do we need to do, doctor?"

I still couldn't move a muscle or respond in any way. I just stared straight ahead. In a nightmare, your brain helps you flee the dreamscape. There was no such rescue here. My fear was unabated, only now I knew I wasn't dreaming and reality was more terrifying.

"I'll need to admit her to the hospital immediately."

The next thing I knew we were walking across the pedestrian bridge to Hartford Hospital, Bruce on one side, Dr. Horowitz on the other.

Bruce handled all the admission paperwork and got me settled in my room. Technicians took vials of blood and I was quickly wheeled off for an angiogram to see if other perils lurked within my broken heart.

After a few hours, a tall, fit man wearing blue scrubs entered the room, his wavy gray hair combed straight back over a high forehead. He appeared to be in his sixties, a few years older than us, not quite grandfatherly in appearance. After introducing himself as the surgeon on call that Christmas weekend, Dr. Humphrey pulled up a chair beside Bruce at the side of my bed. "I have the results of your angiogram and everything else in your heart looks good," he said. "Unfortunately, your low white blood count will prevent us from operating before Christmas. So, we'll plan for the day after."

"Have you seen a myxoma before?" Bruce asked the questions I would have asked under normal circumstances.

"They're very rare. I've known of only one during my time practicing. But the procedure involves the same technique I use for repairing congenital holes in babies' hearts, and I've performed the technique many times."

As Dr. Humphrey described the operation, he pointed to the top of his breast bone, just below the throat, and moved a finger down the center of his chest stopping about four inches above his navel. The path of the scalpel. I tried not to visualize my ribs being cracked open, a bypass machine pumping blood that would keep me alive while Dr. Humphrey and his team cut the tumor out of my heart.

"As with all surgeries, there are risks."

I had heard this before, but the potential complications had always been so rare that I had dismissed those warnings as something that surgeons were legally required to divulge but were of no real consequence to me.

After a pause to make sure I was with him, a more somber Dr. Humphrey continued. "There is a small chance that you could suffer severe and permanent side effects . . . or that you won't survive the operation. The risk is less than five percent, but it is real."

A 5 percent probability for most things——the chance of a thunderstorm spoiling your picnic or getting stuck in a traffic jam on the way to an important meeting—seems inconsequential. A 5 percent chance that you'll never see your husband and children again, that you'll never get to meet your grandchildren, that life will end—that's an enormous risk to face, even for someone like me who had always felt invincible.

"What if I don't have the operation?" I asked.

Bruce looked at me when I said this. I wasn't sure if he was shocked I was considering not having the operation or if he was wondering the same thing.

"A piece of the tumor could break off and kill you instantly," Dr. Humphrey said.

Bruce looked as shaken as I felt. Genetics and a healthy lifestyle predicted I could thrive for another thirty to forty years if I could just get this disease out of my body. I decided to take my chances with the surgery rather than live with a ticking bomb in my chest. I looked at Bruce and he squeezed my hand. I knew, based on our loving thirty-three-year marriage, that Bruce's decision would be the same. I signed the paperwork, acknowledging that I understood the risks Dr. Humphrey had described and agreed to the operation.

Finally alone, my eyes and Bruce's met and I felt a tsunami of emotions, some new and frightening, some known and comforting. Bruce climbed on to my hospital bed, pulled me close, and tenderly held me as he repeatedly kissed my bald head.

All my life I had imagined, and then realized, my version of the perfect life. But I had never been good at imagining my death. It was too scary. How could it be possible that I'd cease to feel anything? Would it be fast or slow? Would I know it was happening? I didn't want my body to be consumed in flames or to rot underground. But why even worry about that if I wouldn't be aware of either? I'm not a fearful or morbid person, so these thoughts were rare, usually arriving late at night in bed. They invariably invoked a dread that shook me to my core. I had always been able to force my mind to think of other things, mundane things like the following day's to-do list or what I'd have for breakfast. But my death no longer felt abstract. How would I control my mind now?

I loosened my embrace and pulled back to look at Bruce. "If anything happens," I said, "I don't want to be kept alive as a vegetable." The timbre of my voice belonged to someone else.

As I had aged and watched family members die, I knew logically that these were my wishes, but I finally had the need, and the courage, to voice them in a way that left no doubt about my fully informed conviction.

"You're going to be fine," Bruce said, trying to reassure me, and possibly himself. I had been so shocked and overwhelmed by what might happen to me, that until this point I hadn't given thought to the loss that Bruce could be facing.

"I hope so, sweet love. But I need to know that you'll be able to make the tough decisions if it comes to that."

We had discussed my end-of-life wishes and contingencies with Dr. Humphrey, but the full magnitude of those decisions had not sunk in. Now, after time for both of us to process the day's events, it was very real.

"I will. I would feel exactly the same if it was me." This clearly was not easy for him to say, but even so, I knew I could count on him.

We lay together a while longer, sometimes reminiscing about our wonderful life together, but mostly in quiet reflection and the comfort of each other's bodies. Even though my labored breathing was a nagging reminder of my illness, I didn't feel like I should be confined to a hospital. But here I was. In the span of eight hours, we had gone from joyously preparing for Christmas celebrations with family to facing the very real prospect, however small, that I could be dead in a matter of days.

Both of us exhausted, physically and emotionally, it was time for Bruce to go home and prepare for the arrival of our children from their homes in Tennessee and Maryland. I walked him to the elevator, arm in arm. As a soft ping announced the arrival of the elevator, I gave him a big hug and a kiss, and said, "If I survive this, I'm going to throw the best party ever!"

***

Six months later, I made good on my promise.

During a lifetime, some are fortunate enough to experience an event that causes us to look at life anew and realize how precious it is. Having been "doubly blessed" in the last year, I promised that when I made it through, I would have a party to celebrate life. The time has come!

Celebration of Life Party
Saturday June 23, 2001
3 P.M. until ????

Come early to swim, play volleyball, badminton, croquet, and assorted games of strategy and skill.

Stay late for dinner, fireworks, dancing, and surprising entertainment and amusement.

Come with a skit, a poem, a musical performance, a dance, a lip synch (my personal favorite is Barry White), or any other "artistic" expression in the spirit of the celebration. I happen to know the guest list is rich in talent—hidden or otherwise!

I hope you will join us!
Sue & Bruce Hoben

The day of the party was perfection, warm sun on my skin, a light wind gently evaporating the moisture. I walked out to our meadow, neatly mown and smelling faintly of hay. In one area, Bruce was playing bocce with his business partners. The shiny metal balls did not roll across the grass as smoothly as they had glided on the bocce courts of Italy, where we had purchased the beautifully boxed set, but they bumped along well enough for a rousing match. Walking up behind Bruce, I put my arm around his waist and my lips to his ear. "When you're done, would you help me round people up? The caterers are going to begin passing hors d'oeuvres at six."

Giving him a kiss on his freshly shaved cheek, I made my way to the middle of the two-acre meadow where a game of croquet was underway among our children and other assorted Gen Xers. Our daughter, Sasha, and John, her husband of less than a year, were visiting from their home in Nashville. My Celebration of Life party was the capstone of their week-long stay. We were just beginning to navigate the new reality of needing to share our daughter, and her limited vacation time, with her in-laws, but there was no debate that this celebration was of the highest priority. Two of Sasha's close friends and high school field hockey teammates were demonstrating the skill and competitive drive that had won them state championships. Our son, Justin, was "home" from Brookline, Massachusetts. He had finished his degree in English and philosophy and was working just outside of Boston at an independent bookstore. His vacation allotment only allowed for a long weekend with us.

Beer was the beverage of choice for this hip young group. Each player held a Rolling Rock or Heineken that they balanced on the grass when it came their turn to grasp the wooden mallet, thumbs pointing down, and take a shot at the metal wicket. Above the whooping and hollering, I called out, "Hey guys. That's a lot of trash talk for a genteel English garden game. When you wrap up this round, would you start making your way to the lawn for cocktail hour?"

At the top of the meadow, a more energetic game of volleyball was underway. Groups of people who weren't engaged in sport were talking and laughing, either waiting their turn to play or just enjoying the warm sunny day. As I made my way through the meadow and back to the front lawn, I stopped briefly to let guests know it was time to start moving toward the pool for hors d'oeuvres. I thought of our three cats who had likely herded themselves away from the rowdy game scene to some quiet spot in the woods that surrounded the house and pool.

The guest list was rich and varied. I felt honored that my cardiologist, my heart surgeon, and my primary care doctor had accepted my grateful invitation to join the celebration. I appreciated that my IBM Consulting Group colleagues had travelled from near and far to be with me, given the demands of the job and how we all prized our time at home. In one way or another, I owed my life to these friends who had gathered around me, whether figuratively or literally, physically or emotionally.

As I reached the front lawn, the caterers were efficiently and methodically setting up eight round tables, each with eight white wooden chairs, and were dressing them with crisp, white floor-length linens, creating an elegant contrast to the vibrant green backdrop of nature. All that remained was to put the white tapers under the hurricane lamps and they would be ready to pass the savory and fragrant hors d'oeuvres. Everything matched the mental image I had been carrying. The scene could have been a painting in a museum or the film of a luscious garden party. Energy sparked every cell in my body. I closed my eyes and breathed it in.

Bruce and I entertained often. Whether small dinner parties, summer cookouts, or large Christmas parties, our gatherings always ended in dancing, and often included hot dogs on the grill at midnight.

I had begun honing my party planning and social skills since eighth grade. Almost every other week, my parents bought cases of Coca-Cola in glass bottles and made pizza for my friends and me to enjoy as we played forty-fives and danced to Johnny Mathis, The Everly Brothers, and Ricky Nelson. My yearbook is full of classmate comments about the parties in my rec room. At our fiftieth high school reunion, they were still reminiscing about my "make-out parties," which I had called dance parties, especially when talking to my parents.

This dinner for over sixty-five people was our most ambitious party yet. I wanted to savor every minute, so we had decided to splurge and have it catered, something we had only previously done for Sasha's wedding. I floated from group to group on the warm summer air, on the love of friends, on the joy and gratitude of being alive.

As the caterers poured champagne, guests made their way from the pool to the enchantingly decorated lawn to choose their seats for dinner. Bruce asked everyone to gather around as we stepped onto the low deck that separated the lawn from the house. He stood at the edge, the toes of his sandals almost hanging over. He had planned a very short speech, in hopes that he could make it through without falling apart. He had cried during my chemo treatments. He cried at happy movies, at sad books, at uplifting music, and when he had held our newborn babies. That emotional openness was one of the many things I loved about him.

With the tips of all ten fingers, Bruce delicately held his glass of champagne as he began to speak.

"Thank you so much for coming." His eyes were glistening already. "It's been a tough twelve months." Taking a deep breath, he glanced over, catching my eye as I smiled. "But I'm sure you all agree that Susie has emerged stronger and even more beautiful!" Applause. Whistles. Catcalls. Music to my ears.

I was, indeed, feeling more beautiful, inside and out, than I ever had. Ten pounds over my hospital discharge weight, but ten pounds under my precancer weight, I was the happy recipient of many compliments throughout the afternoon. Inspired to show off sculpted muscles, the fruits of my labor at the gym, I posed Wonder Woman style. Skinny black mid-calf silk pants fitted my form perfectly. Sasha's gift of a shiny silver and black geometric-patterned halter top showed off my shoulders and neck, two body parts that I considered some of my best physical assets, while covering the foot-long scar that traversed the front of my chest. Dangling silver earrings and black sandals completed a look that telegraphed *This is a woman who is celebrating life!*

With his left hand flat across his middle, tears of joy and pride swelling, Bruce raised his champagne glass with his right hand. "To Susie!"

I felt the heat and blood rushing to my cheeks. Standing off to the side with Justin and Sasha, I raised my glass, looked Bruce in the eye, heart full of love and gratitude, and took a sip.

"To Susie," our guests echoed.

My turn to speak. I walked over to Bruce. As I went to start my speech, one I had not rehearsed, I felt the blood draining from my face as my throat tightened. I put my left hand over my heart, took a deep breath, and exhaled slowly, my lips parted. I looked at Bruce, who rested his hand on my shoulder as our eyes met. The summer evening was completely silent for what seemed like minutes, but the pause must have been only a few seconds. I turned to face our guests and started to speak.

With some lingering constriction in my throat, my voice sounded unfamiliar. "I've always been a pretty happy person, but I didn't RE-ALLY appreciate being alive until this year." My now-healthy heart was beating powerfully. "Having two things that could have killed me within a six-month period has truly been a blessing. I don't think it's possible to appreciate how beautiful life is until you've faced death. I almost feel sorry for people who haven't."

Realizing how inappropriate that probably sounded, I clarified. "I'm not wishing that any of you go through what I did." I heard a chuckle. "And, I'm definitely not volunteering to do it again!"

I raised my glass. "To all of you, my beautiful friends and family, I can't thank you enough for your love and support."

Loving energy emanated around me, feeling as though it was touching me physically.

"And Bruce." Beaming, I turned to look at him. "The love of my life, my best friend, my soul mate. I couldn't have made it without you."

Bruce and I gently cried with joy as our glasses clinked. "To life!" everyone said.

I turned to Sasha and Justin, and other friends standing nearby, and touched glasses with them before we all drank champagne in honor of the beauty and wonder that surrounded us. I was consumed by gratitude—for being alive, for all that had come before—Bruce, our children, our friends, who we had become—and for all that was yet to be.

The caterers lit the slender white candles on each table, brought the elegantly presented food to the buffet table, and began serving. As guests filled their plates and took a seat, I turned on the strings of white lights we had threaded through the branches of four large maple trees that lined the front lawn. With the sun inching toward the horizon and a glow of pink just starting to tinge a few low clouds in the sky, the atmosphere was magical.

As sunset approached and wanting to complete the promised "surprising entertainment and amusement" before it was too dark, I looked for my sister, Jane. "I'm going to help Bruce get ready. Are you all set?" I said.

"I am," she replied, an uncharacteristic twinkle of mischief in her eyes.

"This is going to be so much fun!" I said and beamed.

Next, I found Justin and quietly told him to be ready to cue the music in about fifteen minutes. Last stop was Bruce. I whispered in his ear and he followed close behind me, up the stairs to our bedroom.

Bruce took the shiny black and white, abstract-design halter dress off its hanger. He stripped to his briefs and slipped the dress over his head. The back plunged below his scapula. The hem stopped just above his knees, showing off the shapeliest calves I've ever seen, male or female. He slid on Sasha's low-heeled black sandals.

I got down my Rachel wig. When the time had come to buy a wig to cover my chemo-ravaged head, in addition to one that most closely mimicked my current hairstyle, I bought an auburn, shoulder-length shag wig that transformed me into my alter ego, Rachel. I put the wig on Bruce's head, adjusting it so the bangs fell just right on his forehead, and applied red lipstick along with a swath of blue eyeshadow. He was now Charmaine. We stood arm in arm facing the mirror and giggling as we shared the moment. Our outfits were perfectly coordinated. We looked fabulous!

Bruce and I snuck down the stairs, hid behind the fireplace with Jane, and cued our niece Beth, who stepped onto the deck that spanned the front of the house. Only four inches above the lawn and without railings, it was the perfect performance stage. Beth began:

It's so nice to see all of you here for the first Celebration of Life. In that spirit, I would like to say a few words about family, specifically about the way we learn by example.

I have been very lucky to have strong female role models at every turn, starting with my grandmother, the amazing Minnie Johnson Ducharme Wilder.

Minnie's equally amazing daughters, my mother Jane and my Aunt Sue, provided a shining example to their daughters: They are so beautiful, so accomplished, so academically dominant.

It's a challenging legacy for a young girl, and sometimes I wondered at my grandmother's success—the two perfect daughters and of course her handsome and successful son George. It all seemed a bit . . . Stepford.

But recently I learned something that made me see the situation quite differently.

You see, there is a third Ducharme sister, one who wasn't a model of feminine grace, who didn't measure up to the strict ideals of industriousness and modesty New England then demanded.

And while Sue and Jane were nurtured and educated here in Canton, Charmaine, the third daughter, was disinherited and shipped off to Europe, where she found work in a disreputable establishment. Eventually, the talent and charm which is Charmaine's birthright overcame her poor circumstances, and through hard work she became quite a famous cabaret star.

Though celebrated and internationally renowned, Charmaine still couldn't stop thinking of the hometown that had rejected her. She knew she could not rest until she had made her family and their friends love her as the world did.

She's here tonight but reluctant to perform. Would you like to see her dance? . . . Let's encourage her!

Beth clapped loudly and the audience joined in. Justin started the CD that Sasha had burned for the occasion and turned the volume of the living room speakers all the way up. The introductory instrumentals played. As Chaka Khan began to sing, *"I'm every woman . . .,"* I walked across the deck, pivoted three times, and swayed to the music. On the next stanza, Jane joined me, and we swayed together, arms right, left, right. We flawlessly executed our choreography to the amusement and delight of our audience.

Then Charmaine made her entrance. The crowd went wild. Jaws dropped, people roared with laughter and exclamations of surprise. Charmaine got caught up in the moment, to the detriment of the choreography we had so carefully practiced, but no one cared. Bruce basked in the adulation of a standing ovation. Charmaine had, indeed, made her family and her friends love her as the world did.

I had been in several high school plays, and Bruce's ad hoc antics often made him the life of the party, but we had never aspired to be Ginger Rogers and Fred Astaire. I couldn't believe how much fun it was.

We had worked on the routine for weeks. When the memorization wasn't going well, Jane typed up a two-page, large-font, very-detailed description of the moves and corresponding lyrics. Jane and I have a natural sense of rhythm, and although Bruce loved music, and loved to dance, I would classify him as rhythm challenged. For many years, it bothered me that he couldn't dance at (or even near) a level of competency that met mine. At times, I had even felt embarrassed to be on the floor with him. Fortunately, I had learned the irrelevance of dancing skills when compared to all of Bruce's other wonderful qualities. I learned to change my attitude, relax, and be proud to be with someone who danced through life with such exuberance. And I had fun.

Bruce, Jane, and I went out to the audience and pulled people up on stage to join us as we danced to "He's the Greatest Dancer," "I Will Survive," and "Good Times." The dancing continued for the rest of the night and ended with a launch of a colorful fireworks display from the driveway.

I will always remember that night as a special moment of pure joy and lightness, of being carried on music that held a special place in my life, of release from the burden of just trying to survive. It was a celebration of life that would inspire and nourish me forever. My brush with death had changed me profoundly for the better. I would never again take for granted the smallest pleasure that life had to offer.

I thought this feeling would last forever.

THERE IS A TUMOR

Friday morning, August 29, 2008

Bruce was in the first bay in a corner. The bay next to him was empty. The curtain around his bed was pulled partway out, providing some privacy while still allowing the nursing staff to observe. A small monitor, dark and dormant, hung on a wall to the right of the bed. Windows high above his bed let in the morning sun and softened the glare of the overhead fluorescent fixtures. The bay was just big enough to hold one brown vinyl visitor chair, a small bedside stand, and the single bed on which Bruce had been wheeled.

As I neared his bed, I could see that Bruce was in distress. Having known and loved him for over forty years, I still saw him as the handsome, robust young man I married. Here though, a smaller, more fragile Bruce lay in a hospital gown, his thin frame covered with a white sheet pulled up to his chest. Pillows elevated his head slightly. He was shaking, his color ashen, a sheen of sweat on his forehead, his eyes glassy.

I rushed to the bed and hugged him close. "What's wrong, sweetie?" His gaze was unfocused. He wasn't responding. I put my face close to his and pleaded, "What can I do?"

Was he in shock? Was he having a reaction to the anesthesia? I frantically looked around. Midway down the recovery room, on the opposite side, there were two small nursing stations each with a desk that neatly overflowed with procedure manuals and patient files, a phone,

17

and a computer. With my focus away from Bruce for the first time, I was aware of a cacophony of accents and laughter. Concurrent and loud conversations were underway as resource staff called doctors, procedure nurses delivered new patients, and recovery nurses reported status updates. Six nurses were milling around. I knew endoscopies were low-risk procedures compared to open surgeries, but why were there no nurses attending to Bruce?

By the time I turned back to Bruce, he was calm enough to speak. "I have a tumor." Desperation and confusion clouded his eyes.

"Have you already seen the doctor?" I asked. I tried to appear calm, but I was confused and furious that Dr. Murray would give Bruce this news without me. He must have known I was in the waiting room and would want to be there, supporting Bruce, when he was given the results.

Bruce shook his head. "I overheard two nurses . . . wheeling me back," he stuttered. "They thought I couldn't hear . . . I couldn't say anything. . . . I couldn't move." He spoke slowly and haltingly, as though trying to reconstruct a bad dream that just didn't make sense.

Sitting on the bed next to him, I held him tight, now both of us crying. I felt helpless. This should never have happened. The nurses should have known better.

As his breathing steadied, I let go of my embrace and looked around. I noticed the discharge paperwork on the bedside stand. Sitting on the chair next to his bed, I silently read it. In the top left corner was the Hartford Hospital logo. In the top right corner was an identifying sticker that read:

14590749
HOBEN, BRUCE 67 07/13/1941
ATN: MURRAY JR, JAMES H. 08/29/2008
PCP: ABRAHAM, RICHARD

At the end of the expected list of things he could and couldn't do, item four on the discharge paperwork confirmed what Bruce had heard. Handwritten in large print I saw the sentence: *There is a tumor in your esophagus—biopsies taken and sent to the lab.*

As we waited for Dr. Murray to come speak with Bruce, we sat quietly on the bed, holding hands, hugging when Bruce started to tense, my anger rising. No one should have to hear a diagnosis the way Bruce had.

Dr. Murray arrived about fifteen minutes later. Medium height and weight, in his early seventies with gray hair, he was wearing a blue button-down shirt, a red and blue striped tie, and the standard white hospital coat. He looked the part of an experienced and confident doctor. Standing at the foot of Bruce's bed, Dr. Murray briefly described for me the twenty-minute procedure he had just performed, during which he lowered a tube through Bruce's esophagus to get a look at the obstruction. He then turned to Bruce and his voice became quietly compassionate, more slowly paced and gentle. "We found a tumor where the esophagus joins your stomach."

Unaware of the hospital staff's indiscreet chatter or of the fact that I had already read the discharge paperwork, he must have thought we were taking the news very calmly. Still stunned, and not knowing how much new information he might give us, I didn't interrupt him.

"I took a biopsy for analysis," he continued.

Dr. Murray had no way of knowing we had already been through the leading front of the storm. Hearing this officially, from him, was anticlimactic.

"Is it cancer?" Bruce's voice was shaky, asking a question he didn't want to ask and bracing for an answer he didn't want to hear.

"We won't know until the biopsy results are in." This was technically true and yet not very forthcoming. I knew from my experience with breast cancer that the color and texture of biopsied tissue can be a strong indicator of cancer.

"We understand," I pressed, "but what are the odds?"

"It's very likely. . . . We should know in a few days," the doctor responded. I could see he was uncomfortable with the question. Was it because I was forcing him to speculate or because he knew the answer?

"Once we have the biopsy results we'll decide the most effective treatment."

Why Bruce? My logical mind wanted an answer. But then, why anyone? Cancer really is just a one-cell mutation that can be caused by almost anything.

After Dr. Murray left, I drew the curtains around Bruce's bed. He was still a little shaky as I helped him get dressed. "We're going to get through this," I told him. I stared intently into Bruce's eyes, holding his gaze, willing my love and support to permeate his body.

"I know," he responded with the best smile of acknowledgment he could muster. I hugged him, trying to make him believe that what I had just said was true.

As I retraced my steps through the waiting room and crossed the road to the dark musty parking garage to retrieve the car, I thought back to July 2000 when my breast cancer diagnosis had come in a call from my surgeon while I was working in Providence, Rhode Island. I had handled everything matter-of-factly, scheduling surgery around my upcoming business trip to London. But after hanging up I'd found myself needing to take a few deep breaths before calling Bruce. As I began to talk, my voice faltered, my stomach tensed, and adrenaline flowed. Saying it out loud made it real. Bruce offered to come immediately, but ever the stoic and feeling a little more in control, I told him he didn't need to, that I'd be home in two days and would call that night when I finished work.

I thought I'd be able to get back to work but my subconscious did not cooperate. *This isn't fair! I'm fit and healthy.* Although I had known I was at high risk—my mother and grandmother were breast cancer survivors and I had taken hormone replacement therapy for three years after a hysterectomy—I still somehow never thought that I would get breast cancer. I thought my sister would be the one to draw the short straw, if either of us did, because she physically favored my mother's side of the family and I physically took after my father's. *What if my genes had been different? What if I'd done self-exams every month? What if I'd gone for that three-month follow-up the way my OB/GYN had wanted me to?*

After another hour or two of trying to focus on work that day, I gave up and headed back to the hotel. Opening the door to my room, I was assaulted by the musty staleness that characterizes a hotel room with no functioning windows. My senses longed for the familiar smells and sounds of home.

Standing at the white marble counter in the bathroom, I looked into the mirror. Same blond hair. Same blue eyes. Same toned body. But transformed. No one else would see it, and I couldn't attach a word to it, but something had changed. Now I was someone with cancer. I tried to convince my image in the mirror of what my doctor had said. *Luckily breast cancer is often curable, and we caught it early.*

I lay down on the bed and pulled the feather pillows close around my head. Emotionally spent but not sleepy, I don't know how long I had been lying there when I heard a knock at the door. I ignored it at first, but the knock came again.

Looking through the peep hole, I recognized the warm brown eyes and out-of-control eyebrows that belonged to my husband, rogue hairs spiraling into his eyes. I opened the door and Bruce enveloped me in his arms. For the first time since my surgeon's call, my tears flowed freely.

When Bruce released his embrace, he held my shoulders and looked into my eyes. "I didn't want you to be alone, and I didn't want to be alone."

Of course, he had come. Joyfully married for thirty-three years, we had done everything together. We laughed, cried, danced, and sat quietly together. We swam, sailed, and traveled. We savored good food and wine, and shared books. We made babies, built two houses, and looked forward to welcoming grandchildren. This would be something else we'd do together.

As the afternoon sun faded, we went to the lobby bar for a glass of wine and some snacks. We talked about everyday things, our children, my upcoming trip to the United Kingdom, and Sasha's wedding in two months. Life goes on, even in the face of cancer.

When it was time for bed, I nestled into a comfortable spoon, Bruce's hand cradling my traitorous left breast. Our heartbeats and breathing slowed and synchronized, and I felt myself drift into that same kind of drugged sleep state that had lulled me on more than one occasion by a baby asleep on my chest. Bruce was there for me, and no matter what happened he would always be there.

Now, as we began our second journey through cancer, I would be there for him, trying to provide for him the same comfort that he had given me that day in Providence eight years earlier. At the hospital entrance, Bruce was delivered to the car in a wheelchair while I waited by the open passenger door. His color was better, but fear and foreboding still lingered in his eyes. I was trying to be upbeat but a terrible premonition of things to come flashed through my mind.

CHAPTER THREE

RESUME USUAL ACTIVITIES

Friday morning, August 29, 2008

On the thirty-minute ride home we said little but communicated volumes through touch and gaze and pure loving energy. I rested my right hand on Bruce's thigh. I was sure he was trying to process what we had just learned. I know I was. Bruce was by nature not talkative. He never felt the need to fill a silence. After forty-two years of a happy, loving marriage we could sit together in silence and not feel alone.

Arriving in Canton, we passed the bandstand on the green, the quintessential emblem of a small New England town, a town that I couldn't wait to leave as a senior in high school but was happy to return to six years later. We passed the little red school house where my mother had spent her grammar school years. I turned left on East Mountain Road and took the first right into our driveway—the driveway where to this day I live.

Our lot, part of 200 acres that had belonged to my grandparents, sits at the top of a mountain, or at least what passes for a mountain in Connecticut. A two-acre meadow gently slopes downhill to our driveway. Most of the surrounding acreage is woodland and wetlands, what we called swamp. Many of the trees have been there since my childhood, when the meadow was a source of constant fun and intrigue: pretending to be a cowgirl as I rode my quarter horse, Texas Star; sending our white-throated black border collie, Bobby, down to the meadow to herd the sheep and cows back to the barn; eating sweet, crisp apples picked directly from the trees lining the meadow.

Tall native plants and shrubs bordered the one hundred-yard driveway on the left. Wild Concord grapevines were completing their annual rite of taking over, and a faint scent of ripening fruit was in the air. Halfway up the drive, forsythia and ferns formed a border between the woods and a ten-foot strip of grass I had planted. The obligatory suburban basketball hoop sat at the end, patiently waiting for a game of horse.

As I turned into the driveway, the first sight of our house, a passive solar contemporary with fifty-five feet of floor-to-ceiling glass, filled me with joy and gratitude. I lived in a stunning home on beautiful ancestral land. But on this day, every glorious detail was in exquisitely high definition. I wanted to hit pause. I wanted the joyful sense of living and loving to hold back the shock, fear and sadness. I wanted the impossible.

I pressed the garage door opener and entered the right bay. Once inside, while Bruce went upstairs, I quickly went to my office and started Googling, my natural inclination leading me to seek facts and analysis in times of crisis. Everything was happening so fast. Just a few weeks earlier, Bruce had begun experiencing some discomfort swallowing and brushed it aside, thinking he might have strained a muscle when he started a new regimen of pushups. Now I was researching esophageal tumors.

Finding that less than one percent of esophageal tumors are benign, and that those are found in patients between the ages of twenty and fifty, I searched the phrase *esophageal cancer*. We knew the cancer drill. But this time, there was no doubt in my mind that the tumor in Bruce's esophagus was much more serious than the tumor in my breast and the fact that it was hidden deep within his body meant this would probably not be a case of early detection. Hoping for more encouraging statistics than the overall 15 percent five-year survival rate, I was shaken to learn that many patients die within a year of noticing the first symptoms, but hung on to the fact that if it was confined to his esophagus then the prognosis was good. At this point we knew nothing more than that there was a high probability of a cancerous tumor in his esophagus. Despite a gnawing unease, I was determined to be optimistic.

Up until now, our lives had been blessed. No time for tears. Given that we didn't yet know any specifics about Bruce's diagnosis, I decided this was not the time to tell him what I had learned. The biopsy would provide critical information on the type of cancer and whether it had metastasized. For the moment, we would focus on absorbing what we did know.

When Bruce came downstairs, we went out the living room slider and sat together on the edge of the deck, our thighs touching. We looked out across our lawn to the meadow beyond, and across the street to our neighbor's pond shimmering in the sun. The adjoining brick patio was ringed with large pots of deep scarlet geraniums and impatiens, Bruce's favorite flower, in a mix of red, hot coral, lilac, and blush pink. Baskets of cascading flowers hung from the roofline just behind us. Beneath them were four large jade plants that had been "part of the family" for over forty years. Our bare feet in the grass, it was impossible not to feel the energy of our life together that had been lived on that lawn. Our children's soccer celebrations, my mother's sorority lunches, our daughter's wedding parties, her best friend's rehearsal dinner, grand-children lying on blankets in the shade of the trees, annual summer parties with food, wine, dancing, fireworks, and Charmaine.

We sat in silence for a while. *How could this be happening?* Bruce was one of the healthiest people I'd ever known. He was an avid runner, cyclist, and swimmer. He had a special fondness for good wine and dark chocolate, but we generally ate very healthy foods. Forty years after leaving the service, he could still comfortably and proudly fit into his army uniform. He was never one to let stress get to him. He had a loving family, good friends, and colleagues who enjoyed and respected him. He smoked when he was young (as many did in the 1960s and 1970s) but had not had a cigarette in thirty-five years. *This was not fair.*

"I won't get to meet the twins," he said, tears in his eyes.

"We don't know that." I put my arm around him. "Sasha's due March fifth. That's only six months away."

Bruce looked out to the meadow, his gaze fixed.

"I'm retiring," he announced, his voice gaining confidence as he made the first decision of the rest of his life.

I had retired in 2003, shortly after my cancer and heart surgery, and was glad that he would be joining me. I felt a spontaneous and hopeful smile emerging as we looked forward to planning something positive. "We'll visit the kids and do all the things we love."

Another period of silence.

"I thought we were going to have at least twenty more years together," he said quietly, his face close to mine, somber yet not desperate.

"We've had a wonderful life," I told him, slipping my arm around his, smiling and snuggling close. "And we're not done yet!" I spoke deliberately, emphasizing every word.

There were so many good times to remember, and Bruce loved to recount stories of significant moments in his life. Some tales, of his childhood, the grandchildren begged to hear every time they saw him: taking the train to Waterbury as a boy with his friends; the nuns rapping him on the knuckles for misbehaving; getting bitten by a dog when he was roughhousing on a raft in a lake and jumping, bleeding, into the water to escape; falling out of a tree near his house while trying to get a bird. As a young boy, he had been so excited to take out his first library book that he was hit by a car as he ran from the library, forgetting to look either way, let alone both ways. As a teen, he and his brothers trapped his oldest sister's fiancé in the family garage by putting him in the sub-floor oil pit and driving the car over it. Indeed, he'd had a colorful youth!

But his favorite story by far was how we met. His brother, John, married my sister, Jane. My family (including sixteen-year-old me) had gone to Naugatuck to meet John's family (including twenty-one-year-old Bruce). Although Bruce originally had other plans for that night, when he saw me he immediately cancelled them and spent the evening with his future in-laws. We soon began dating (what were my parents thinking?) and the rest is history. We married four years later during spring break my junior year of college.

We were now on the verge of a whole new era of our life together, making new memories in uncharted territory. We vowed that no matter what the future held, we would continue to celebrate life and live every day to its fullest.

What a start to the Labor Day weekend, a time we had planned to spend at our pool, reading, sunning, swimming, listening to the radio, sharing a Sunday *New York Times* crossword puzzle, playing with the cats, barbequing. We could and would still do all that. Item two on the discharge paperwork: *Resume usual activities tomorrow.* We'd just start a little early.

Ready to resume daily life, including the chores, we walked up the steps to the pool. The pool was constructed in the middle of nature with woods on two sides, the meadow on one side and, on the fourth side, steps to a brick walkway to the house. The result was our own mini-resort, removed enough from the rest of the house and grounds to make it feel as though we were away from home yet close enough for every-thing to be accessible.

I started to weed and deadhead the spent blossoms in the flowering pots that surrounded the pool. Bruce got out the equipment to vacuum the pool. He paused and took a deep breath.

"You'll need to learn how to do the pool," he announced.

I had tried vacuuming before and found it tricky to get the vacuum hose properly attached to the opening in the skimmer basket. Bruce had a good point. As much as I didn't want to think about it, there were many maintenance tasks I might have to learn.

Although we had always shared most household and childrearing tasks, Bruce did not sew, and I didn't do anything mechanical. I knew I was able to learn how to do anything if I wanted to, but rationalized avoidance of all things mechanical by saying it just didn't interest me.

Bruce, on the other hand, had grown up tinkering with cars and became a model homeowner who could solve virtually any home maintenance problem.

Happy to have something practical and tangible to think about, I went down to the house to get something for taking notes while Bruce continued to set up the pool equipment. I found a five and a half by eight and a half-inch loose-leaf binder with a padded burgundy cover and clear pockets on the inside front and back. Back at the pool, Bruce walked me through the vacuuming process. He attached the hose, disconnected it, and watched as I did it myself. When my first attempt was unsuccessful, he patiently positioned my hands and held his hand over mine as I tried again. At the completion of each step I took notes. I drew a schematic of the five valves that controlled the flow of water between the filter and the pool, and the settings required for various functions. When he explained how to run the attached hot tub, he watched as I correctly repeated his moves. The hot tub was simple compared to vacuuming, a much-needed boost to my confidence. We finished with a tutorial on testing the water and adding chemicals.

Over the next months, I was to take many such notes as Bruce showed me how to drain water from the hot water heater, charge the battery of the riding mower, check the oil in both mowers, and do various other maintenance tasks. The binder would become my repository for all notes, diagrams, and schedules of indoor and outdoor maintenance tasks that I might need to handle, though I hoped it would never be necessary.

After I finished vacuuming the pool, we sat side by side on chaise longues and planned out the rest of the weekend. Normally it would have been walks, chores, meals, maybe a bike ride, but on this Friday, we planned how we would tell those we loved that Bruce had cancer.

CHAPTER FOUR

WE HAVE SOME BAD NEWS

Friday afternoon, August 29, 2008

Bruce took his cell phone from the kitchen counter and intently held it as he put it on speaker and dialed. "Hi Tom. It's Bruce." His tone was strained, his words careful. This was not the usual lighthearted social call. Bruce looked to me for encouragement as he continued. "I need to talk to you about something. Could you stop by?"

"Sure. I'm in Avon now." Tom responded warily, sensing something wasn't right. "I'll be there in a few minutes."

Although Bruce's biopsy results, which would be used for staging and treatment planning, wouldn't be available for several days, we felt we needed to begin telling our family and friends what was happening. Our children would still be at work, not an appropriate time or place for this conversation, so Bruce started the process with a call to his good friend Tom Francoline, a successful builder of high-end custom homes in the Farmington Valley. Bruce and Tom had been friends and business associates for thirty-four years, beginning in 1975 when Bruce became the town of Avon's first Town Planner. When Bruce began his consulting practice in 1987, Tom had been Bruce's first client and their friendship flourished.

Having attended many Planning and Zoning public hearings together in front of anxious and angry neighbors, Tom valued Bruce's ability to appreciate the other person's point of view and address it with

29

respect. Bruce was skilled at getting people to calm down, so they would listen and comprehend how to move forward with solutions that all could accept.

Bruce and Tom also knew how to celebrate a victory. On the night of a successful public hearing in Salisbury, Bruce had danced in the front seat of Tom's car all the way home to a blasting "Burning Down the House" by the Talking Heads—with Tom's eighty-two-year-old father dancing along in the back seat.

The two shared a great admiration for each other's talents, integrity, and humanity. They both enjoyed running, loved good food and wine, met often for lunch, sharing hearty laughs and witty banter. I can honestly say that they loved each other—and I delighted in their friendship.

As we waited for Tom to arrive, we continued tackling our outside chores. Amid illness and fear, life goes on. That life included all those things that give us pleasure as well as the mundane activities that keep things flowing smoothly. The western side of our driveway was teeming with native Connecticut flora: trees, grape vines, flowering shrubs, briars, ferns, and assorted wildflowers and weeds that Mother Nature had thoughtfully and abundantly provided for us. They were lovely and hardy, but needed regular taming to prevent them from completely reclaiming the strip of grass that I had painstakingly planted.

I was halfway down the driveway, beating back the vines with a bypass pruner and plant shears, and Bruce was near the house working on the lawn mower when Tom pulled into the driveway. He slowly approached and stopped his truck next to me.

"He OK?" Tom's head was cocked to one side as his eyes moved toward Bruce.

"You'll need to ask him," I gently replied.

Tom continued down the driveway. As Tom slowed and pulled nearer, Bruce stopped what he was doing. I had begun walking up the driveway and arrived just as Tom was getting out of his truck. His new Labrador puppy, hoping it was time to play, leapt out of the cab of the truck.

"Everything OK?" Tom asked, this time of Bruce directly, his gaze trying to discern what was wrong.

"Not really," Bruce answered, speaking slowly. "I have some bad news. I've got cancer." No sugar coating here.

The air was sucked out of the atmosphere, replaced with an electrical charge of emotion. Tom didn't know what to say. As Bruce began to cry, Tom's tears of sadness, fear, and compassion also flowed, and they embraced.

We hadn't rehearsed, or even discussed, exactly how we were going to reveal what was happening. After a long hard hug, we started with the details that we knew, most of it conveyed by me because it was just too difficult emotionally for Bruce to speak. We had always been a good team with complementary strengths. We learned quickly that a helpful role for me, the logical, analytical one, would be covering the facts and next steps.

After offering his love and support, and volunteering to do whatever he could to help us, Tom didn't stay long. Seeing the horror on Tom's face, and remembering our own reactions during the preceding hours at the hospital, I was beginning to realize that people would need time to reflect on and process this kind of life-altering news. In addition to the anguish felt for Bruce, his news would likely bring their own mortality to the forefront.

Bruce was totally involved raising the children, a hands-on father in the '70s, long before it was expected or fashionable. He regularly braided our daughter, Sasha's, long hair, not just in braids but in French braids. He packed lunches for Sasha and our son, Justin, every day, coloring the brown paper bags with birds and airplanes. On holidays, as an extra treat, he packed holiday-colored SnoBalls. The lunches were so envied by Sasha's friends, who referred to Bruce lovingly as Mr. Mom, that he packed an extra fully stocked and decorated lunch as gifts for their birthdays. Every Columbus Day, he took both kids to the air museum where they boarded a small chartered plane that took them on a flight path over our house. His legacy as "Crazy Pa" began early when he would drive the kids to school down East Hill Road, coasting and pumping the brakes (actually, the clutch), yelling, "Oh, my God! —The brakes have failed!" Sasha and Justin caught on quickly but played along for years.

We had just seen our children two weeks earlier for their summer visit, our days filled with swimming, playing, and cookouts, including the eighth annual Celebration of Life Party. Throughout the preceding weeks of diagnostic testing, we had talked about when to let our children know that something was wrong. We didn't want to alarm them. Nor did we want them to think that we had been withholding important information. The secrecy was weighing heavily. We'd come to a difficult crossroad with some news that would profoundly affect our children.

A few hours later, we decided the time had come to tell them and went to the kitchen to make the calls together. Like many homes, our kitchen has always been the hub of activity. Our spacious kitchen looks through a greenhouse area of glass walls and vaulted ceilings, where pots of mature geraniums blossom through the winter, waiting to be moved back outside when spring arrives. Shelves over the desk cradle worn cookbooks, and sundrenched pictures of smiling and teary children and grandchildren, and feline family members at various ages. Commanding a place of honor is a framed poem Bruce had written for me on the occasion of our thirtieth wedding anniversary. It accompanied his gift of two intertwined bracelets.

BRACELETS
FORMS ENTWINED,
CIRCLED ROUND,
INEXTRICABLE,
BOUND BY METAL AND SPACE,
A METAPHOR FOR YOU AND ME.
EXCEPT OUR METAL IS LOVE,
AND OUR SPACE IS TIME.
THIRTY YEARS

The cream-colored paper had faded and there was a water (or white wine) spot. I'd had to replace the frame when the original fell, and the glass broke, but the poem, for me, was eternal. On the wall was a framed print that Sasha gave me after my illnesses. *Everything changed the day she figured out there was exactly enough time for the important things in her life.*

Our first child, Sasha was born in 1972 after a five-year extended honeymoon with all the passion and joy of newlyweds. She was an easygoing baby who matured into a loving and accomplished adult, a beautiful young woman inside and out.

After graduating from Vanderbilt University in Tennessee, Sasha stayed in Nashville. When she married John, a North Carolina native, we only half-jokingly tried to negotiate a prenuptial agreement that they would move north in five years. Unfortunately, the agreement was all in our minds. Their daughter Mae was now eighteen months old and they had recently learned she would be joined by twin girls in March. We decided to call Sasha first.

Because we talked to Sasha almost daily, we were keenly aware that, during the preceding days of less than full disclosure, virtually all telephone calls with her had started with the generally innocuous question, "How are you?" We were counting on this time being no different.

I took two glasses down from the racks of wine glasses hanging on hooks from wide beams above the island, and poured us each a glass of red wine. Sitting at our usual seats at the counter, me on the leftmost end and Bruce next to me, I put my cell phone on the counter between us. We left the screen door of the kitchen slider open so that our three cats, Spenser (For Hire), Kinsey (Millhone), and Jake (of no particular detective series significance), could come and go without interrupting us. The room was filled with the rosy, muted light and warm, fresh air of a late summer evening.

Allowing for the change in time zone, Sasha would just be getting home after picking up Mae at daycare. With the phone on speaker, I dialed.

"Hey, Mom," Sasha answered breezily.

"Hi, sweetie," I responded with my usual greeting, my stomach in knots, trying to mask a shaky voice.

We looked at each other as Bruce, probably feeling the same sensations, chimed in, "Hi, Sash,"

"How're you doing?" Sasha began the conversation with the question we had anticipated and hoped for. That was usually followed by "Good. How are you? How was your week? How's Mae? What are you having for dinner tonight?" But not this time.

"Not good, actually," Bruce answered, his drooping shoulders reflected in his voice.

In the background, I had heard the noises of Mae's school bag being unpacked and the dishwasher being unloaded. "What's up?" Sasha asked uncertainly.

"I've been having some trouble swallowing lately, so I went to see Dr. Abraham and he ran a few tests." Bruce paused allowing it to sink in. "Unfortunately, they found a tumor in my esophagus."

"Oh no." John must have detected the worry in her voice because the next sound I heard was him scooping Mae up and leaving the kitchen so that Sasha could continue the call without distractions.

We went on with more details about the tests, the diagnoses, the doctors, the next steps, everything we knew at the time which, as it turns out, was not a lot.

"Is there anything I can do?" Judging by the tone of her voice, Sasha's stomach was in as much of a knot as mine was, and distance prevented the soothing hug we all wished for.

"Not now, sweetie," I answered, putting my hand on Bruce's arm as he tensed. "We'll call as soon as we know more."

"OK. Love you."

"Love you, too," Bruce and I answered in unison.

Since we didn't talk to Justin daily (I like to attribute this largely to the communication patterns of sons vs. daughters), we hadn't needed to hide anything from him during the preceding days of tests. Justin, two years younger than his sister, is the artist of the family. After graduating college cum laude with a double major in English and philosophy, he went to work at an independent bookstore in Brookline, Massachusetts. Finding Boston "too boring" he soon moved to Washington, D.C., and got involved in music while bartending to pay the bills. He performed and recorded under the name John Bustine, an anagram of Justin Hoben. A skateboarder since junior high (when he built a skate ramp in the back yard), he was still skating at the age of thirty-five. Now living with his wife, Kylie, and their six-year-old daughter, Ruby, right outside of Washington, he was in the middle of courses for a two-year master's program in special education. I was amused and proud when I thought of his students having a bright, literate, handsome, six-foot-four tattooed musician skateboarder for their teacher.

After a break of only a minute or so, with the phone on speaker again, we called Justin. Opening the same way, the conversation flowed as expected. Justin responded with shock, disbelief, a request to keep him informed, and an offer that he would be there for whatever we needed.

"Love you, Just," we both told him, willing our voices to sound more energized than we were feeling.

"Love you, too," he answered, probably trying to do the same thing.

I hit the red off button on the phone, inhaled deeply and took a sip of wine. We were done and done in for the day. Saying it out loud had made the cancer diagnosis real, as if there had been any doubt. I was not yet thinking in detail about what the next weeks and months might hold, but I was beginning to internalize that our lives had changed forever.

Still at Bruce's side at the counter, I put my right hand on top of Bruce's left thigh and let it rest there for several minutes as the adrenaline rush in my body ebbed. I was concerned not just about Bruce's future, and mine, but also that of our children. The thought of hurting our children was excruciatingly painful.

"How're you doing?"

"OK, I guess. I don't know who it was harder on—them or us."

"I know," I said. My body slumped in weary resignation. As straightforward and optimistic as I'd sounded on the phone, I lamented being the bearer of painful news.

I raised my glass toward Bruce. He lifted his glass to meet mine.

"I love you. We're gonna be OK," I told him.

CHAPTER FIVE

WE WERE NEVER CLOSE ANYWAY

Saturday afternoon, August 30, 2008

I was not looking forward to talking to my sister. I'm told, and have photographic evidence, that Jane pushed my baby carriage (with me in it) into the woods. My earliest memories are of her pushing me away. She wouldn't allow me to be with her or near her, especially if she was with a friend. I have no childhood memories of play, laughter, or affection with her. That situation changed when I married Bruce, her husband, John's, brother. We lived next door to each other for eight years, during which the four of us spent many happy times together.

Their two daughters, Beth and Aimée, and our children were close in age. There was a well-worn path through the woods between our houses. We have many photos of Aimée, Sasha, and Justin playing together. Most holidays were at our house and in later years we hosted virtually all family gatherings.

Jane and I both inherited the travel bug from our mother. When our children were grown, and Bruce and I began to travel more, Jane often came with us since John did not like to travel. She joined us for two weeks in Italy; she and I house-sat an apartment in Paris for a month; we went on sailing trips in the Caribbean together; and she sailed with us in the British Virgin Islands on several occasions. Using the small amount of money that we had inherited from our mother's estate, Jane and I formed a travel-related business, Wilder Adventures. Our mother's name was Minnie Johnson Ducharme Wilder, and we prided ourselves on the play on words.

After a house fire in 1992, Jane and John had lived with us for several weeks until they were able to rent a condo while their house was repaired. There were the normal tensions that arise when people with different lifestyles are forced to share living space, but the relationship survived and snapped back to normal as soon as we were no longer living under the same roof.

Thirty-six years after marrying Bruce, I thought Jane and I had finally become sisters and friends. But in 2003, everything changed.

As part of our ongoing celebration of life, Bruce and I had bought a forty-one-foot catamaran sailboat in the British Virgin Islands, naming her, of course, Celebration of Life. Most people buying a forty-one-foot boat started sailing smaller vessels when they were younger, graduating to progressively larger boats over a period of years. We had started big, especially for novice sailors, but with our newly adopted philosophy of life, we decided that if we wanted to learn to sail then we had better do it now, and we might as well go big.

Celebration of Life was twenty-seven feet wide with four staterooms and four heads. Before taking delivery on our boat, we spent a week on a similar model with instructional skippers who taught us to sail. We invited Jane to come along. The first day out, after a few hours of basic hands-on instruction, our instructor threw a fender off the side and yelled, "Man overboard!" That set the tone for the rest of the week during which he pushed us hard and expected us to be self-sufficient. By the end of the week, we were feeling very good about our sailing abilities.

For our maiden sail on Celebration of Life, we had asked John and Jane, who had owned smaller sailboats for many years, to be our backup crew as we learned the ropes (literally and figuratively). Leaving base that first morning, Bruce and I were nervous yet determined to do it ourselves. John seemed OK with the role of observer, but Jane was clearly frustrated, wanting to be more actively involved in the sailing. While we had let her learn and practice some on the training runs with the instructors, we did not want any help this time unless we asked. Knowing that the next time out we would be solo or with guests, we felt it was critical to make all our own decisions and mistakes.

After sailing for a few hours, we decided to pull into one of our favorite spots, Cam Bay, to anchor and relax for the afternoon while we debriefed and planned the rest of the trip. Outside the bay, as we turned into the wind to drop the sail, Jane offered to help. Thanking her, I nicely explained that we needed to be able to do it ourselves. Bruce and I then muddled through, discussing what we'd do differently the next time.

We then turned to enter the bay as we steeled ourselves for the hard part, navigating an eight-ton boat through a fifty-foot opening between a reef on one side and the rocky shore on the other. Bruce was positioned on the trampoline netting at the front. I was at the helm, twenty-five feet back, yelling to him to let me know what he was seeing and if I was keeping the boat in the channel. The wind was at my back, blowing directly at him and carrying his voice away from me as he attempted to answer. Between the wind and our inexperience, we were both highly stressed. During all this maneuvering and yelling, Jane and John, as we had requested, sat silently on the bench at the back of the cockpit.

We cleared the coral and rocks, slowly motored to a sandy-bottomed spot and dropped the anchor. Then, out of nowhere Jane erupted, yelling at me. I don't remember exactly what she said, just that she was cursing me. I was speechless. Unable to connect her actions with the sailing maneuvers we had just completed, I looked at Bruce who was as shocked as I was. Jane, not willing or perhaps not able to tell me exactly what had just happened, made it clear she wanted to leave the boat right away. Bruce managed to calm things down and they agreed to stay, albeit in a cloud of tension that never dissipated.

With time, as things did not improve, I asked Jane to talk with me about it. I suggested we go to counseling, but she declined my offer, saying, "We were never close anyway." I couldn't believe what I was hearing. It shattered a belief of closeness I'd held for over thirty-five years. Our discussion ended with no resolution and apparently no desire on her part to fix the relationship. In December of that year, unable to work together, we dissolved what had been a successful business partnership.

In addition to the pain and sorrow I felt, my estrangement with Jane was hard on Bruce. Most days, at the end of his run, he would stop in to visit John and Jane on his way home. That ended. He didn't even call John, fearful that Jane would answer.

Now, on this afternoon, over five years after Jane's eruption, and one day after Bruce's cancer diagnosis, I was not looking forward to seeing her, but our life was changing and our relationship with them would need to change as well. As the perfect summer weather continued to hold court, we walked the half mile to their house, past my parent's house, and past our first house. The old path between our houses was now overgrown but still visible, a reminder of an earlier and happier time. We turned left into their driveway and walked across the lawn to the side entrance that led into the laundry room. Once at the door, I inhaled deeply, trying to relax a stomach that was already tightening. Turning to Bruce, I saw my sense of foreboding mirrored in his face. I took another deep breath and exhaled slowly and audibly, then said, "Here we go."

I knocked, hesitated at first, but then, as was our family's custom, entered without waiting. "Hello," I called out, announcing our arrival. Their traditional cape house had been remodeled to an open floor plan after the fire. We walked through the kitchen area. A dining area, where we used to be welcomed, extended from the far end of the kitchen. At the other end of the kitchen was a fireplace with a couch and built-in cabinets that held framed family photos, photos we had replaced for them from our personal copies after their fire.

Entering the living room, Bruce and I sat next to each other on the first of two white couches positioned at right angles. Jane was sitting on the other one. John pulled up a rocking chair across from us. My body was in a self-protective fight-or-flight mode, as it always had been whenever I was with Jane after her tirade in 2003. On this occasion, I would have happily chosen flight but that was not an option. Bruce, looking and sounding strained, related his symptoms, the tests of the previous days, and the resulting diagnosis, while I quietly sat close to him. Then, uncharacteristically angry and aggressive, Bruce said, "This has got to stop. We've wasted too much time." Still shaken by the news of Bruce's tumor, Jane and John silently nodded agreement.

John cleared his throat, lowered his voice, and leaned forward slightly. "Do you want me to tell anyone?" he asked deliberately. "I can call our sisters."

"I'd rather call them myself," Bruce responded. "But would you tell Beth and Aimée?"

"Sure and let me know if I can do anything else."

Walking up the driveway, Bruce asked, "Do you think anything will change?"

"I don't know. I'm not optimistic," I answered, wishing I could have confidently said yes. Although I hoped for the best, I was skeptical that a relationship that had been broken for years, and whose basis for estrangement seemed to be deep seated, could be completely repaired, even in the face of life-threatening illness.

Arriving home, exhausted both emotionally and physically, we took a short break and then began calling Bruce's sisters. Bruce was the sixth of seven children in an Irish Catholic family whose grandfather emigrated from Ireland in the late 1800s. Bruce called Marion and then Barbara, both of whom lived in Connecticut. Keeping our tag team intact, he broke the news and then I provided the details and answered questions. Other than *I'm so sorry* and *Please let us know what we can do*, there are few words to say at a time like this. Our call to his sister Sandra in California proceeded along the same lines.

The call to Suzanne, who lived in Georgia, was a little harder. She had recently been treated for breast cancer and either the treatment or her advancing age had left her occasionally out of touch. She had never been chatty, but this was an unusually clipped conversation. "I'm sorry to hear. Take care of yourself. I love you. Our prayers are with you," she said. She hung up before we knew what happened.

My brother, George, is five years older than I am, but as a child I played more with him than I did with Jane. He loved sports and there were many times when we had played basketball on the third floor of our barn. Actually, I think he was playing "coach" and I was doing as told, but I loved it. In warm weather, he had "coached" me in softball. For the last twenty-five summers he had hosted a clambake at his house for our family, Jane's family, and his children. At first, the intent had been to celebrate my birthday. As the years went by, it became harder to get us all together for July 26. We had seen him a few weeks earlier at our Celebration of Life party. Although our relationship was good, other than those two annual occasions, and exchanging Christmas cards and the occasional email, we rarely talked. So, it was a bit unusual for me to call him now. Since it was my brother, we dispensed with the tag team and let Bruce have a rest. I informed George about Bruce's diagnosis and assured him we would keep him up to date.

Ready for some relaxation, we put on our bathing suits, grabbed some reading material and headed to the pool. As Bruce swam laps, I tried to read for a while before dinner, but Jane's comment kept replaying in my mind: *We were never close anyway.*

CHAPTER SIX

EARLY RETIREMENT

Sunday morning, August 31, 2008

The day began with our usual Sunday morning routine. After staying in bed long enough to play the puzzle with Will Shortz on NPR's "Weekend Edition," I walked out to get the *Hartford Courant.* I sorted the paper into one pile of ads and newspaper sections that would go straight to recycling, the comics for Bruce, coupons for me, and a shared pile of the remaining newspaper sections. After a quick browse, I took Bruce's breakfast order, offering a well-deserved treat of poached eggs on English muffins.

Bruce had called his business partner, Glenn Chalder, on Saturday, hoping to meet with him. Glenn was a workaholic who loved what he did and was exceptionally talented at it. Bruce had assumed he would be in the office, as he often was on weekends; instead we caught him on his cell phone on the way to do some shopping with his wife, Holly. Without giving a topic, Bruce set a meeting time for 10:00 AM Sunday at their office. I'm sure Glenn thought it a bit strange—it was Labor Day weekend—but he didn't say anything. He probably thought Bruce wanted to talk to him about retiring, which, as it turns out, he did. We left home at 9:45 AM for the six-mile drive, a trip we had made many times but which felt very different this time.

Bruce and Glenn had been friends, colleagues, and business partners for over thirty years. They met in 1977, when Glenn interned for Bruce with the town of Avon. When Bruce left Avon in 1980 to become Town Planner for neighboring Farmington, Glenn was hired as Bruce's replacement. In 1983, Glenn left to work for a real estate development firm and then a consulting company. In 1995, they joined together to form Planimetrics, a land use and planning consulting firm that became a leader in Connecticut. Glenn concentrated on public clients, doing plans and regulations for towns, while Bruce specialized in private clients, helping individuals and companies through the land use approval process. They were professional equals now, but to the younger Glenn, Bruce was a mentor, and to a degree, a father figure. Glenn had become a family friend early on and had known our children from the time they were small.

We pulled into the parking lot, quiet and empty on this Sunday morning. When Bruce and Glenn first formed Planimetrics they were in a small dim and nondescript office. Later, when they added staff, they had moved into this lovely old brownstone building in a bucolic setting among towering scented pines and mature landscaping.

Leaving the parking lot, we walked up the sloping path and entered the double-locked doors. To the left was Glenn's office. To the right was Bruce's office, its walls, bookcases, and desktop filled with professional awards and photos capturing our travels—like one of me posing in front of our hotel in Venice with a backdrop of the Santa Maria della Solute across the Grand Canal, Bruce in Paris in front of a statue of his hero, Winston Churchill, the night-lit Eiffel tower from our hotel balcony. There were photos of his beloved cats and, of course, our granddaughters. Work-in-progress binders filled bookcases, echoing years of Bruce's presence in this room.

Walking through the light-filled common space, we passed the five staff cubicles on the left, a cubicle on the right, a printer/plotter/scanner station, and a kitchen area that also housed the fax and copier. Filling the walls were clever and funny Planimetrics advertising posters that Glenn had designed and framed. Puzzles, games and playthings littered the large common workspace in the middle of the office—a Connecticut version of a Silicon Valley planning firm designed to spark creativity and foster fun.

Entering the conference room at the back of the office, we sat in the nubby beige chairs, positioned with a view of the woodland beyond. Glenn entered with his upbeat and energetic personality, not sensing the timbre of the meeting.

"Hey Bruce. What's up?" Glenn asked as he reached into his brief-case for a pad and pen.

Solemnly, Bruce rose to his feet and opened his arms. "Give me a hug."

Without hesitation, Glenn stood up and wrapped his arms around Bruce. Glenn is well over six feet; Bruce's claim of five feet ten inches may have been true in his younger years, but did not allow for the inch or two he had lost to age. Most times a hug between the two of them would be comical. As they separated, Glenn looked at Bruce warily.

"I've been diagnosed with cancer," Bruce said. With practice Bruce was getting better at getting out the words, but the emotion was still raw each time he said it.

As they cried together, Glenn hugged him in a protective embrace. They shared a sentimental and compassionate side that neither was afraid to show. When they sat down, all three of us dabbed our eyes with tissues that I now carried with me.

"I'm retiring," Bruce said, his voice shaky.

Through tears, Glenn responded, "Just tell me what you need me to do. We'll handle whatever it takes."

We didn't yet know exactly what the treatment would be, but from my cancer we knew there would be an intense focus on medical care for months. After a run-through of clients and outstanding projects that Bruce would need Glenn's help to complete, Bruce committed to pull together all the materials needed so someone could take over for him by the end of the week. Glenn didn't hesitate to step up. We never doubted he would. An abrupt retirement from the successful business they had built was never in the plan, but Bruce had made the decision with clarity and conviction.

"How're you doing?" I asked Bruce, taking a deep breath as we walked down the path to the parking lot.

"I feel like I've been hit by a bus," he replied.

"Me too." Over the last few days I had repeatedly felt the rush of chemicals and hormones released with sustained stress. My muscles ached from all the tension.

"I'm going to change how I approach people," he informed me. "If I don't cry, then maybe they won't cry."

I marveled at his compassion for others and hoped I could follow his example. I was going to try.

CHAPTER SEVEN

NO MORE TEARS

Sunday evening, August 31, 2008

It was time to start telling friends. I went to call the Kidders and the Christophers to invite them for wine and hors d'oeuvres at the pool. Thanks to a combination of my retirement, to a new housing development up the road and some turnover of older houses, we now had developed relationships with new neighbors whom we really enjoyed.

Marty and Becky Kidder moved in next door to us in 2005. I say, "next door," but next door is really not all that close unless we were to build a path through the woods—something we had joked about on more than one occasion. We first met them when Bruce and I, on a walk, had stopped by to introduce ourselves. I had brought a carton of blueberries freshly picked from our bushes and a large slice of Bailey's white chocolate cheesecake, one of my signature desserts. It quickly became clear that we shared a love of food, travel, and grandchildren. Busy schedules kept us from seeing each other on a daily or even weekly basis, but the friendship was always solid, and we enjoyed each other's company whenever we could.

We met Kay and Todd Christopher that same year at the annual neighborhood "block party." Kay and Todd were in their forties when we met; their only child was six. They lived in a new development of large homes called Hoffman Farms. It was a little further up the road on the former site of the original Hoffman farm where, as a child, I had ridden my horse through the woods and meadows.

The first time we invited the Kidders sailing on our boat, Celebration of Life, we also invited the Christophers. The six of us had a raucous time—with lethally delicious frozen Bushwackers, bras on heads (actually, only Kay), straws up noses (more than Kay), and general craziness. We began a supper club, rotating hosting duties. Becky and I are both very good cooks and Todd, who was trained at the Culinary Institute of America, brought our pot luck gatherings to a gourmet level.

When Marty and Becky arrived at 6:00 PM, we were in the kitchen plating the hors d'oeuvres. It was not unusual for us to issue an impromptu invitation for cocktails, so there was no reason for them to think that this was anything but a pool-side evening among friends. After hugs all around, we took the two bottles of wine Bruce had chosen, a terra cotta cooler for the white wine, glasses, and snacks, and headed to the pool.

Following the brick walkway that curved from the house to the pool, Becky and I, both gardeners, couldn't help but pause to admire my kitchen garden. My mother's heirloom irises lined the edge of the house. In front of the speared iris leaves, chives, green onions, garlic chives, lavender, thyme, oregano, basil, and tarragon created an herbal bouquet that supplied my culinary needs. Irish moss, carnations, and white bleeding hearts had worked their best reproductive magic, but couldn't come close to the early spring forget-me-nots. Snowy clematis climbed from the corner of the screened porch over the door, while red Oriental poppies were budding in preparation for their second blooming of the season.

Taking the wide bluestone steps up the berm, we pushed open the hinged gate to enter the pool area, a nature preserve for butterflies, various insects, occasional snakes, and many birds. Rambling blush pink roses, grown from thorny cuttings from my mother's garden, intertwined silver, weathered lengths of a split-rail fence. Surrounding the bluestone pool deck, varieties of tall waving ornamental grasses, yellow

Stella Dora lilies, forsythia, burning bushes, purple coneflowers, and black-eyed Susans attracted beautifully-winged insects and birds and the occasional shy snake or frog.

The generous-sized pool was custom designed, shaped somewhat like a kidney bean, with a Jacuzzi spa at the shallow end nearest the woods. From the spa, we could watch bats dip and dive at twilight, with the backdrop of a western horizon lit with burning oranges and pinks, and later, in the evenings, the arching Big Dipper in the starry night sky.

The four of us took a seat at the wrought iron table under the wisteria-draped pergola. As Bruce poured the wine, we caught up on kids and travel. When Kay arrived, I poured her a glass of wine, we all toasted, and then Bruce dropped the bombshell. This time he didn't cry.

It was getting easier for us—we now had some experience—but we knew that for those on the receiving end it was a terrible shock. They showered us with loving words and offers of help. I would have many occasions over the next months to take them up on their generosity.

We steered the conversation back to more pleasant topics as quickly as we could. Unlike previous experiences when we had told people our bad news, this time nobody left after only a short time. Maybe this was a testament to our understanding of how to help people process the shock. John stopped by unexpectedly, though Jane wasn't with him, and joined us for a glass of wine. It was a beautiful summer evening with just a hint of dusk in the air as the temperature began its gradual descent to the evening coolness. We poured another glass of wine, happy to enjoy the rest of the evening talking about things other than cancer.

Over the rest of the long holiday weekend, exhausted from the emotional conversations with family and friends, we didn't talk a lot about what the future might hold. For now, we were content to live in the moment. We celebrated Labor Day at the pool, reading and working on the *Sunday Times* crossword puzzle that was still waiting for us after a weekend consumed with delivering bad news. I made my much-requested sour cream potato salad recipe, we grilled hot dogs and savored the sweet local butter and sugar corn on the cob, whose season would sadly soon be coming to an end.

There was nothing we could do, and nothing more we would learn, until our appointment with Dr. Abraham the next morning.

CHAPTER EIGHT

TO WHOM IT MAY CONCERN

Tuesday morning, September 2, 2008

In preparation for our appointment, I again Googled *esophageal cancer*. I gathered up my folder with printouts of the explanations and diagrams I had reviewed with Bruce, and a pad for notes, and we made the five-minute drive to Dr. Abraham's office. The waiting room looked exactly as it had for all the years we had been patients of his predecessor. A bit dim, even with the two windows, the chairs were threadbare, and the cushioning worn thin after years of use. A fireplace, from the original New England house that had been converted, was no longer in use but called to mind the physical warmth if not the reality. As a clinical professor of internal medicine at the University of Connecticut and solo practitioner of many years, his small office was a layered accumulation of family photos, current textbooks, and other medical publications.

Dr. Abraham had been our trusted and respected physician for over twenty years, treating our entire family. Knowing all of us gave him context, to treat the whole person, not just a symptom or an illness. Since he'd often had students shadowing him, over the years I had come to appreciate first hand his teaching and mentoring skills. His thorough explanations and conservatively prescribed treatments, coupled with our active involvement in medical decisions complemented our values of knowledge, honesty, and balance. During our long relationship, we had gradually, strand by strand, grayed together (though I was still magically a blond).

We checked in with the receptionist, and after a short wait, his nurse ushered us to his office. Normally, we would first chat about family and upcoming trips to exotic locations, but these were not normal times. Dr. Abraham was the clearinghouse for all tests and results, and as we expected, he was more forthcoming about the situation than Dr. Murray had been. He knew we welcomed honesty and details.

Bruce took the lead. "So, what do you think?" he asked.

"I'd say it's virtually certain you have esophageal cancer." Dr. Abraham's frankness was not harsh, but a relief. Drawing a picture of the stomach and the esophagus, he pointed at the junction and said, "The tumor is right here. If it hasn't metastasized, you'll have surgery."

Then Dr. Abraham patiently and thoroughly described the mechanics of the surgery, the risks associated with it, and the recovery process. I took detailed notes. As it turned out, this would not be an easy operation. The surgeon would remove part of the stomach and esophagus where they joined and then three to four inches of esophagus above the juncture. Risks and side effects were significant and even in the best case there would be a long-term impact on his life.

"The cancer can be cured by surgery half the time. The other half, it can't be cured because cells have spread to the lymph nodes or liver," he solemnly told us. With more optimism in his voice he added, "I have a patient who had this surgery fifteen years ago and is doing fine."

"What happens if it's spread?" Bruce asked. From my cancer, we knew about stages and how staging determines treatment and prognosis.

"Then you could have a less invasive palliative surgery to keep the esophagus open, so you can eat. You'd also probably have chemotherapy and/or radiation therapy."

We also knew about chemo and radiation. I found myself wondering how patients without prior experience and/or access to online information would process all this information and uncertainty.

While we waited, Dr. Abraham called the Hartford-area surgeon most experienced doing this type of procedure and got Bruce an appointment for Friday afternoon. Dr. Murray had already ordered a CAT scan for Thursday morning and the results would be available within twenty-four hours.

I took a deep breath, feeling some relief that we had a plan and were moving quickly. It all felt like an out-of-body experience, as though we were observing some other couple having this discussion with their doctor.

Then Dr. Abraham cautioned us. "Be aware there's a limit to what a CAT scan can pick up. It can detect small masses but not areas where there are only a few cancerous cells. A clean scan will dictate next steps but does not guarantee that the cancer has not spread."

I didn't remember reading that on the internet! Would there always be uncertainty? Would we never be able to rest easy? That must be why survival rates are measured over five years.

Turning to what changes we might have to make to accommodate Bruce's treatment, I asked, "We're scheduled to go to the Grand Canyon in a few weeks and sailing at the end of October. Should I cancel these trips?"

Dr. Abraham smiled—we always had trips planned. "Hopefully, Bruce's surgery will take place quickly. The Grand Canyon is definitely out, But you may still be able to sail as long as Bruce doesn't have to do any heavy lifting."

"Since the Grand Canyon trip is an organized tour, I assume I'll need a letter from you for the organizers to cancel it."

"I'll have one typed up while Bruce is getting his blood work done."

With all our questions answered, I thanked Dr. Abraham for his honesty and thoroughness and Bruce went to have the blood tests that would guide the scan technician in determining the amount of contrast material to use. On the way out, we picked up the travel letter. It was very difficult to read the dire language that Dr. Abraham used in this formal letter to strangers. The written word somehow made our situation real.

To Whom It May Concern:

My patient, Bruce Hoben, has just been found to have an advanced cancer of the esophagus. He will, therefore, be unable to proceed to a planned trip to the Grand Canyon.

Richard Abraham, M.D.

As soon as we got home I read my notes and Bruce let me know where he had a different understanding or had remembered things that I neglected to write down. I put my notes in a Word document, researched the internet to make sure I accurately described medical terminology and procedures, and put it in an email to Sasha and Justin who were waiting for news from Bruce's appointment. The next time we talked, they told me that they found the detailed and timely communication helpful in understanding, without being there, what was happening to their dad. They also appreciated that they could forward the information to friends who knew Bruce and wanted to be kept updated.

My years as a manager, and later as an executive consultant had taught me much; my project management skills would be heavily utilized over the next months. Once again, I was struck by how difficult it would be for someone without my skills and experience to navigate the health-care system, especially if the patient did not have a healthcare advocate. Everyone with a serious illness would benefit from having a project manager. I was proud to be Bruce's and glad I could do something useful for him and the kids.

The monthly meeting of my book club, the Page Turners, was scheduled for the following day. The founding core was a group of women from neighboring towns whose husbands worked for United Technologies. Several lived in the same area of Simsbury; some lived in Farmington. Over time, a few of us without UTC connections were added. Living in Canton, I am the lone geographic outlier.

The Page Turners were all fascinating women, many of whom had lived abroad. Their children now ranged from young teens to college grads, but when the book club first began meeting, several members still needed to be home in time to meet the school bus. As the oldest of the group, and the only grandparent, I was looked up to as the "sage" who had successfully raised her children to middle age. I watched as the younger members each encountered the turns and stages of family life that I had already navigated.

It had been a stable membership of close-knit friends. The range of professions within our group—a lawyer, a master gardener, an English teacher, a librarian, an interior designer with clients in Manhattan and Connecticut, a fashion designer who was featured in *People* in 1987, a mentor for inner-city schoolchildren, a housekeeper, and a few stay-at-home moms involved in many community volunteer activities—made our group interesting. The few who had left the group did so because they moved out of state or out of the country. They remained on our email distribution, enjoying the banter that took place as we planned our books and menus. Cathie, Carol, and Beth occasionally made the trip from Houston, Philadelphia, and Toronto, respectively, to join us for a meeting.

We were all passionate about our families, reading, and cooking. We only saw each other monthly, but fed off each other's unique personalities and experiences, sharing stories and laughter. Most times we met for lunch, but opted for evening soirees at Christmas and during the summer. I always hosted the July gathering, with cocktails at the pool followed by a candle-lit, flower-filled dinner on the screened porch.

When possible, we added extracurricular restaurant luncheons, dinners, or coffees, even an occasional weekend getaway.

We also supported each other through the inevitable crises that happen in all lives: illnesses, the care of aging parents, and the behavior of teenage children who think they're adults. They would be my biggest support group.

September 4, 2008
Subject: Sad News

> *My Book Club Friends,*
>
> *I have gone back and forth on how to break this sad news— send an email in advance or "drop the bomb" at our meeting tomorrow. I've come down on the side of an advance email. Bruce has just been diagnosed with esophageal cancer. He had a CAT scan this morning to see if it has spread but we don't yet have the results. Either way, it is not a good cancer to have (if there is such a thing). We expect that he will have surgery as soon as it can be scheduled, hopefully next week. It still doesn't seem real but I'm sure it will once things start moving.*
>
> *I am planning to come to book club tomorrow, but will be leaving at about 12:30 for an appointment with the surgeon. I will certainly welcome your support and good wishes, but I hope you/we can also enjoy the good food, insightful discussion, and, of course, warm friendship that makes these monthly meetings so special to me. We are hopeful—he's a strong and positive man!*
>
> *See you tomorrow.*

By the end of the day, Dr. Abraham called to tell us the CAT scan had shown no evidence of a spread of the cancer to sites outside of the original tumor. He cautioned us again that it was not a guarantee that there would be no cancer elsewhere in the future since a small number of cells might be lurking somewhere, but it made survival much more likely. I emailed my second update of the day with the good news.

Even though Bruce and I had a full dance card, including the surgical consult that afternoon, we agreed it was important for me to not miss book club. It was great to see everyone, if only for a brief visit, and I was glad that I had sent the note in advance. Through the ages, from childbirth to death, women have circled around their own to support their sisters in times of need and tragedy. Now, in this tradition, I received comforting hugs and words of support and we were able to get on with the business at hand: lunch and *The Space Between Us* by Thrity Umrigar.

CHAPTER NINE

THE PROGNOSIS IS NOT GOOD

Friday afternoon, September 5, 2008

The receptionist greeted us, and I gave her the CD with Bruce's CAT scan. With its muted rose walls, nondescript artwork, and spare modern furniture lining the perimeter, I could have been in any of the many doctors' waiting rooms I've visited. We were the only ones there. Perhaps that was typical for this type of surgery or maybe scheduling was light on Friday afternoons. I was just glad Dr. Abraham had gotten us in on short notice.

After completing the obligatory paperwork, we were led to an examining room. Dr. Piorkowski appeared shortly. He was about the same age as us, perhaps a few years younger. His graying, sandy blond hair framed a long face that tapered at the chin. In his blue scrubs and tan, rimmed glasses, he looked very professional but not formal or stiff. Bruce and I were both comfortable with doctors, and for that matter, people in general. Like my mother, I often strike up conversations with strangers. And we'd had at least our share of interactions with medical professionals.

Bruce hopped up on the examining table without benefit of the step stool. Dr. Piorkowski took Bruce's medical history and did a physical exam.

"You're young, fit, and otherwise healthy—not the typical patient we see with this diagnosis," he said with a smile. "I haven't gotten the pathology report yet, but based on the CAT scan I feel surgery will be the best treatment plan."

Dr. Piorkowski explained the surgery and drew a picture of the anatomy involved, including where a feeding tube would be inserted if necessary. The image of Bruce with a feeding tube brought me back to the endoscopy a week earlier and our short wait in the reception area. We had overheard a doctor describing how the patient's esophagus would have to be opened again to make him comfortable and able to eat. Bruce and I felt bad for the patient, a little nervous that this could be in Bruce's future, and surprised that such a discussion would be had in public. Little did we know.

Dr. Piorkowski continued, "Some good news . . . The location of Bruce's tumor is the best place to have it." I was on alert. When someone begins with the good news, it usually means there's bad news coming. "Although the first scan was clear, it was only of the pelvis and abdomen. This type of cancer is aggressive, so we need a second CAT scan, this one of the chest, and a PET scan to see if it has spread."

"What do you think about a second opinion?" I felt a little hesitant asking, not wanting to insult him, but my niece Beth had just told us about a friend who survived stage 3 esophageal cancer after being treated at MD Anderson.

Dr. Piorkowski was not at all defensive. "The two premier cancer hospitals in the United States are Sloan Kettering in New York and MD Anderson in Texas. They're both fine hospitals. You just need to be aware that if you're treated there, you're not guaranteed of getting a top surgeon at either location." That made sense. I was lumping together all the doctors in a premier cancer center as being premier surgeons, but of course some would be less experienced and/or less skilled. Another lesson learned in this grim tutorial.

We opted not to explore other hospitals, at least for now. Dr. Piorkowski had spent several years doing surgery at MD Anderson, and his partner Dr. Jimenez, who would be the one doing the surgery, had worked in surgical oncology at Sloan Kettering. We left confident and fortunate that we had the best surgeons.

Arriving home, buoyed by confidence in our surgeons, we saw the message light on the home phone blinking red. "You have two new messages," the computerized voice informed me.

2:21 PM.

This is Dr. Murray. The pathology report was not what I was expecting. It shows you have a neuroendocrine tumor which does not usually arise in the esophagus or stomach. I've consulted with an oncologist who feels that surgery is not the best way to treat this type of tumor. Chemo and radiation are the best way to go. Give me a call if you want to discuss this.

We had just left a doctor who was moving forward on the path to surgery. No one had mentioned it depended on whether it was a neuroendocrine tumor. I retrieved the next message.

2:41 PM.

Dr. Murray again. I just spoke with Dr. Piorkowski. We discussed the biopsy at some length and I agree with what Dr. Piorkowski is considering. If the tumor is not neuroendocrine then there is no question that surgery is the best way to go. The pathology report did contain some language about the limitations of having "suboptimal material" and Dr. Piorkowski feels it's still possible he may find a squamous cell carcinoma or an adenocarcinoma when he operates. The chest CAT scan and PET scan will help clarify. I'll do another biopsy if needed.

We looked at each other, confused. *What is suboptimal material? How will they determine what type it is? Why does it matter?* This was clearly not as simple as my cancer diagnosis where there had been no disagreement over type of cancer or recommended treatment.

I greatly appreciated the amount and timeliness of communication, both between our doctors and with us, and I was glad the doctors reached an agreement, but there was a lot of complex information that we didn't yet understand. Although I wanted to know all the gory details as they unfolded, the mathematical analyst in me would have preferred a more precise process with unambiguous results. Welcome to the real world. We'd be seeing Dr. Piorkowski in a few days and would get a better understanding.

We then did our standard debrief with one another and our support community. I compared notes with Bruce, augmented them with internet research, and documented the results. I sent an email to my "Bruce's Medical Update" distribution list, which now included our extended family, the Page Turners, and my friends from the gym.

We needed to absorb a huge volume of complex information to make good decisions, but I knew not everyone would be interested in all the details. I introduced a five-sentence executive summary and followed it with two pages of detail, complete with embedded links, for those who wanted to know everything. At a minimum, I knew that would include our children.

I felt useful researching and documenting Bruce's situation as it unfolded, both for our understanding and discussion and to keep family and friends updated with timely consistent information. Even with my professional knowledge of healthcare and my personal experience with cancer diagnosis, prognosis, and treatment, it felt overwhelming. I wondered how those without my background and access to technology could understand their options well enough to make informed treatment decisions.

We were surprised and grateful for the responsiveness of our medical system and the quality of the team that was being put together to support us. Bruce's second CAT scan on Monday morning in Avon was uneventful except that the contrast material caused an allergic reaction resulting in a rash and itching. We left the lab with a CD of the results to take with us for our appointment with Dr. Piorkowski the next day.

The PET scan was that afternoon in Hartford. Surprisingly, we enjoyed our conversation with our radiology technician, talking about everything except cancer. We could have been at a cocktail party, minus the wine. Actually, wine would have been quite welcome! Bruce was getting to be a pro. Our attitude towards the tests made the drill seem routine. It was just part of the process required to determine what our future might hold.

The following morning, we were back at Dr. Piorkowski's office for our second surgical appointment, this time with Dr. Jimenez, who appeared to be about our son's age. When did we get to be so old?

After briefly examining Bruce, Dr. Jimenez told us, "I've personally looked at the biopsy material with the pathologist, and agree with the diagnosis of a neuroendocrine tumor."

I was glad to hear there was consensus, but since the first CAT scan indicated the cancer hadn't spread, we weren't too concerned about what type of tumor Bruce had. We went into an adjoining room with several computers and a large light box where Dr. Piorkowski joined us. As Dr. Jimenez led us through the pictures from the second CAT scan and the PET scan, a very different and disturbing picture arose.

"We can see here the tumor in the esophagus," Dr. Jimenez showed us, pointing to the screen on the right. Though I didn't know the significance of it, I found it interesting to be looking at Bruce's innards.

"Unfortunately, the scan done last week didn't use the right contrast material that would have let us distinguish normal from abnormal conditions, so we were more optimistic than was warranted," he added. I bristled at the sentence that started with *unfortunately*. "We see, on this scan," he said, pointing to the screen on the left, "that there is also significant disease in the lymph nodes around the stomach, at the primary tumor site, and at least four nodules on Bruce's liver."

Dr. Jimenez pointed to each of the spots on the liver as Bruce and I sat in stunned silence. It was one thing to try to decipher the text of pathology or scan report. It was quite another to be looking at actual tumors on Bruce's organs, visualizing cancer cells spreading through his body, and reacting to the growing fear of what that meant. We looked at each other, like deer in the headlights.

"Given that removal of the tumor would not slow the spread of the cancer, Bruce is no longer a candidate for surgery." The treatment we had been hoping would give Bruce a 50 percent chance of being cured was now off the table.

"However, the lungs are clear, and it is good news that the PET scan didn't light up in the liver the way it did in the esophagus and lymph nodes."

A thin ray of hope.

"I want you to get a biopsy of the liver nodules."

"What if the liver is cancerous?" Bruce asked.

"Then treatment is chemotherapy only. You could survive for years with alternating chemo and rest cycles, but cannot be fully cured."

Sitting next to each other, I put my hand on Bruce's leg. I could feel the current of tension flowing between our bodies. I sensed they were being more optimistic than realistic, but I grasped at any anchor to hold on to.

We came into this room full of optimism. Now the future was looking bleak. Where had the contrast CAT scan order and/or execution gone astray? Many people would have reacted differently to this error, which had given us false hope and then dropped a bomb, but we knew it was not a good use of our time and energy to worry about something that was past, and over which we had no control. I had learned a valuable lesson about acceptance years earlier: I cannot change someone else's behavior; I can only change my reaction to it.

Having been raised in a family where being on time was valued and expected, it used to annoy me that Bruce, raised with no concept of timeliness, was habitually late. Once I decided that when Bruce and I were going out together, I would wait and not get ready until Bruce's preparation was well under way, and I coupled that behavior with a change in my irrational belief that I alone would be judged irresponsible if we, as a couple, were late, our issues disappeared. That approach to conflict was sorely tested during my tumultuous relationship with my sister, but being angry made me feel terrible and had no impact on the target of my anger. I also found it helpful to keep this perspective when confronting life's tendency not to play fair, such as when I got cancer.

Now, knowing we couldn't change Bruce's diagnosis, we would have to focus all our energies on how we responded to it. We still had age, health and an indomitable spirit on our side. We had already learned the value of celebrating life every day and were accomplished practitioners. At home I sent out my second update that day.

CHAPTER TEN

THE CALM BEFORE THE STORM

Thursday, September 11, 2008

After two draining weeks on an intense roller coaster, we needed to rest and reflect. Block Island fit the bill. September found the island surrounded by the summer-warmed Atlantic Ocean but vacated by the clamoring seasonal crowds. The hotels and restaurants remained open, hoping to catch the last customers before closing for the winter. We first went to Block Island together for the twenty-fifth anniversary party of Bruce's niece and her husband in April 2000. We biked in the salt air, exploring the small island from end to end, and enjoyed sunset cocktails and dinners with family. Later, when we returned in September 2007, we stayed at a charming cozy New England bed and breakfast and we knew this would become a regular destination for us.

With a forecast for the next few days to be sunny and bright, we drove to Rhode Island, parked our car and boarded the Block Island Ferry for the windy trip across Long Island Sound. We had stayed at the same B&B in the same room as the previous year. It was a restful haven with no TV, no phones, and no news, giving it the kind of serenity that can emerge only when electronics are not present. The backyard of the inn, edged with tall blue hydrangeas, overlooked a marsh of velvety cattails and out to the expanse of ocean. Hawks and peregrine falcons soared overhead as warblers, flickers, catbirds, and scarlet tanagers darted among the reeds and shrubs. We sat out back at sunset, sipping wine and nibbling on nuts, sometimes reading, sometimes chatting with other guests. In an unspoken agreement, we did not talk about the tests or the possible prognoses. We had learned through experience that we can't ever know what's going to happen or when. Worrying about it is a waste of precious time. We breathed in the salty ocean air and celebrated life in the moment.

For dinner, we took a short walk up the hill to the Spring House, the grand Victoria-era hotel where we had attended my niece's anniversary party. Our food was scrumptious, the candlelit tables romantic. The dining room was quiet with very few other guests, so there were no distractions but our own thoughts. Bruce was having some discomfort swallowing but still managed to enjoy his meal, or at least made me believe he was enjoying his meal. We would normally exchange blow-by-blow commentary, critiquing the courses and wines as we sampled each other's choices. This time, however, there was noticeably less of that. I put my hand on Bruce's and we quietly smiled at each other.

Morning brought an al fresco breakfast of fresh fruit, warm muffins, and rich coffee followed by a walk down the hill to Ballard's Beach. During the high season, the Ballard's Inn hosts live music and a rowdy bar scene, but this time of year the main attraction was the nearly deserted white sandy beach. We relaxed on the beach, walked a little bit, picking up interesting shells and stones for our expanding collection, and enjoyed a sundrenched seafood lunch on their deck. Pretty much a perfect day.

Monday morning, it was back to reality as we arrived at Hartford Hospital for Bruce's liver biopsy. I continued to be impressed by and grateful for the efficiency and humanity of our care providers. After checking in and answering a few questions, Bruce changed into the wrinkled and softly worn hospital robe, while I settled into the guest chair with my tote of papers. Various staff came in and out, performing their individual duties in the overall process. After the doctor explained how the biopsy would be done, I gently kissed Bruce on the forehead and he was wheeled away.

Because we were told it was a quick procedure, I stayed in my chair and read. I began to get concerned as the time lengthened. When Bruce was finally wheeled back, I learned the biopsy was harder than expected but that he had tolerated it well and was doing fine. They wanted him to rest for a while to make sure he did not experience any bleeding or dizziness. They offered to bring us sandwiches. Bruce did get one, but I opted to stretch my legs and walk to the cafeteria to pick up something better.

By now, we'd been to Hartford Hospital enough that I knew my way around. It felt strangely comfortable to navigate. Bruce never felt that ease, spending his time in treatment rooms and waiting rooms. Away from Bruce, I could almost forget why I was there. I felt a certain sense of accomplishment that comes with learning the layout of a new place and feeling like you belong, even if this was a place I didn't want to belong.

Next day, the pathology report came back: *Metastatic high-grade tumor.*

Bruce was stage 4, no longer a candidate for curative surgery or radiation. I thought back to my first research into esophageal cancer just eighteen days earlier.

Patients with distant metastases (who are not candidates for curative surgery) have a less than 3 percent five-year survival rate.

Well, someone's got to be in that 3 percent who survive. It could be Bruce.

CHAPTER ELEVEN

DECISIONS, DECISIONS

Tuesday, September 16, 2008

Dr. Nerenstone gave a quick knock and entered the examining room. With straight, sandy brown hair parted in the middle and flowing down her back, in a different setting and another era she could have passed for a hippie. But in her white coat, laptop under her arm, and with her self-assured demeanor, it was easy to believe she was a nationally recognized expert in ovarian and breast cancers. A trim woman, she had delicate features, kind eyes, and a smile that belied her fierce intellect and passion for advancing cancer treatments. Now in her early fifties, with five children, she looked much younger.

Dr. Kern, my surgeon during my breast cancer, had recommended her, telling me that she was not only a great medical oncologist but also a good match for my personality. He was absolutely right on both counts, and over the eight years since my diagnosis and surgery, we had developed a close relationship with her and her amazing team of oncology nurses. As Dr. Nerenstone examined my breasts, the three of us would chat about medical and nonmedical topics, Bruce just as likely to ask a question as me.

Dr. Nerenstone smiled in greeting as she set her laptop down. "You're looking well. How are you feeling?"

"I'm doing fine," I replied, my normal enthusiasm muted a bit, but not enough for her to take notice.

As Dr. Nerenstone conducted her exam we talked about family and travel plans. Eight years out, with no cancer recurrence, this was just a routine annual checkup.

"Any problems with the Femara?" she asked as she scanned my file on her laptop.

"No problems. I'll just be happy to be done with it."

Three years earlier, when I had been near the end of the recommended five years' daily dose of Tamoxifen, the proscribed treatment had been changed to include taking Femara for five years. I had two years left and my ten-year treatment, along with the daily reminder that I still lived under the cloud of cancer, would be done.

"Then we'll stay with the same dosage and I'll see you in a year," Dr. Nerenstone said as she handed me a new prescription and began to pack up her laptop.

"Actually, we'll be seeing you sooner." I paused. "Bruce has been diagnosed with neuroendocrine cancer and we want you to be his oncologist."

Setting her laptop back down and shifting her gaze to Bruce then back to me, her reply was slow in coming. "I'm so sorry to hear that." She paused and looked at us both and spoke slowly. "But the slow-growing type can be treated fairly well."

I took a deep breath. "Unfortunately, Bruce has the fast-growing variety."

Her countenance changed. I gave her a synopsis of all the tests and diagnoses.

"I'm afraid I'm going on vacation, so I won't be available to see you until October seventh," she told Bruce, "and time is of the essence." How often do we hear that? How often does it really apply to life and death? Could this be one of those times?

"I really don't want you to wait until then to start treatment." Her gaze scanned from Bruce to me and back again. "My partner, Jeff Baker, is excellent and he sees more of these cancers than I do. He could see you next week and then, if you want, you can continue with him or have me take over."

Bruce didn't hesitate. We knew that a three-week delay was not acceptable, especially with a fast-growing cancer. "I'm sure Dr. Baker is great. I'll start with him, but I already know I'd like you to treat me."

"That's fine. I can take over when I get back."

Comfortable that Bruce would be treated by a trusted doctor who knew us well, we left her office feeling hopeful.

The following Monday afternoon, we were back at the same offices for Bruce's appointment with Dr. Baker. After stopping in the lab for routine blood work, we were shown to an examining room that was almost identical to Dr. Nerenstone's. Windows looked out on a meditation garden. After a short wait, we heard the noise of rustling papers on the other side of the closed office door, followed by a click and the turn of the doorknob.

"Hi. Jeff Baker," he extended his hand. His longish face was framed by wavy brown hair parted on the side. In his late forties, his youthful appearance was not diminished by the emergence of a few gray hairs at the sides. I liked his energy. He was, as it turned out, the next-door neighbor and good friend of my book club friend, Alex, who had already confirmed he was brilliant and an all-around good guy. All characteristics normally considered when sizing up a date, but over time I had begun to see that many qualities are as important for medical relationships as for romantic ones.

"Hi, Dr. Baker. Nice to meet you," Bruce responded as he stood up and they shook hands.

"I understand you have a history with Stacy, but you want to begin treatment before she's back from vacation."

"That's right, but we're planning to transfer to her care when she gets back," Bruce replied. Starting our relationship by announcing our plan to transfer care could have been awkward, but he was fine with it.

"High-grade neuroendocrine tumors are aggressive cancers, so we'll use aggressive treatment."

I took notes as Dr. Baker described the current "gold standard" for treating neuroendocrine cancer. During the diagnosis debate in early September, I hadn't been concerned about the difference between neuroendocrine and esophageal cancers, but we now knew that it mattered.

"The good news is that neuroendocrine tumors are more responsive to chemo than other cancers," Dr. Baker continued.

"That's encouraging." We glanced at each other with cautious optimism.

"Sometimes, but not often, the chemo will cause a complete remission." I squeezed Bruce's hand as I allowed myself a little smile.

"What happens if it doesn't?" Bruce asked.

"We can try a second line of treatment, probably using other drugs."

I wasn't encouraged by his answer. If we were to begin with the drugs proven to be the most effective, it was hard to believe that a second line of treatment would succeed where the first had failed. I reminded myself there was no reason to anticipate the worst when I could hope for the best.

"I want you to have a brain MRI tomorrow." Noticing our surprised and apprehensive look, Dr. Baker quickly added, "It's standard for this type of cancer and is used for staging to see if the cancer has metastasized to the brain."

Standard? This was the first we'd heard about the possibility of metastasis to the brain. I didn't even want to ask what that would mean. Bruce was already Stage IV based on the known metastases to the lymph nodes and liver. I knew he could handle the corporeal part, but cancer in the brain, impacting his thinking and feeling? That was a much more frightening prospect for both of us. As I began to understand the implications of Bruce's late-stage cancer, I was unprepared for the growing trepidation about our future.

"Because the type of cancer is so rare, I think it's a good idea to contact a national cancer center for a second opinion on the chemotherapy regimen," Dr. Baker advised.

"As a matter of fact, I've already been in touch with MD Anderson in Houston. A friend of my niece credits them with saving his life after he was diagnosed with Stage III esophageal cancer."

I relayed to Dr. Baker what we had learned during the previous week. Unfortunately, my experience dealing with MD Anderson had been stressful rather than encouraging. They did not do second opinions, only treatment, and it would be seven to fourteen business days before a doctor would be able to review Bruce's file. They wouldn't discuss treatment options over the phone, so we'd have to fly down just to hear if what they would offer was any different than what we'd get locally. Looking at it objectively, I could understand their rationale for being so restrictive, but on a personal level it was putting us in the terrible position of having to decide if we should delay three weeks just to hear about treatment options, with no way of knowing if it would improve Bruce's prognosis.

Now, sitting in Dr. Baker's office, it had come down to us making a life-or-death decision with incomplete information. And what if we chose wrong? How would we even know what would have happened had we chosen a different path? There was consensus, including from MD Anderson, that the treatment for stage 4 esophageal cancer is chemotherapy only, and that there is a gold standard of drugs that any good oncologist would administer. We knew Bruce should start chemo ASAP, but that choice would eliminate MD Anderson as an option. *Time is of the essence.* Bruce opted to start treatment, thereby shutting the door to MD Anderson.

"I'll schedule you for chemo next Monday, if that's OK."

Hearing this, Bruce looked at me and nodded.

I felt a huge weight lifted from my heart. There was no turning back on the treatment decision. There was no turning back on anything. We'd never return to the blissful ignorance of that warm summer day five weeks earlier when we had celebrated life with friends and family.

The email updates were now going to an ever-expanding distribution list. A happy byproduct of our open and honest communication was that friends and family made an effort to reach out, whether in person or electronically. My email traffic was definitely picking up with outpourings of love and support. That evening Bruce added his own personal message to my update.

P.S. I feel fine, I am eating well, can't find a glass of wine that isn't worth drinking, and my daily increase in chocolate consumption is astounding. I am deeply touched by the support I am getting from all of you.

Love,
Bruce

CHAPTER TWELVE

LET THE POISON BEGIN

Monday morning, September 29, 2008

"You could still get a second opinion if you want. Dana Farber and Sarah Cannon, and I'm sure other national cancer centers, would be happy to see you," Dr. Baker told Bruce. "Since there are no clinical trials, and the protocol used elsewhere is the same one you'll get here, it would be mainly for peace of mind."

Peace of mind was feeling very elusive right about now. If peace of mind meant freedom from worries or an absence of stress and anxiety, it was hard for me to imagine anything like that until Bruce had successfully completed treatment. If, however, peace of mind was being comfortable with "what is," then that was attainable, albeit in fits and starts. We'd had plenty of practice being comfortable, and even celebrating life, as it is.

"I'll do chemo here," Bruce told Dr. Baker, making the decision official.

"Any more questions before we get started?"

"I'm a runner. Can I exercise?" As a diehard runner, being deprived of the endorphin-fueled runner's highs would be a blow to Bruce.

"Exercise is good. You'll know what's right for your body."

"Can he hot tub?" Even though we were nearing the end of the pool season, an early evening soak was a treasured part of our daily ritual, and I wanted to hold on to as many of our daily rituals and pleasures as I could.

"Once you start the chemo, you shouldn't hot tub. You'll need to be extra careful about the impact of germs on a suppressed immune system." I remembered when, in the middle of my chemotherapy, I had worn a surgical mask on our flight to Portland for the wedding of our niece Beth.

"What about wine? Susie couldn't have wine while she was on chemo."

"Wine in moderation is fine. One glass a day, but not during the days you're actually having the chemo treatment. . . . Anything else?"

We turned to each other, silently questioning if there remained more to ask. After signaling to each other that we were ready to begin this new chapter, Bruce looked back to Dr. Baker. "Nope. Let's get started."

Entering the treatment room down the hall from Dr. Baker's office, Bruce chose the first recliner he saw. His view, through a wall-length expanse of windows, was of the meditation garden, with its pergola and cedar benches, and the surrounding flowers, shrubs, and trees still lush on this late summer morning. Below the windows, a desk held well-worn books donated by previous occupants and extra pillows meant to keep patients and visitors comfortable during the four hours it took for treatment.

On the wall to the left, an organized and functional countertop was framed top and bottom by cream-colored cabinets on which nurses had taped the artwork of children who wished the temporary residents good luck. In the corner, a lone, leggy schefflera plant sent an anemic eight-foot branch toward the window on the opposite wall, calling out to me to cut it back and move it across the room into the bright light; it was testing my self-control as a gardener who has been known to weed public plantings. The light mauve walls, hung with large, framed floral prints, attempted to fulfill the presumed design objective of a neutral yet soothing décor.

Despite the room being long and narrow, and lacking individual privacy curtains, the just-opened facility had managed to create the most inviting space possible for the delivery of toxic chemicals.

I scanned the room for a comfortable place to sit, but only found a round blue backless stool on wheels, a drab green cushioned chair with chrome legs and armrests, and a decidedly uncomfortable armless purple plastic chair. Since Bruce was the only patient, and my relationship with these nurses went back eight years, with their consent I made myself comfortable in the plush dark brown recliner next to Bruce.

I couldn't help thinking back to 2000, when we had nervously arrived for my first chemo treatment with Dr. Nerenstone. After completing my mandatory lab work, her oncology nurse, Helen, had led me to the larger of two treatment rooms where I took the first recliner, a piece of furniture I would never allow in my home, but I had to admit looked really inviting and was perfect for its intended purpose. Helen moved at a crisp pace, but not hurriedly. Her voice was calming, her demeanor upbeat. She put a pillow under my arm, cushioning the bones and skin that would need to be held still for several hours. She tightened the blue elastic band around my bicep and put a warm compress on my hand, deftly encouraging the vein to swell and make itself accessible. I barely felt it when she inserted the needle. The fluid felt ice cold as it entered my vein and burned for a minute or two. She had warned me, but I hadn't been ready.

After the initial jolt, there was no pain and I calmly spent the next several hours just doing what had to be done, sitting still as I alternated between reading and chatting with Bruce. It had been hard on him to watch me in the recliner, poison being forced into my veins and carried throughout my body. For years after, he cried every time the subject of my chemo came up. Nevertheless, he was faithfully by my side at all appointments.

Now, eight years later, Bruce and I had traded places. I sat by Bruce's side as he began his own journey, the first day of his first chemo cycle and the rest of his life.

Bruce had already made himself comfortable in his recliner when the oncology nurse who tended Dr. Baker's patients checked in before going to the supply room. On his lap rested an extra-large fluffy feather pillow covered in a crisp white pillowcase, a pillow that I coveted for our bed at home. She set him up with another pillow under his arm and a blanket in case he got cold. Returning from the supply room she hung a bag of saline and a bag of Bruce's chemotherapy cocktail on a pole with a drip chamber that would control the flow of delivery while preventing air from entering the blood stream. Having been at my side and witnessing all my chemo treatments, Bruce knew exactly what to expect though he hadn't experienced first-hand how skilled oncology nurses are at painlessly inserting a needle. After rubbing the palm of her hand back and forth on the top of his hand to warm the veins, she turned her hand over and used her knuckles to gently strike his veins, coaxing them to rise. She deftly inserted the needle, secured it in place with tape, and started the flow of steroid-infused saline.

Once Bruce was settled, I inspected their large, diverse selection of reading material and made myself comfortable with the latest *People*, a guilty pleasure that I reserved for doctor's offices and nail salons. Bruce lifted the tote bag we had brought from home and took out Sue Grafton's *T Is for Trespass*, opening it to his bookmarked page. Quickly exhausting the supply of trashy magazines, I retrieved my current book club selection, Erik Larson's *The Devil in the White City*, from the bag. We repeated that pattern for two more days.

***

By the end of the three-day cycle, Bruce was pretty worn out. But on Friday morning, after just a day of rest, we started the six-hour drive to Justin's house in Silver Spring, Maryland. Over the previous month, we had talked with Justin often, but this would be the first time we would see him in person since Bruce's diagnosis. On previous trips, although I always offered to take a turn each time we made a rest stop, Bruce loved to drive and would not always accept. This time, we stopped every two hours and swapped driver/passenger roles.

We arrived at Justin's house at 3:30 PM. Kylie was still at work, but Justin and Ruby had just gotten home from school and Ruby was playing soccer in the street, her tall, lanky frame and long legs already showing the budding muscles of an athlete. Ruby had been playing soccer from the age of three, coached by Austin, the boy next door. When she saw our car, she stopped mid-kick and started to run towards us, her strawberry-blond ponytail bouncing with each stride.

"Wait for them to park, Ruby," Justin loudly cautioned from his wicker chair on the front porch. Looking toward her dad, she silently froze in place.

As Bruce emerged from the driver's side, she joyously flung herself at him. "Hi, Pa," she said, using the moniker she had coined as a toddler, presumably a shortening of Grandpa, that would be used by all future grandchildren. She ran full force at Bruce who scooped her up in his arms and held her tightly. By the time she wriggled down and headed for the passenger side to hug me, Justin had walked from the porch to the curb.

"Hey, how's it going?" Justin's tall, lanky frame engulfed Bruce, holding the embrace longer than usual.

"Good," Bruce responded, beaming. "How about you guys?"

"We're good. Ruby's enjoying kindergarten. I'm busy with teaching and schoolwork, but we're doing well." He was working on prerequisites for a two-year master's degree in special education at Johns Hopkins University. After helping us carry our bags inside, including the cooler of food that we always brought, the four of us went back outside so Ruby could rejoin her soccer buddies.

I was fifty-seven when Ruby was born in 2003. I hadn't thought of myself as old enough to be a grandmother, but once Ruby entered our lives I was besotted. As much as I had loved being a mother, I now had a fresh and glorious perspective on infants and toddlers. I actively observed and noted every new concept and ability Ruby acquired, marveling at her brilliance. When Sasha became a mother in 2007, we stepped up our visits to Nashville, astonished at our good fortune to have two totally different yet equally fascinating granddaughters. Now, we had an additional motivation to spend as much time with them as we could. Fortunately, retirement allowed this.

When Ruby was born, her parents had already started looking for a place to live, but their search to find a suitable apartment that would take Miko, their ninety-pound lab/shepherd mix had proved difficult. So, we bought a house in Silver Spring, an 832-square-foot, three-bedroom, one-bath ranch, that we rented to them at cost. When that house got too small for a toddler, a large dog, and grandparents, we found a larger one a few blocks away. This new house had three good-sized bedrooms, two baths, a living room, and a large sky-lit family room.

Our visits were always fun-filled. But this one, the first time we'd seen each other since Bruce's diagnosis, was especially sweet. On the Friday we arrived, after grilling hot dogs for Bruce and me, and "not dogs" for Justin and his vegetarian family, we visited Ruby during her bath. I then read her a book and Bruce told stories from his childhood, stories that Ruby begged for every time even though she could recite them verbatim by now.

With Ruby tucked in, Justin and Kylie joined us in the family room. We had talked often and kept Justin updated on medical issues so there was no reason to have long conversations about that, but we were uncertain about Ruby.

"What have you told Ruby?" Bruce asked Justin, feeling no need to clarify the subject.

"We told her you were sick, but not how serious it is."

"That makes sense. She's probably too young to understand, and why frighten her if we don't need to?" Bruce said, reassuring Justin.

After the long day of travel, we retired early, read for a little while, and drifted off to sleep in each other's arms.

In the morning, Ruby knocked on our bedroom door, as instructed by her parents, and upon hearing a joyful chorus of *"Come in,"* she pushed open the door and leapt on our bed, snuggling in between us as we put our arms around her and each other.

"Good morning, sweetheart," Bruce told her, beginning our morning ritual.

Ruby turned to me. "He called me *sweetheart.*"

Playing along, I answered, "Do you know why?"

"Because he loves me!" she enthusiastically and loudly responded.

We laughed and snuggled some more.

That morning, we went to Ruby's soccer game. They start young in the sports-obsessed Washington, D.C., metro area. At the age of five, Ruby's games more closely resembled a pack of young girls moving as a unit, often sidetracked by giggles and chatter, than a serious game that justified the uniforms and referees. She loved it and her individual abilities had been well honed through street soccer.

Later, as Bruce relaxed on the deck and Ruby played in the back yard, I got the gardening gloves and pruning shears that I kept in their shed. I border on being a compulsive gardener. It's the perfect activity to soothe my Yankee work ethic (inherited from my mother), my passion for being outside, and my artistic sensibilities. It was also a calming way to deal with the stress of the current situation, especially beneficial for the times I didn't have access to yoga.

I had been extolling the physical and emotional benefits of yoga for six years. I hadn't liked yoga when I first tried it, but when retirement afforded me the time and luxury to work out daily, I gave it another shot, augmenting my spinning and body bar classes. Once I found the right yoga teachers, I discovered that its benefits went far beyond improved flexibility.

I doubt that I am alone in this, but I often feel that my mind goes a million miles an hour 24/7. For me, yoga, especially the aptly named corpse pose, slows down the mental loops of frustration, regret, anger, fear, and more mundanely, my current to-do list. The relaxation effect is so complete that, unlike any other time in my day, I feel I could lie quietly forever, without moving a muscle.

Through yoga I had also developed more compassion for myself and others by taking the invaluable lessons I learned on the mat to my world off the mat.

Live in the present. Be grateful for what your body can do today; not what it could do yesterday or what it will be able to do tomorrow. It is easier to achieve a pose if you ease into it rather than try to force your way into it. Whatever your expression of a pose looks like, it is exactly right.

***

On Tuesday we were back at Dr. Nerenstone's offices for Bruce's first weekly post-infusion checkup. As soon as Dr. Nerenstone entered the examining room, Bruce couldn't wait to share his good news. His symptoms were gone! He could eat! Dr. Nerenstone was delighted. We were exhilarated, surprised by how quickly his body had responded to treatment. Surely this was an omen of (good) things to come. That evening, I added more people to the distribution list—neighbors, nieces, nephews—and sent out the latest update. We were celebrating life and basking in the kind words, thoughts, and prayers of friends and family.

Amid all the hopeful medical news and joyful visits with loved ones, we carved out time to complete some critically important business. We had done wills after our children were born, but we had first gotten serious about estate planning, living wills, and health-care directives after my cancer and heart surgery in 2000. Now, with the need for good end-of-life planning once again in the forefront, we met with our lawyer to make sure everything still reflected our desires. We updated our wills for the addition of grandchildren and gave each other a general power of attorney to make financial and personal decisions on the other's behalf.

Bruce's mother died when he was seventeen. Hospitalized due to a fall down the stairs at home, she died shortly after, not from the fall, but from cirrhosis of the liver. A decade later, despite attempts by firemen to revive them with mouth-to-mouth resuscitation, Bruce's father and stepmother died of smoke inhalation in a late-night fire that swept their apartment. The tragic nature of their deaths made their end-of-life wishes a moot point, but I was aware that their sudden deaths had sadly cut off the opportunity for closure of outstanding family issues.

Having watched my father suffer needlessly at the end, we made sure our living wills clearly documented our desires. In the nine months preceding his death from emphysema, my father had endured four hospital stays and three nursing home stays. It was heart-wrenching to see the vibrant, gregarious, and generous man, who had taught my mother to dance, literally and figuratively, and who had danced with me on many happy occasions from the time I was a child, wasting away and fearful that he would stop breathing.

During his hospital stays, in addition to the pills, IVs, x-rays, and EKGs, each day he underwent multiple nebulizer treatments to temporarily clear his lungs. On at least one occasion, there were nine treatments in one day. On the day he died, my mother, my sister Jane, and I were visiting him when the nebulizer therapist entered the room with his equipment. My father was unconscious and clearly, even to my untrained eyes, did not have long to live. Before the technician could start the treatment, my mother ordered him to leave the room. I was stunned. It hadn't occurred to me that this was an option. I admired my mother for taking charge on my father's behalf. Jane and I sat with him a while longer and then, at my mother's suggestion, went to the hospital cafeteria to get something to eat. When we returned, my father had died. Over a long slow decline, emphysema had destroyed his quality of life long before it killed him. We learned that it was possible to exert control over medical procedures that you or a loved one have, and that it is an act of love and compassion to intervene.

Now, as we updated our living wills, we reaffirmed that if we had a condition that was deemed terminal or would leave us permanently unconscious, we wanted to be allowed to die and not be kept alive through life support systems. The documents specifically laid out the life support systems we did not want and our desire to be given sufficient pain medication to maintain physical comfort.

We appointed each other our healthcare representatives, authorized to make any and all health-care decisions, including the decision to accept or withhold treatment and to withhold or withdraw life support systems if our physician determined we were unable to understand and appreciate the nature or consequences of healthcare decisions or unable to reach and communicate an informed decision. We appointed our children as backup in case we both became incapacitated at the same time.

We then took the critical next step that too many people skip. We talked to our children and all our physicians about our end-of-life wishes and gave them each signed legal documents for their files.

CHAPTER THIRTEEN

WE ARE FAMILY

Saturday, October 11, 2008

My body was on high alert as we approached John and Jane's house. A sunny October afternoon with the temperature close to 70 degrees was all the incentive we needed to leave the car at home. It was the first time back to their house since August 30th when Bruce had given the ultimatum that ended our estrangement with Jane. It was also the first time since Bruce's diagnosis that we'd see other family members in person.

For as long as we'd been living in Canton, John and Jane had hosted a family pot luck dinner on the Saturday before Christmas, but when we had started our annual Celebration of Life party eight years earlier, they had stopped their annual gathering. I guess they decided one family party a year was enough, until now. With Bruce's diagnosis, they didn't wait for Christmas to revive the tradition.

By the time we arrived, most of the family was already there. As I opened the door and we moved toward the kitchen, I caught snippets of hushed conversation. "How sad about BruBru." "I hope he's OK." "Remember when Richard had cancer?"

Richard died in 1998 at the age of sixty. His death was not sudden, but it was secretive. After he had moved with his wife to Florida many years earlier, we had not seen him often. When he called his sister Barbara to let her know he would be coming to Connecticut, I don't know if he requested that she have a family party, or if she just knew we would want to see him. On a sunny Saturday afternoon, we gathered in her backyard, admiring her garden of lush ripe tomatoes and shiny green peppers as we feasted on hot dogs and hamburgers. Richard arrived emaciated and frail, and spent his time sitting in the shade while we informally took turns visiting with him. There was no mention of his physical condition, no acknowledgement that he was gravely ill. It was surreal trying to keep up small talk when it was clear there was so much of importance being left unsaid. When he left, on his way to visit someone else, I was baffled and disturbed that no one had mentioned what had just taken place. He died of cancer one month later.

From this experience, we learned firsthand the impact of not being open with those who care about you. Not everyone chooses to communicate about their terminal illness, but the imposed silence took a toll on Bruce and on me. There was no opportunity for Bruce and Richard to express regrets, tie up loose ends, or share what they had meant to each other.

Bruce had chosen to be open about his cancer, wanting to put people at ease, and it had worked. Once his siblings, nieces, and nephews noticed our arrival at the party, the conversation ebbed as they took turns hugging Bruce and me.

In addition to the regular roster of relatives, Bruce's younger sister, Sandra, had flown in from California for the occasion and "little" Richard, the only child of Bruce's late brother Richard, had traveled from Virginia to join us. Anything but little now, he was part of the Navy Seal Team Six that would later kill Osama bin Laden. He couldn't tell us about the many hot spots around the world where he'd been deployed, or he'd have to kill us (his words), but Somalia and maritime incidents came up in conversation. We had seen Richard very little as a child and young adult, but now in his forties, he seemed intent on establishing a closer relationship with his extended Hoben family. He and Bruce shared a special connection; they were brothers-in-arms even though Bruce had left the army over forty years earlier.

As we circulated from group to group, catching up on family news and gossip, Jane put out the buffet. Over time we had all settled into our regular culinary contributions. Jane made the turkey; John made sautéed kielbasa with peppers; Bobbi brought the ham as well as an apple pie, still in the grocery store box, which was a running joke in the family; Marion contributed her surprisingly delicious and rightly famous lima beans; the nieces filled in the menu with inventive vegetarian sides and salads. I made my signature Bailey's White Chocolate Cheesecake for dessert. With his tumors continuing to shrink, Bruce happily and heartily ate abundant helpings of everything.

We talked little of Bruce's cancer, but not because of an uncomfortable "elephant in the room." There may have been a bit more reminiscing than usual, but most conversation was about other topics. Bruce was on a high—eating comfortably and enjoying food, surrounded by love, a beautiful fall day, and a firm plan in place. It was just like old times, but on steroids—literally for Bruce and figuratively for the rest of us.

I had first met Bruce's six siblings at a Jack-and-Jill party a month before John and Jane's wedding in 1963. I felt at ease with them now, but as a naïve sixteen-year-old I had been overwhelmed at being thrust into this noisy, brazen, rambunctious tribe of adults. It was the baby of the family, Sandra, who most intimidated me, perhaps because she was only one year my senior, yet so different.

Sandra had just graduated from a private high school, and in a few months, would be starting at St John's College in Annapolis, a private liberal arts college with a curriculum, known as the New Program, centered on reading and discussing the great books of Western civilization. I was fascinated by her bohemian, pleasure-seeking lifestyle, and probably more than a little envious that her father was rich enough to support it.

I was still early in my coming-of-age story, sheltered in my small-town life of cheerleading, proms, listening to the latest 45s with friends, and sneaking the occasional cigarette. I was a confident teenager: smart

enough to graduate valedictorian and go to Cornell University on schol-
arship, and pretty enough to be the runner up in the Connecticut Miss
Jantzen competition, but not aware enough to question who I was. Although I had not yet decided on Cornell, I already knew my major would
be math, not because I loved it but because it was my easiest subject.
At the same time I was put off by Sandra's insolent and cocksure attitude, I wondered if she was judging my naiveté and lack of
sophistication. In all likelihood, she probably hardly noticed me, and if
I had been more mature I might have appreciated how difficult it must
have been for her after losing her mother at the age of fourteen.

Over the years, Sandra had mellowed, and I had matured into a comfortable kinship with her. She had become a published poet and studied
with U.S. poet laureate and Pulitzer Prize-winner Phillip Levine. Single
until forty-one, she was now living with her husband and twenty-year-
old son in Mill Valley, California, fourteen miles north of San Fran-
cisco.

In the past, when Sandra visited, she had stayed at John and Jane's.
We were pleased when she asked to stay with us this time. Marion, who
lived only an hour's drive away, decided to stay in our other spare bedroom and make a party of it.

We were three weeks away from the 2008 presidential election, an
election of historic significance that generated enormous enthusiasm for
potentially our first black president with the highest voter turnout in
forty years. George W. Bush's popularity was among the lowest of any
modern president up to then. The Dow had dropped 26 percent. Sarah
Palin, McCain's vice-presidential candidate, judged incompetent and
unprepared even by Republican commentators, provided abundant fod-
der for the blogs and 24/7 news cycle. We knew she was scheduled to
be on *Saturday Night Live* that night, but all of us were too tired to stay
up, so I recorded it.

My first recollection of political awareness was during my senior
year of high school. I had heard about JFK's assassination as I sat, ap-
propriately enough, in my Problems of Democracy class. Shocked and

saddened, but young and naïve, I had mourned the end of Camelot, and the loss of the magnetic, well-educated man with a beautiful family more than the president and his policies. When I began college at Cornell, my horizons were expanded. A child of the Sixties, I stopped short of attending a march on Washington, but strongly supported civil rights for all and decried the war in Vietnam. Bruce and I had even talked of moving to Canada if he had been forced to stay in the Army for a tour of duty in Vietnam.

Bruce and I were staunch supporters of Obama. It had been a long time since we had held such hope for a president, and we were energized by his continued rise in the polls and the prospect of his winning. Fortunately, everyone staying in our house felt the same way. On Sunday morning, coffee in hand, we gathered in the living room to watch Colin Powell's *Meet the Press* endorsement and the now-famous *Saturday Night Live* skit with Tina Fey as Sarah ("I can see Russia from my house") Palin. We loudly cheered and clapped for Powell, and replayed Tina Fey's skit over and over. It was the most one-on-one time I had ever spent with Sandra and Marion and I was genuinely sad to see them leave that afternoon.

***

On Tuesday morning, October 21, we arrived at Dr. Nerenstone's office, reading material in hand, and ready to start the second cycle of chemo. Bruce was a little tired but feeling upbeat, savoring every morsel of food he was now able to eat without discomfort. Dr. Nerenstone gave a quick knock, entered the examining room, and opened her laptop.

She seemed a bit more restrained than usual, especially in contrast to Bruce's high spirits. "I've got the results from your bloodwork yesterday. I'm afraid your white blood cell count is dangerously low."

We knew that a low white blood cell count would leave Bruce more open to infection, and if an infection did develop, he would be unable to fight it off.

"We'll have to postpone this cycle for a week." Bruce slumped slightly in his chair, hands limp, high spirits waning. "I want you to get a shot of medication on Friday to increase production of white blood cells so you'll be strong enough to have chemo next Tuesday."

I guess we should have anticipated it. One of my chemo cycles had been delayed a week, but after that I had stayed on schedule. I hoped this would be the case for Bruce, too. We were disappointed to delay, but it didn't feel like a huge setback.

"Your blood work also shows a problem with creatinine," Dr. Nerenstone continued.

"What's creatinine?" Bruce questioned, puzzled. We hadn't heard of this potential new problem.

"It measures your kidney function. If your kidneys aren't able to cope with the toxins created by the drugs, then that would also prevent you from having chemo."

"What do we do for creatinine?" I asked. She'd had a solution for the white count problem. Surely something could be done for creatinine.

"The most important thing is hydration to help the kidneys flush out wastes as fast as possible."

Although Bruce, with my insistent prodding, had been drinking the copious amounts of water that had been prescribed, it was not enough. He would now be given fluids intravenously one day before, each day during, and for several days after each treatment in order to flush the toxins out of his kidneys. I told myself extra days at the oncologist were not a big deal in the overall scheme of things.

"Unfortunately, once you have a problem with creatinine, it's likely to get worse each time. Since alcohol dehydrates and interferes with the drug, you'll have to give up wine until your treatments are done."

Bruce was crestfallen as he turned to look at me. This was a blow, not because he needed the alcohol, but because it was an enjoyable part of our daily schedule to sit together in the early evening, sipping wine and talking about our day and the world. I felt bad for him and for us, as I saw another familiar and comforting routine slip away. More worrisome, it was becoming clear to me the treatments were taking a physical toll on his body, especially on his kidneys, a toll that may not be reversible. My ability to maintain a rosy outlook was being sorely challenged, but I was determined to persevere.

As if the stresses of having chemo weren't enough, we now had the stress of *not* having chemo. The time required at Dr. Nerenstone's offices had expanded significantly since his first cycle. With more days of infusion, shots to boost his white and red blood cell production and IV hydration before, during, and after treatment, he was required to be at the oncologist's all five days of a weekly cycle as well as several days during intervening weeks, and with the additional blood tests and IVs, his veins were getting harder to find.

Bruce started his second chemo cycle two weeks late with hydration on Monday November 3 followed by chemo. Hydration again and shots to stimulate his bone marrow production rounded out the week. Although it had taken longer than hoped to get his white count back to an acceptable level, Dr. Nerenstone was pleased with the progress of his symptoms. The overwhelming likelihood was that, even though Bruce could only feel the shrinkage of the tumors in his esophagus, the liver and lymph nodes were responding as well. The good news made all the extra time and injections worthwhile. I sent out another medical update, the first in a month, to which Bruce attached a note.

P.S. We continue to celebrate life each day, visiting children, grandchildren, family, and friends, eating chocolate and drinking an occasional "medicinal" glass of wine. Your visits, cards, calls, prayers, and concern propel my days and really, as Mr. Rogers would say, make me feel special.

Bruce

The hair on Bruce's head was gradually thinning, but he still had eyebrows, eyelashes, and body hair. My hair loss during chemo had been immediate, total body, and devastating, fundamentally shaking my sense of identity. As winter approached and his head got cold at night, he started wearing the soft white, pink-trimmed cap I had used to shelter my own bald head. It was quite a sight that gave us both a good laugh. Well, maybe I laughed a little harder.

We had a huge boost of optimism at the beginning of the week when Barack Obama became the first black American president. Yes, We Can! Barack and Bruce!

We continued to talk to Sasha daily, mostly about Mae's new and marvelous accomplishments and how Sasha was feeling as the twins continued to push the limits of her uterus and her abdomen. We sent medical updates as necessary, but in general our communication was of our respective every day, mundane (and glorious) lives.

The plan of an aggressive schedule for injecting the strongest drugs possible was slipping from our grasp. I stayed optimistic about the outcome but worried about the toll it was taking on Bruce. Fortunately, living in the present was at our core, defining us both as individuals and as a couple. We'd had a lifetime of practice and our ability to celebrate life in the face of adversity had only been strengthened by my brush with death in 2000.

***

Justin and Kylie were still living in the second house we had bought as a rental for them, but now, after two years there and without the dog, they were moving to a two-bedroom apartment in a beautiful converted seminary surrounded by parkland. I wished, for Ruby's sake, they could have stayed in a house with a yard, but we couldn't compete with the $500/month reduction in rent.

Having decided to keep the house as a rental property, we met with our realtors on Thursday. There was a lot to do to get it ready to rent again. All four of us painted the walls, covering the turquoise and bright orange that Justin and Kylie had favored with a neutral white. I cleaned up the yard, raking, pruning, and dragging debris to the curb for pickup. It was very much a working visit. We drove back to Connecticut on Sunday after an exhausting week, Bruce still taking turns at the wheel but happy to let me take on more of the driving.

Between working on the house and playing with Ruby there had been little time to think, which was fine. We'd had enough drama to last us a lifetime, or at least a week or two.

CHAPTER FOURTEEN

LET US GIVE THANKS

Thanksgiving Day, November 27, 2008

"Mama." Mae's sweet baby voice echoed down the hallway only to be met with silence.

"Mama! Mama!" She upped the decibels and the urgency.

Bruce looked at his Timex, pressing the tiny button that activated the Indiglo backlight behind the display.

"Six-thirty," he said, answering my unspoken question. "The sun hasn't even started to come up."

I was already awake, my sleep interrupted by the distant sound of a train whistle, repeating at frequent intervals. The tracks were several miles from Sasha's house, but the whistle was loud enough to be heard through closed windows. When I'm not trying to sleep, I love the plaintive sound and the images it conjures, but this was an active rail line and I'm used to sleeping in a dark, quiet room.

I heard footsteps on the oak floor, followed by excited squeals and some murmuring as Sasha lifted Mae out of her crib and changed her diaper.

Bruce and I, now wide awake, smiled at each other, like children waiting to open a birthday present, listening for Sasha's knock on the guest room door.

"Come in," I called. "We're awake."

Sasha sat at the foot of our double bed, Mae on her lap.

"Good mooorning!" Bruce greeted them with cheery exaggeration.

"Did you sleep well?" Sasha asked me.

"Pretty good. It always takes me a while to adjust to the trains."

"That's funny. I don't even hear them anymore. How about you, Dad?"

"I did sleep well. . . . I'm a little tired, but it's no big deal."

I was a little tired myself, after driving home from Justin's on Sunday and then flying to Nashville on Wednesday.

Mae stared at Bruce, and then pointed to his reading glasses on the nightstand.

"On!" she commanded, with an excited smile. Bruce put the glasses on.

"Off!" She giggled as Bruce shook his head, raised his eyebrows, opened his mouth with a gasp, and took the glasses off.

"On!" Mae laughed at Bruce's show of shock.

This went on for a few minutes until Bruce hid his glasses under the comforter. Her gaze went next to Bruce's wrist.

"I see?" she asked, pointing at his watch and wriggling off Sasha's lap to crawl up next to us.

Bruce unbuckled the worn and cracked brown leather strap and passed the watch to Mae. He then lifted the covers for the three of us to slide down and cover our heads. As he helped Mae push the button on the side of the watch, a soft glow faintly illuminated our makeshift cave of sheets. This had been a part of Ruby's routine when she was little, and Bruce now carried the ritual forward to Mae, becoming part of who "Pa" was to all his granddaughters.

"Come on MaeMae. Let's go get some breakfast." Sasha held her arms out, but Mae didn't move.

"Go ahead, sweetie. We'll be right there." Bruce seemed to hold the most sway in this situation.

After they left, Bruce gave me a snuggle and a kiss on the shoulder before climbing out from under the warm comforter. He pulled on his plaid flannel PJ bottoms and gray long-sleeved thermal top and started down the hall to the bathroom. I got up and slipped into the flannel bathrobe that Sasha hung in the guest room for winter visits. After weeks of daily photos of Mae, it was a joy to be with the flesh-and-blood object of our adoration.

Thanksgiving is my favorite holiday, a day-long culinary extravaganza with none of the pressures of Christmas, just a long, slow, gentle day together in a toasty house, swaddled in memories and traditions. We had begun hosting the family feast in 1982 when we moved into our current house. My mother, who had cooked the Thanksgiving meal for the previous twenty years, was happy to pass the baton. When we held our first Thanksgiving, the adults were wowed by the turkey that Bruce had cooked, especially the gravy, and wanted to know how he made it. As he listed the ingredients, ten-year-old Sasha asked, "What are giblets?" The adults smiled discreetly, looking at each other over the table. Realizing it would not be wise to tell Sasha the graphic details, Bruce attempted to evade the question by simply ignoring it. But Sasha was like a dog after a bone. The more she and the other kids pressed, and the adults resisted, the more we laughed. Not a Thanksgiving went by without someone asking about the giblets.

At our 2002 Thanksgiving, ten of us were squeezed around a dining room table meant for six, four odd chairs from various rooms pressed into service to accommodate the overflow. After everyone had finished their "just one more bite," there was a lull.

"What are we going to do when someone has a baby and we need to add a chair?" Jane inquired, tongue in cheek, with a sideways glance at her oldest daughter, Beth.

"We'll find room," I replied, not worried about having to deal with that issue anytime soon. "Eventually we'll probably have to start a kids' table." I had loved sitting at the kids' table until I decided I was no longer a kid but there was no room at the grownup's table.

"I'll bet Sasha and John will be the first," Beth said, deflecting Jane's gaze. "They've been married the longest." Technically true, but they had only just celebrated their two-year anniversary in September.

"It should be Beth. She's the oldest." Sasha deftly passed the "hot potato."

"Not me," said Mike and Aimée in unison. They had been married only one year.

Without a word, Justin got up from the table and headed to the bedroom wing. He returned less than a minute later, holding a small piece of shiny paper.

"As a matter of fact . . ." He held up the ultrasound image of a three-month-old fetus.

We were speechless. As far as we knew, Justin was still a footloose and fancy-free bachelor. Suddenly Sasha, John, Mike, Aimée, and Beth all seemed to have an urgent need to clear the table. I have never seen so many people get up at once to take dishes to the kitchen. Their voices were not loud enough to hear every word, but the tone of surprise and confusion was clear. Bruce and I eventually managed to get out a stunned but heartfelt, "Congratulations." After a few minutes, when everyone had returned to the table, Justin passed around the sonogram, told us about Kylie and launched a new era in our lives. I wonder when or how he would have announced his impending fatherhood if the conversation had not played into his dilemma.

This 2008 Thanksgiving at Sasha's house would hold no such surprises, no drama, just a celebration of times together, past and present, and that was perfectly fine with all of us.

As I entered the kitchen, John had already retrieved the massive Thanksgiving Day newspaper from the sidewalk and was standing at the black and gray-flecked granite island, sports page open, dark roast coffee with lots of cream and sugar in hand.

"How about those Titans?" I said as I passed behind him to make my cup of green tea in the microwave. I am not a football fan, or a sports fan in general, but I try to make an effort for my son-in-law. John is a sports junkie in general, but his passion is football, with North Carolina college basketball a close second. His Tennessee Titans were kicking off against the Detroit Lions at 11:30 AM. John excitedly relayed to us the expert opinions and predictions as he sipped his coffee. A selling point of living where they did in East Nashville was that it was walking distance to the stadium where John held two season tickets.

Sasha was preparing to make fried egg sandwiches. As I manned the toaster, she cooked the eggs, one at a time, flipping them without benefit of a spatula. She made it look so easy, but not easy enough for me to want to try. Bruce and I took our sandwiches and sat at the island across from John. Sasha stood next to John, offering him a bite, but he declined. John rarely had more than coffee and a banana for breakfast, except on home game days when he invited his friends and fellow ticketholders for southern sausage and biscuits.

Breakfast done, Bruce was ready to put on his apron and start cooking. "Hey, Sash. Would you get me the turkey recipe?"

She rifled through the cookbook shelves on the end of the island and laid out all the meal's recipes on the countertop. Without waiting to be asked, she consulted the turkey recipe and got out the stuffing ingredients.

Bruce's legendary Roast Turkey with Two Stuffings was based on a recipe from a 1977 James Beard cookbook that had long since fallen apart. He now worked from a two-page printed Word document enclosed in a protective plastic sleeve. As he hoisted the eighteen-pound turkey out of the stainless-steel, side-by-side refrigerator, he asked Sasha to put on some cooking music: Eagles, Bruce Springsteen, and Bob Dylan. It was a large turkey, considering there were only four of us, but running out of leftovers, before we ran out of an appetite for them, was not an option.

Bruce used his hands to blend sausage, ground ham, fresh thyme, coriander, tabasco, parsley, and pine nuts for the stuffing that would go into the neck cavity. Then he folded thinly sliced green onions, along with tarragon, parsley, and water chestnuts, into the butter and water-softened bread stuffing mix for the body cavity stuffing.

After sliding the turkey into the oven, Bruce took a break, making himself comfortable in one of the two armless club chairs in the kitchen sitting area on the wall opposite the stove. I sat in the other chair, resting my cup of tea on the table between us. Reaching his arms out to Mae, who was playing on the floor nearby, he lifted her up with a "Booga, booga, booga," moving his face close to hers, looking into her eyes, and shaking his head, lips pursed. Smiling proudly, looking around the kitchen to make sure we were all watching, she then put her finger in Bruce's mouth, so he could loudly pretend to eat it, just like he had done thirty-five years earlier with Sasha and Justin.

When Bruce went to the fridge, I coaxed Mae onto my lap. Startled by a loud pop, we looked up from her book to see Bruce holding a bottle of champagne, a mist of tiny bubbles flowing out of the top. He opened the oven and carefully poured some of the festive fizzy wine along the turkey breast. In past years he would have been "basting" the chef at the same time, but his compromised kidneys required a modification to that particular custom.

I was drinking in the delightful aromas that would deepen as the morning went on, from the tangy raw green onions and warm spices to the deep brown butter and champagne-basted skin. I found myself smiling involuntarily, anticipating the wonderful day to come.

Even though there were only four of us, we made the complete menu. Sasha had added a side or two over the years, in deference to John's parents when it was their turn to visit for Thanksgiving, but she put her foot down when I suggested we might take one of our traditional sides away. We each had our defined responsibilities that had not changed over the years. One of mine was the turnips. Turnips were part of every Thanksgiving dinner when I was growing up. I had never developed a taste for them, but it didn't seem right to ban them from the harvest table. Some traditions we carry forward through generations simply to have voices from our past join us at the table. Fortunately, my turnip aversion was overcome when I found a delicious recipe for Smooth and Chunky Turnip Puree with Caramelized Shallots. I take comfort in knowing that the family turnip tradition will endure at least one more generation.

Thanksgiving is a family effort that requires coordination and coop-
eration and we'd had many years of practice. The recipes were
displayed on the island countertop so any one of us with some spare
time could check the recipe and jump in to help. I think a case can be
made for a new slogan: *A family that cooks together is hooked together.*

Once the culinary tasks were under control, and Mae was tucked in
for her nap, we took turns showering and donning our holiday finery.
Sasha, in her maternity jeans and long red sweater, looked beautiful as
always, but I could almost feel the weight of the twins pushing on her
belly. Doctors measure the size of a pregnant uterus—the distance from
the fundus to the pubic bone—to determine the gestation. Thirty-one
centimeters, for example, would imply thirty-one weeks gestation.
Sasha had fifteen more weeks until her due date, but had already measured forty centimeters (full term) at her last checkup. She would
measure fifty-three centimeters by the time the twins were born.

With everyone back in the kitchen, John mixed mimosas and Sasha
put out the bacon-wrapped water chestnuts. Bruce allowed himself a
token sip of champagne as we touched glasses and I offered a toast, "To
life . . . and my favorite holiday." The sensory prompts of Thanksgiving
call forth a flood of memories of past celebrations and this year, with
Bruce's medical situation, I was much more deliberate in recalling and
savoring the many traditions that defined our family. We had so much
to be grateful for. I gave Bruce a kiss, moved to John for a hug, then to
Sasha for a hip-to-hip embrace that would accommodate her large belly.

When Bruce took the turkey out of the oven, we all stopped what we
were doing to admire his masterpiece, leaning over the sizzling crispy
brown bird and inhaling deeply. As Bruce carved, I stole pieces of turkey as I had done as a youngster when my father carved the
turkey.

We sat down to the feast shortly after Mae got up from her nap. Before we began eating, we paused a moment for another round of toasts.
To the chef! Cheers! Happy Thanksgiving! Then, while Mae daintily
ate her small bits of turkey, potato, and peas, the adults lustily downed

multiple servings of everything. Conversation came to a temporary standstill, other than *This gravy is amazing! I don't know which stuffing I like better! Would you pass that delicious turnip?* The hours of cooking were a lot of work for something that was consumed so quickly, but the result, and the time spent together preparing it, were well worth it.

Our family's Thanksgiving tradition includes a sport walk that takes place between the turkey and dessert. As we stepped out onto the front porch, and I surveyed their neighborhood, I understood why they loved where they lived. An eclectic, historic, and hip neighborhood, East Nashville attracts a diverse mix of residents that includes many musicians and visual artists. Italianate, Renaissance Revival, and Queen Anne homes coexist alongside bungalows, ramblers, and craftsman homes. A low-key neighborly personality thrives along streets where virtually all houses have a well-used front porch.

A slow meandering walk would not do. We needed football and soccer to shake off the tryptophan-induced fog. We carried the balls to the middle of the street. A normally quiet neighborhood anyway, on this Thanksgiving afternoon there was virtually no vehicular traffic to interrupt our play. None of the houses on their block have a garage so we had to retrieve the occasional ball from under a car parked on the street or from someone's lawn. Bruce and John were very good at passing and catching the football. Sasha held her own. I made a few throws but no successful catches. I prefer kicking the soccer ball—less dangerous. I was a cheerleader in high school, an accomplishment that had won no points from the teenage Sasha, a field hockey player, but was the best I could hope for in a high school that didn't have girls' sport programs.

On one of our past Connecticut walks, in a year when winter had come early, Sasha had thrown the football to John who had leaned out to catch it and fallen in a snow-filled ditch on the side of the heavily wooded road. We had laughed so hard it was several minutes before we could pull him out.

There was no such danger here in Nashville. After running, kicking, passing, and catching our way through Sasha's neighborhood, we went inside for small slices of apple pie a la mode, and moved to the living room to crash. According to tradition, we were to have turkey sandwiches that night, but John was the only one who managed to find room.

We went to bed early, exhausted and happy. Passing Mae's room on the way to ours, we couldn't resist peeking in, as we had done every night when our children were little. She was sound asleep in her crib, her arm around UrfUrf, a small plush dog given to her by Ruby. Resting on Mae's other side was Gunny, a well-worn and oft-repaired pink bunny that a boyfriend had given to me when I was fourteen, and which years later I had lovingly gifted to my newborn Sasha. The eponymous two-foot-tall Panda, our present to Sasha on her first Christmas, stood watch from atop a bookcase beside her crib, the guardian of memories passed from one generation to the next.

Bruce gently rested his palm on Mae's back. As he stepped away, I moved closer to touch her silky-haired head. Sated in body and soul, grateful for every moment with our family, we climbed into bed, snuggled into a spoon, and fell asleep immediately.

After a very busy couple of weeks of travel and medical appointments, it was a joy to just relax. Mixed in with all the normal emotions of Thanksgiving, I felt a more conscious giving of thanks for what I had now. There was no talk of cancer. Sasha and John were up-to-date on everything and, although Dr. Nerenstone had not yet restaged, Bruce appeared to be in remission. The only faint reminder of his diagnosis was uncharacteristic fatigue and thinner hair. We were filled with optimism. Statistics I had googled three months ago were pushed to the recesses of my brain. Survival was still a long shot, no matter what the interim indications of remission, but, in the euphoria of disappearing symptoms, I put it out of my thoughts.

CHAPTER FIFTEEN

A CHRISTMAS MIRACLE

Friday, December 5, 2008

"Hey, John. What's up?" Answering my phone, I glanced at Bruce who was sitting next to me reading the morning paper. We expected a daily call from Sasha, along with a photo of Mae, but it was rare for John to call.

"I'm at the doctor's office with Sasha," John answered.

Instantly fearful for the babies, I asked, "Is everything OK?" Bruce laid down the newspaper as I put my phone on speaker.

"No, it isn't. Sasha woke up early this morning in pain. We dropped Mae off at Larry and Michelle's, so we could be here when the doctor's office opened. They're trying to figure out what's going on. They're still running tests but think it may be appendicitis."

"I can get on the next plane." I looked at Bruce who nodded his agreement with my unilateral offer. At least one of us needed to be there with Sasha, and whatever the diagnosis, John would need help with Mae.

"I'll call as soon as I've booked my flight." We had just flown home from Nashville Monday morning and now I was on my way back.

"Give Sash our love," Bruce shouted into the phone.

I managed to get on a Southwest flight at 11:40 AM. My years of business travel had made me an expert at packing quickly. I had no idea how long I would be gone but packed light, knowing that if I needed anything Sasha would have it. While Bruce drove me to the airport, we went over what he might need while I was gone. Since Bruce had just finished cycle three of his chemo the day before, I wouldn't be away during a critical part of his treatment. He felt comfortable driving himself to hydration, which was scheduled for Tuesday through Thursday.

As I boarded the plane, I called John for an update.

"It's appendicitis. We're at the hospital now waiting for emergency surgery." I could hear the worry in his voice. I felt it in my bones.

"I'll check in when I land in Baltimore." I tried to stay calm, for his sake and mine, but I couldn't fathom how they would do an appendectomy on someone who was six months pregnant with twins.

Landing in Baltimore at 12:45 PM, I called John again as I rushed to make my connection.

"How is she?" I wondered how we managed in the days before cell phones.

"She still hasn't gone into surgery. Another emergency bumped her."

"You're kidding! How can they do that?" It was a rhetorical question, of course, that needed no answer, but I didn't know what else to say. I was frustrated, still hundreds of miles away and unable to help.

I normally read or solve Sudoku and crossword puzzles when I fly, but all I could do was run through the possible "what if" scenarios. Most of them were not good.

When I finally landed in Nashville, they still had not operated. I took a cab to Sasha and John's house and let myself in. I put on my best, calm, loving Grandma face when, shortly after, their friend Larry dropped off Mae. Because I had only been gone three days since our Thanksgiving visit, I knew Mae's routine well and she was comfortable with me. She had wanted to know where Pa was, so I called him and let her say hi.

Sasha didn't go into surgery until 5:30 PM. The doctors had hoped to go in with a small incision on the side of her abdomen but were unable to because her extra-large uterus was in the way. Instead, they had to make a large incision down her middle through her belly button. An operation that should have taken an hour went much longer than expected. By the time they got in, her appendix had ruptured leaving them with a lot of cleanup to do, all the while needing to be very careful with the twins.

John got home late that night, after I had already fed Mae and put her to bed. The doctors had needed to manually manipulate the uterus to get at the appendix and the surgery had caused some small contractions. Sasha was in the hospital's neonatal intensive care unit, where they planned to keep her until Monday, to make sure the pregnancy was proceeding normally.

The next morning, I brought Mae to visit her mom. John had gone in earlier, wanting to spend the day with Sasha and knowing that Mae would come later. After getting our visitor's badge, I let Mae push the elevator button for the sixth floor and we found Sasha's room quickly. All the NICU rooms were private. Hers was spacious with light streaming in the windows.

"Hi, sweetie." I walked to her bed. She looked exhausted.

"Hi MaeMae," Sasha called out, radiating a spark of energy at the sight of her daughter's sweet face.

Mae nervously eyed the narrow bed with side rails that kept her mom confined. A wide blue cuff on Sasha's right upper arm started to automatically inflate, monitoring her blood pressure. A finger device measured oxygen levels in her blood. IV pumps delivered antibiotics and morphine. Two belts, placed around Sasha's abdomen to monitor fetal heartbeat and preterm contractions, were connected by wires to a bedside device that displayed the results in real time and printed them at intervals. Mae tightened her grip on my hand as we slowly edged closer.

"It's OK, sweetheart. Mommy's fine."

As Mae clung to me, anxiously reacting to a nurse entering the room, John came over and picked her up with a big hug. She declined to sit on the bed with Sasha and was nervously silent when Sasha attempted to engage her. Recognizing that Mae was overwhelmed, we cut the visit short, so I could take her back to the familiarity of her home. The next day, Mae knew what to expect and we stayed for longer, much to Sasha's delight.

I stayed in Nashville for ten days, mostly taking care of Mae, doing laundry, and holding down the fort. Even though I knew Bruce was able to take care of himself, and we both agreed on where I needed to be, I felt torn. He had adapted to being alone when I travelled weekly for business, but that had ended five years earlier when I retired. In fact, I had stopped work specifically because I hadn't wanted to be away from him Monday to Thursday every week. I remembered how important his daily presence had been when I was sick, the healing touches, and the simple comfort of his being at my side. His therapy was much more difficult than mine had been, physically and emotionally, and I felt I was abandoning him. We talked several times a day, continuing with daily photos of Mae, but hands-on love and moral support was what I missed giving.

We got by with a little help from our friends—actually a lot of help from our friends. We were fortunate to have a robust social network that provided essential care and support. They reached out to us daily, with a card, a call, an email, a visit, and sometimes chocolate or other goodies. They graciously helped care for Bruce when I couldn't be there. I always felt good when I could help a friend; I was confident they felt the same.

It takes mutual experiences, shared interests, and time to develop close connections, and during ordinary times, it's easy to take those friends for granted. These were not ordinary times and I was not taking them for granted.

Bruce's sisters, who had always been close to him, called regularly. Although Jane and I had ended our estrangement, John was making more of an effort to reenter our lives than Jane, whom I did not yet fully trust. I wondered if perhaps our struggle was that our only connection was genetic and had, apparently, never been based on mutual affection.

I envied people who had loving relationships with their siblings and hoped that my children would continue to like and respect each other as adults.

***

After spending ten days in Nashville, Sasha's mother-in-law, Diane, arrived and I flew home, where I would stay for nine days until our scheduled Christmas visit. Sasha was on disability leave for a month and still needed a lot of help, not just for herself but also for the health of her unborn babies. She was banned from picking up anything over five pounds for six weeks and would not be able to pick up Mae for the duration of her pregnancy.

December 16, 2008
Subject: Bruce's Medical Update—Great News!

Bruce had a CAT scan on Monday to "restage" his cancer after three cycles of chemotherapy. His diagnosis in September had been a stage 4 cancer, meaning it had metastasized, beyond the original site in his esophagus, to his liver and lymph nodes.

On Tuesday we learned that this latest CAT scan was clear, i.e. it showed no evidence of cancer in his liver, lymph nodes or esophagus!! Pretty amazing news. The caveat is that a CAT scan's ability to detect cancer cells is limited by the current technology, so there could be some cells that would cause the cancer to reoccur in the future. However, the oncologist is delighted with the results, as are we. Bruce will have one more cycle of chemotherapy the first week in January, hopefully to eradicate any stray cells that could not be picked up on the CAT scan.

Our heartfelt thanks go out to all our friends and family who have sent their prayers, good wishes, love, cards, chicken soup,

and, yes the occasional chocolate and wine. We look forward
to continuing our daily celebration of life with each of you.

Have a joyous New Year,
Sue and Bruce

We knew Dr. Nerenstone had expected a clear scan but were euphoric when it was confirmed. Bruce had made it through. We threw all caution to the wind. The caveat about a CAT scan only being able to detect cancer deposits of a certain size felt like the fine print of contract terms when downloading the latest version of Windows. You mark the box that says *I agree* and never consider it again.

Arriving home from Dr. Nerenstone, we hastily put together a celebration, inviting Jane and John, Kay and Todd, Becky and Marty, and Aimée and Mike to join us. I got out the Perrier-Jouët crystal champagne flutes. This was exactly the type of special occasion we saved them for. Once everyone had arrived and were gathered in front of the roaring fireplace, Bruce popped the cork on a 1500 milliliter bottle of Moët & Chandon Brut Imperiale champagne that we fortuitously had in our cellar and filled the beautiful glasses with the bright elegant effervescent champagne.

It was a Christmas miracle. We were the perfect picture of good friends enjoying life. The fine print attached to the scan results was too small to see in the glow of celebration. Those details were for some other poor soul. Bruce's hair was thin, but I still saw my sweet handsome husband. This was indeed a reawakening of joy and hope.

When the bottle was empty, I got a black felt marker and we all signed the label. I felt the joy and exhilaration of that first Celebration of Life party. I was intoxicated with the love and hope that permeated the air I breathed.

I left the warmth of this celebration to attend our book club's annual Christmas event at Lisa's, feeling blessed to have such a wonderful group of close friends with whom to celebrate. Lisa's house was magical. A cluster of four-foot-long bare branches, decorated with mini-lights and glittery holiday sprays, hugged the kitchen ceiling. In the living room, every square inch of the eight-foot-tall tree, nestled in a well of brightly-wrapped presents, was covered with ornaments and lights. Reflected in the mirror that hung above the fireplace mantel, a swag was punctuated by more festive sprays, thick with lights and sparkle. The decorations in her house represented a week's worth of work, lovingly undertaken every year and shared with us. Saks Fifth Avenue could not have competed with Lisa's spectacular and tasteful displays.

We drank champagne and wine and ate Lisa's Chicken Tetrazzini, made only once a year from the handwritten recipe passed down from her grandmother. Though traditions are often associated with families, our book club was a tribe of its own, with important memories and traditions that bound us together. Lisa stoked the fire, as laughter and our mutual love and admiration fed my soul. This was truly a blessed holiday season.

As I toasted my dear friends, thanking them for their love and support, I was reminded that celebrating life must be active and continuous. It's not enough to casually or silently observe life's joys. Years earlier I had learned a valuable lesson from an article on communication. The author talked about the importance of not leaving things unsaid. Although it was written in the context of being honest with loved ones about your needs and feelings, I extended the message to expressions of gratitude. I did not want to find myself, at some point in the future, when it was too late, wishing I had told someone how much I cared about them. I try to remember that in my daily life, from thanking someone for good service, to telling a friend, out of the blue, how much I appreciate them, or telling Bruce *I love you*, not in response to something specific, but just because he is in my life.

***

A week later, Bruce and I continued our holiday celebration in Nashville, arriving the afternoon of December 23, as Sasha's mother-in-law,

Diane, was leaving. We'd had a dilemma with the timing of Bruce's next chemo cycle. It needed to be four days in a row (including the shot for red blood cells after the treatment) and Christmas fell in the middle of it. When the original schedule showed that his treatment would be complete the week after Thanksgiving, we had made plans to spend Christmas in Nashville with the whole family. We explored doing some or all the treatment in Nashville and decided against it. In the end, we put it off two weeks rather than cancel our Christmas with the kids. It was frustrating to have the delays and uncertainty, but with Bruce's symptoms at bay, time seemed less critical.

Entering Sasha's festive house, I could feel Christmas; not the Christmas of colored newspaper flyers and mail-order catalogues, or the loud urgent ads on radio and TV, but the Christmas of home and family.

Sasha and John's collection of decorations and ornaments were far less primitive than ours, but just as important to their evolving family tradition. John had brought to their marriage ornaments that his parents and grandparents had given him every year since he was a baby. Sasha brought with her the green felt stocking—decorated with a red tassel across the top, a white felt candle and a red felt tree with sequin decorations—which I had made for her when she was a baby.

I could not help but be swept up in the Christmas spirit.

With only one toddler, the craziness of Christmas morning had not yet taken over. My philosophy of gifting is not to overdo it. As a child, I only got one present, not counting the oranges and nuts in my stocking. As a grandmother I gave books, highly anticipated PJs from BabyGap, and money in a college fund. I left it to the other grandparents to buy the latest toys, which often collect dust after Christmas day. I noticed that John, like Bruce, waited until the last moment to shop, and then appeared with sometimes random gifts that seemed to reflect what was still on the shelves. Was this a male trait?

It would have been Justin's turn to have us visit for Christmas, but with Sasha not able to travel, we all descended on her. Justin, Kylie, and Ruby arrived Christmas day, allowing them to spend Christmas Eve and Christmas morning in Maryland with Kylie's side of the family. They had missed the Christmas Eve fondue, but were vegetarians, so it was just as well.

Although Justin's late afternoon arrival meant we would be eating our traditional Christmas brunch at dinnertime, we still chose our customary menu of quiche, mushroom pie, sausages baked in wine, and a green salad with orange sections and walnuts. Whereas Bruce was the star at Thanksgiving, I have always made our Christmas meal. Given how important food and culinary traditions are to our family, you would think that we would all be overweight, but that isn't the case. We just love the aromas and tastes, the camaraderie of cooking with the kitchen as the center of our home.

The visit was low key. Sasha's body was still fragile from the appendectomy. Bruce's energy had been sapped by three difficult chemo cycles. Everyone was content to relax.

On New Year's Eve, we had one of Bruce's favorite meals, Steak Diane, which he had first made many years earlier to celebrate our anniversary. When we spent New Year's in Nashville, we usually only stayed up until 11 PM Central Standard Time, when the "real" Times Square countdown finished. This year we didn't even try to make it to 11 PM, but that didn't lessen the fact that every celebration had new meaning. A new year. New hope.

When we left for home, I had spent twenty-four of the previous thirty days in Nashville. On the way home from the airport, Bruce stopped to have his blood work done. His creatinine was high, but we were able to go forward with his last chemo cycle the next day. By the time we arrived home there was email waiting for us. Mae considered us to be one unit, GrandmaPa, indivisible.

January 5, 2009

Mae misses you guys. She was in bed with Daddy when I got back and was asking about GrandmaPa. And she wanted me to get in your bed and cover up. We miss you, too!

Sasha

We began the New Year with Bruce's fourth and final chemo cycle. Over time it had been more and more difficult for the oncology nurses to find veins. Sometimes it took multiple tries; sometimes a working IV would stop, and the nurse would have to stick him again. All oncology nurses are expert at finding veins, but Helen was the master. She could always find a vein, even when others failed. We needed her to work her magic for just one more cycle.

By now, little remained of Bruce's hair and he was very tired. But the remission news had given us a (good) shot in the arm and this was to be the end of treatment.

CHAPTER SIXTEEN

THE AUDACITY OF HOPE

Sunday, January 18, 2009

When I had seen a full-page ad in the *New York Times* for the Inaugural Concert, I knew we had to go. We joined the thousands of people spilling out of metro cars at the Farragut West station. It was slow, funneling into lines for the escalators up to the street, but the usual subway rushing and jockeying for position was absent. The streets were jammed, the mood festive. I later read that the Washington Metro had recorded 616,324 passenger trips that day, breaking the old Sunday ridership record of 540,945 passenger trips set on July 4, 1999.

People were cold but excited as the crowd spilled from the sidewalk onto the street, where the police good-naturedly let the throngs flow without incident. I wondered if this was what Woodstock was like, without the rain, mud, drugs, and sex. One-half mile down Seventeenth Street we arrived at the National Mall. To our left was the iconic 555-foot-tall obelisk of the Washington Monument, where crowds were already gathering five hours before the event was scheduled to start. Seeing the memorials, I remembered being deeply moved seeing my reflection in Maya Lin's long dark wall of the Vietnam memorial. Bruce left the Army in 1966, but on more than one occasion we had reverently run our fingers across the names of soldiers Bruce had served with.

As the start time approached, I took in the scene where crowds filled all the space from the Lincoln Memorial, up the National Mall to the

Washington Memorial and a good part of the lawn that stretched beyond, to the Capitol, a total distance of almost two miles. We managed
to find a small patch of brown grass to sit on the side of the reflecting
pool. A thin layer of ice glistened on the steel blue water, but no snow.
The temperature was close to 30 degrees, up from the 17 degrees when
we had arrived the day before, but a blustery wind made it clear that
this was going to be a long, cold wait.

Although Bruce and I voted in every election, and cared passionately
about the values and policies that some candidates espoused, after the
Kennedys were killed, it had been a long time since a president or candidate had inspired me. I was seventeen when JFK was assassinated in
1963. I heard of Martin Luther King, Jr.'s assassination on April 4,
1968, when I turned on the evening news in the apartment where Bruce
and I lived while I finished my senior year of college. On June 6, 1968,
a radio announcer broke in with the news of the assassination of another
Kennedy as we were driving in Bruce's black MGB convertible, top
down, on Route 44 in Connecticut. I had just seen Bobby Kennedy,
striking in a light blue oxford shirt, no coat or tie, that spring at a rally
at Cornell. It had felt then as though all the inspirational advocates for
change and equality were being systematically eliminated. Like many
in my generation, I had lost hope for our country's future.

And then along came Barack Obama and his audacity to hope. Here
was another young, well-educated, principled, compassionate reformer
with a beautiful family. He had demonstrated devotion to fairness and
human rights at a local level early in his career as a community organ-
izer. As a senator, he had voted against the war in Iraq and now
promised to withdraw our troops. His agenda called for universal
healthcare, energy independence, and a decrease in the influence of lob-
byists. I appreciated the historic import of the first black president, but
it was his beliefs and policies that made me
optimistic that the type of change that was important to us and future
generations would come.

I was keenly aware of Bruce's fragility when I excitedly suggested we make the trip to D.C., mindful that in the past four months, while Bruce was undergoing aggressive chemotherapy treatments, we had traveled eight times for a total of forty days away from home (nine trips and fifty days for me). As Bruce became weaker, I wondered at times if I had us doing too much, if all this travel was for me rather than us, but he never wavered in his desire to fully participate in all aspects of life, to be a part of the greater world.

The air was electric, filled with spontaneous singing and dancing, as we waited for the start of the main event. When, after a train ride tracing Lincoln's path from Philadelphia to Washington, the Obamas arrived at the steps of the massive Greek Doric temple with its iconic sculpture of Abraham Lincoln, the crowd erupted. On the jumbo screens that had been placed around the concert space, I could see the Obama family up close. They looked so young, Barack in his black overcoat and bright blue tie, Michelle in her cream coat and a long black scarf. Ten-year-old Malia sat next to her mother, while seven-year-old Sasha squirmed in the chair between her parents, at times leaning on her father's lap as he put his arm around her.

Obama's speech was a call for change. Our nation was at war and our economy was in crisis, but he still had the audacity to hope, believing that "if we could just recognize ourselves in one another and bring everyone together—Democrats, Republicans, Independents, Latino, Asian, Native American, black, white, gay, straight, disabled, and not— then not only would we restore hope and opportunity in places that yearned for both, but maybe, just maybe, we might perfect our union in the process." I wanted to believe him, for the sake of our granddaughters.

The concert, broadcast live around the world, featured musical performances and readings of historical passages by more than three dozen celebrities. Bruce Springsteen took the stage to sing "The Rising," a song he had written in reaction to the September 11, 2001, attacks on New York City. I had been teaching a class at IBM's

Madison Avenue office that day and I remembered how I felt when I saw coverage of the first plane hitting the World Trade Center. Later when I went to an empty Central Park, the only noise was the circling fighter jets. That evening, not knowing when or if I would be able to leave Manhattan, I gathered with my fellow hotel guests in front of the TV at the bar, tearfully applauding President Bush's address to the nation. The hotel staff had spontaneously put together a meal, made from what they had on hand and served buffet style in the lobby. Amid unthinkable terror, everyone in New York demonstrated compassion and a sense of community unlike anything I've experienced. I can still see the black smoke against the skyline and smell the acrid air.

After Springsteen's rousing start, musical performances by Jon Bon Jovi, Mary J. Blige, James Taylor, John Legend, Jennifer Nettles, Herbie Hancock, will.i.am, Sheryl Crow, Garth Brooks, Usher, Stevie Wonder, and Shakira were interspersed with celebrity readings of historical passages of Dwight Eisenhower, Barbara Jordan, Theodore Roosevelt, William Faulkner, Abraham Lincoln, Rosa Parks, Martin Luther King, Jr., Marian Anderson, Ronald Reagan, Thomas Jefferson, Thurgood Marshall, John Kennedy, Franklin Roosevelt, Robert Kennedy, and others.

We had never been to a concert of this magnitude, in attendance, star power, or inspiration. The concert closed with Pete Seeger, Bruce Springsteen and Pete Seeger's grandson leading us in "This Land Is Your Land" after which they were joined onstage by Beyoncé and the entire ensemble to sing "America the Beautiful." So much more than the star power, the songs spoke to us and the performances resonated deeply on an individual and a political level. In this shared experience of hope, these patriotic songs no longer seemed trite or outdated.

This important event of our cultural and political lives would be an experience we'd remember for the rest of our lives, an affirmation of hope as a way of life. Fueled by the powerful songs and fanned by our roller coaster ride over the last five months, tears flowed like a spigot stuck on open. The experience for Bruce and me was transcendent and life affirming, at a time when the healing power of hope and love were particularly relevant to us. I couldn't help reflecting that experiences like these, grand and mundane, historic and ordinary, make up our lives, and sharing them make our lives better. I tried to put out of mind what my life, my experiences, would be without Bruce to share them.

CHAPTER SEVENTEEN

ARE WE THERE YET?

Tuesday, January 27, 2009

"How are you feeling?" Dr. Nerenstone's tone was upbeat as she looked to Bruce, probably taking her cue from our beaming smiles. We were still on a high from Obama's inaugural concert and full of hope.

"Great," Bruce replied. It had been three weeks since his last chemo treatment, a time when, in the past, he would have been starting another round of poison. But his scan was clear. He was done.

She summarized for us what chemo had done to Bruce's body and what that meant for the future, giving us a comprehensive view of the lasting toll chemo had taken. Even if the damage was permanent, Bruce could live with it, literally and figuratively.

Dr. Nerenstone continued, "For these types of aggressive cancers there is a high risk of metastasizing to the brain." She paused for a beat, aware of the tensing of our postures in the face of this new information. "Because of that, I want you to consider having prophylactic cranial irradiation, or PCI, which has been shown to reduce recurrence of brain metastases and improve overall survival."

We were speechless. Seeing the dazed look on our faces, she gave us a few minutes to process what she had just said. I thought we had exited the roller coaster, that our post-cancer life had begun. It had never registered that Bruce's remission was only a milestone, and not the end. Dr. Nerenstone had told us early on that if Bruce went into

123

remission we would talk about additional treatment. I assumed it would be something like the Tamoxifen and Femara that I had taken daily for ten years. I never imagined brain radiation! Why hadn't she told us this at the beginning? In answer to my own question, I was transported to the gym, where my trainer never says, "We're doing fifty pushups." She says, "Twenty-five pushups," to which I think, *I can do that*. Then on the twenty-fifth one she says, "Ten more." Then, "Ten more." Then, "Last five." The keyword is *last*. Dr. Nerenstone had never said we were at the end; she just hadn't laid out everything that Bruce was likely to need. I understood it would have been even harder for Bruce to push through the mental and physical demands of chemotherapy if he had known that at the finish line there would be something even more difficult awaiting him.

"For your type of cancer, five to ten percent of those in remission are long-term survivors. That rate has gone up with the use of PCI." I should not have been stunned by the statistics, but I was. I had Googled esophageal cancer in August, what seemed like a lifetime ago, and knew the five-year survival rate was even lower. I realized that I had been assuming remission would make Bruce one of the lucky ones. I hadn't really processed the high likelihood of recurrence.

"I need to do some research," I shakily told Dr. Nerenstone. "And we need to talk it through together." We were both in shock, not able to think clearly, and not ready to decide. Dr. Nerenstone gave us a forty-page booklet on PCI and recommended we schedule a consult with Dr. Kenneth Leopold, a radiation oncologist. We left her office in a much different mood than when we arrived.

Once home, I immediately Googled PCI, going far beyond Wikipedia and the American Cancer Society sites, to scholarly articles and research papers that I struggled to understand. It was a daunting task, dealing with something so unfamiliar and unexpected, but I educated myself and Bruce on the technique, the side effects, and the possible outcomes. We were surprised, not shattered. We just had to reset our frame of mind. With time to adjust and a better understanding of PCI,

Bruce would be able to face the decision he had to make with more clarity.

That Friday, just three days after first learning of PCI, we arrived for our consult with Dr. Leopold, armed with a spreadsheet of fourteen questions. He was calm and welcoming, even in the face of my silent glare and confrontational stance. After Dr. Leopold finished describing PCI, I pulled out my spreadsheet, cleared my throat, and began grilling him.

"How many PCIs have you done?" I pegged him at being in his early fifties, certainly not a novice, so I questioned his experience.

"About one hundred, but none of them were for neuroendocrine." This was not surprising, given the rarity of the condition.

I questioned his judgment. "How will you establish the optimal treatment for Bruce?"

"I propose lower doses over a longer time, probably fifteen to eighteen days. Cancer cells only 'care' about total dose and our experience shows that higher doses over a shorter time cause more damage and side effects."

Mentally ordering myself to calm down, I pressed on. "Can you give me the name of a doctor who would disagree with you on treatment?" I had never asked this of any physician, but Dr. Leopold took it in stride.

"Not specifically, but some would be uncomfortable with extrapolating from lung cancer studies to neuroendocrine. Dr. Nerenstone is conservative; she is not one to throw everything she can at a cancer, and she thinks Bruce should do this."

Dr. Leopold went into great detail to help us understand the differences between lung and neuroendocrine cancers, small cell and poorly differentiated cancers, primary sites and secondary sites, how and why clinical trials may or may not apply across the various types. I found comfort in the detailed knowledge, especially as it related to our decision making.

When we left Dr. Leopold, we felt comfortable about his qualifications and experience, but Bruce was still not ready to commit. What if this was a phantom risk that would never materialize for him? Would the side effects be so severe as to profoundly damage his quality of life?

Arriving home, I called Dr. Abraham to get his view. We started with a phone conversation, but he made time to see us in his office later that day. He reviewed the articles I had found and recounted his experience with patients who had received cranial radiation. Dr. Abraham's main concern was possible long-term side effects, but after calling Dr. Leopold while we waited in the office, he endorsed the treatment for Bruce. Doing nothing, in the face of overwhelming odds, didn't seem right. Dr. Abraham and Dr. Nerenstone, two trusted medical advisors who had known us, individually and as a couple, for a long time, both felt Bruce should have PCI. We were still apprehensive but had no argument against their shared opinion. In the end, Bruce looked at the odds and placed his bet on PCI.

Decision made, we didn't talk about it again. Pondering *what ifs* was neither productive nor helpful. I called Dr. Leopold's office and scheduled the start of treatment for Monday, February 9, with daily appointments ending Thursday, March 5.

Realizing this would be our last chance to get away, at least for a while, I booked a three-night trip to Puerto Rico. I sometimes had a little gremlin running around in my brain, questioning how much travel we were doing. We loved the beauty and comfort of our home, but also loved people who didn't live there anymore. Since the birth of our first grandchild, we had visited either Justin or Sasha about once a month. There had been no change in the frequency of those trips, but now we were able to stay a bit longer. Some of our recent trips had not been discretionary, for example when Justin had decided to move or when Sasha had her appendectomy. I did schedule more spur-of-the-moment trips to favorite places, but those were much-needed therapeutic journeys of peace and renewal. San Juan was one of these, to which Bruce enthusiastically signed on.

We left early Thursday morning on a nonstop flight to San Juan, arriving at the Intercontinental Hotel before noon. It was one of the

many high-rise resorts on the hotel strip that bordered the beach of Isla
Verde, and appeared to have been recently renovated. From the lobby I
could see the lagoon style pool and waterfalls, surrounded by palm trees
and vibrant flowers.

I had splurged on an upgrade to an oceanfront room with a balcony.
There's no sense in going to the ocean if you can't see it and hear it. We
preferred warm fresh air to chilled stale air, so I opened the slider and
pulled the two easy chairs nearer the balcony where we could hear the
roar of crashing waves and smell the briny water. The room was laid
out so that even from the bed we had an ocean view. We kept the slider
open the whole time, the nonstop wind billowing the white sheers that
covered it.

We didn't partake of the sizzling nightlife, great shopping, or spa,
instead spending our days on the beach reading, swimming, and walking. Needing to protect his head in preparation for radiation, Bruce wore
a hat with a wide brim and a flap that covered his neck and spent most
of his time under an umbrella. I alternated between umbrella and sun,
always at a distance where I could reach out and rest a hand on top of
his. We read a lot. We've both always loved mystery novels and easily
traded reading material, though at home Bruce's taste extended well
beyond that. He loved nonfiction, including some heavy-duty scientific
books. His favorite was *The Making of the Atomic Bomb* about Oppen-
heimer. He idolized Winston Churchill, reading and rereading
everything about him or by him. He religiously and thoroughly read
Scientific American, Atlantic Monthly, The New Yorker, and *Popular
Mechanics,* along with *Newsweek, Consumer Reports* and *The New
York Times.*

On a leisurely walk along the two-mile-long beach, we reminisced
about our first time together in San Juan, trying to remember where we
had stayed. In 1966, Bruce was stationed in the Dominican Republic
with the Eighty-Second Airborne Division. When he got R&R leave,
he flew me down for a weekend visit. The hotel was much more basic
than this one and was not ocean front, but we had barely noticed.

Whenever we went out of the hotel, I had turned my engagement ring so that the diamond was on the inside of my finger, somehow thinking it was important that I appeared to be wearing a wedding ring. I didn't need to use that ruse very often. Other than a few meals and one trip to a beach, we didn't venture out of the hotel, two lovers who could not get enough of each other.

We shared a vivid memory of one meal, a lunch in the high-ceilinged open-air lobby bar of the Caribe Hilton. We were enchanted by everything about it, the spectacular lobby, the buzz of vacationers, the view of the ocean, each other. We held hands as we stared across the table into each other's eyes. When the food arrived, we looked up and both caught sight of an older man and woman at a table across the room. They had nothing to say to each other. Their eyes never met, instead vacantly looking around the room. As we turned back to each other I felt a chill. "We're never going to be like that," Bruce solemnly assured me. I agreed.

Now, here we were, back in San Juan, and in the intervening forty-three years, we had talked about that couple on multiple occasions, and we had never been like them.

***

On the morning after flying back from San Juan, we arrived at Dr. Leopold's office to begin Bruce's treatment. They took Bruce's picture and had him sign some paperwork. I remember looking at that picture a year later and not recognizing him, but in person I was unfailingly able to see the physical form he had always been to me.

We would meet with Dr. Leopold weekly, though there was little to discuss since it was prophylactic. Bruce reported some fuzziness and "chemo brain." Every day, we saw a girl of about ten or twelve getting treatment in the time slot right before Bruce. Her name was Mya. Her treatment was clearly not prophylactic.

Bruce wrote the medical update.

Hi Friends,

I have started phase two of my treatment as of Monday, 2/9/09. We didn't know there was a phase two until recently. It consists of a treatment known as prophylactic cranial irradiation (PCI). High energy X rays are directed at the brain to disrupt the DNA of any possible cancer cells. The treatment is precautionary, as there hasn't been a diagnosis of cancer in my brain. I was hoping it consisted merely of putting a condom on my head, but of course, it is more complicated than that. It seems that my particular cancer has a high incidence of migrating to the brain—PCI reduces this occurrence from about 70 percent to 10 percent, so it's a no-brainer to go forward with this. The treatment lasts for eighteen days and takes five minutes per day. Side effects are typically fatigue, sunburned appearance of the scalp, and hair loss—nothing that I can't deal with.

I'm hoping that the procedure will not reveal what many have suspected—my brain is so tiny that nothing else can fit in it.

I had an appointment with my oncologist today and she said, "You are doing fabulously." I have always wanted to be fabulous.

Will keep you posted.
Bruce

CHAPTER EIGHTEEN

AS ONE DOOR OPENS . . .

Thursday, March 5, 2009

> *To: Friends & Family*
> *Subject: New Granddaughters*
>
> *We joyously welcomed our two new granddaughters today (March 5)! Harper was born first at 12:30 PM. She weighed a whopping 7lbs 11 oz. and measured 19¾ inches. Taking after her mother, she emerged with a full head of brown hair. Bette followed her sister by 1 minute. She weighed 6 lbs. 4 oz. and was 18¾ inches long. She has light brown/blond hair. They each have distinctive personalities that have carried over from the womb. Mother and babies are doing great. Grandparents (both sets) are exhausted. Pictures to follow.*
>
> *Today was also Bruce's last radiation treatment. Lots to celebrate.*
>
> *Sue*

We had all joyously awaited the twins' arrival, no one more than Sasha. The emergency appendectomy and the sheer size of the twins had made it a difficult pregnancy. Arriving in time for the delivery was a treasured bonus for me. Since there were two babies, I had the honor of carrying one of them from the delivery floor to the nursery while John carried the other. I cautiously took a tightly swaddled Harper into my arms, choosing her because she was bigger, if only by one and a half pounds. It had been less than two years since I had helped care for the six-pound-fifteen-ounce newborn Mae, but the fragility and responsibility of a tiny newborn remained awe inspiring.

Bruce arrived at the hospital mid-afternoon, unable to join us until he had finished his last radiation treatment that morning. I gave him a celebratory hug and breathed a cautious sigh of relief that he had made it through the weeks of radiation and had tolerated the side effects well. We more fully understood now where the horizon was and how far we still had to go. We would move in increments of three to six months with the CAT scan being the next milestone on this journey of unknown duration with no GPS. But for now, that was forgotten in the pure bliss of seeing the babies who just seven months ago Bruce had feared he would never meet.

John's parents arrived by car the day before. With creative sleeping arrangements, we all managed to fit in Sasha's house. Mae was thrilled to be holding her baby sisters, oblivious to what lay in store for her as she lost her status of only child.

For the next two weeks after Sasha came home, Mae continued to go to school, staying on a familiar schedule with her teachers and friends. Our days became a blur of laundry and meals and diapers, our nights interrupted by frequent mewls from down the hall where Sasha kept "the girls," as we called them, in her bedroom, sleeping nose to nose in a single Pack 'n Play. Sasha was nursing them, so I couldn't help with feedings, but I was on walking-and-burping duty, singing my secret weapon song for fussy babies, *Hush little baby don't say a word,* on an endless loop.

Sasha had enjoyed breastfeeding Mae, but nursing twins was another experience altogether. She tried to get them onto a shared schedule so that she wouldn't be nursing nonstop. But to breast feed them on the same schedule presented a physical challenge. She resorted to the football hold, one infant in each arm, heads facing forward and feet pointing backward, resting on the double Boppy nursing pillow. It managed to get milk into them but provided little opportunity for the cooing and cuddling of mother/child bonding.

Bruce and I took Mae on one excursion to the Opry Mills Shopping Center. After the obligatory ride on the carousel, we went to the Bass Pro Shops where we threw coins into an indoor pond and watched a big aquarium of large fresh water fish. While there, we bought John's birthday present, a hat just like Bruce's with side and back flaps and a wide brim.

It was nice to have the focus off Bruce's medical regimen and on the joy and wonder of new life, but the entire household was so hectic that Bruce and I had little down time together. Breakfast and lunch were catch as catch can. We tried for nice sit-down dinners with all of us, but they rarely worked out. Sasha had been able to nurse Mae at the table, so long as someone cut up her food, but there was no way to nurse two babies and wield a fork.

Finally, on our last night there, the stars aligned. John made a delicious meal of roasted salmon with rice and asparagus. We all listened to the quiet house, exchanged huge smiles, took a deep breath, and dug in. In this space and time, with the chaos at bay, I noticed that Bruce, who had always loved John's cooking, was not eating with the pure abandon that the rest of us were.

"Hey, sweetie." I took a break, setting down my knife and fork. "You doing OK?"

"I'm fine, just not hungry." His tone of voice lacked conviction. I realized I hadn't observed his appetite. Could this just be a one-off or was it a pattern I hadn't been aware of? He noticed me mulling this over.

"The portions are bigger than usual." His halfhearted response wasn't believable. Looking across the table, I saw that Sasha was also skeptical.

"I don't think so. John always feeds us well, but this is not any more than usual."

The silence ricocheted through my body. I helped John clear the table and would normally have done the dishes, but John motioned for me to go back to the table with Sasha and Bruce. Before long, the girls gave us something-more-urgent-to-deal-with squeals for their dinner.

When Bruce went to get ready for bed, I found Sasha in the kitchen and tightly held her in a long hug, rubbing her back. As I pulled back, her questioning eyes were clouded with concern. I was sure she and John had talked.

"I'm going to call Dr. Nerenstone for an appointment as soon as we get home."

"Call me the minute you know something," she implored, lowering her voice.

"We'll get through this, sweetie." I gently reassured her. "I love you."

"I love you too, Mom." It was clear that between exhaustion, hormones, and worry, she was emotionally drained.

Joining Bruce in bed that night, I didn't question him about his appetite. I took his lead, figuring he would bring it up if he wanted. Now I think that he must have recognized a familiar tightening of his chest but chose not to say anything, or maybe chose not to acknowledge it. Whatever was going on inside him, I gave him space.

Before saying goodnight and turning out the light, I put my book on the nightstand, turned to Bruce, and suggested as gently as I could, "I think you should make an appointment to see Dr. Nerenstone when we get home."

He gave me a kiss on the forehead as I cuddled up to him. "I think that's a good idea."

CHAPTER NINETEEN

ANOTHER DOOR CLOSES

Saturday, March 21, 2009

Our trip home was subdued, with lots of caresses but few words. Even during the days that we waited to see Dr. Nerenstone, I believe we both knew the cancer was back. There was nothing that could be done until we had more information, and this was another time when a gesture, a touch, a look could speak louder than words. I tried not to think about what his life would be like if it were consumed by battling an aggressive terminal cancer.

Our forty-second anniversary snuck up on us. Bruce bought a small Whitman's Sampler and a half bottle of champagne to mark the occasion. We did not have our traditional anniversary dinner of Steak Diane; the important thing was that we were together.

The soonest Dr. Nerenstone could see us was Friday afternoon, at her Hartford office located in a large five-story building that housed the Helen and Harry Gray Cancer Center at Hartford Hospital. There were no meditation gardens or bucolic views like those we were accustomed to at her Avon office. Bruce valet parked the car and we entered the cavernous noisy reception area that was shared by eight oncologists. Before long, we were led down a narrow, windowless hallway to her small office. As we waited, I scanned the room.

In Avon, Dr. Nerenstone saw Bruce in a shared examining room that was devoid of personal objects. This was obviously her private office

from which she not only saw patients but also performed her other duties associated with being a clinical professor of medicine at the
University of Connecticut and President of the Hartford Hospital Medical Staff. The framed photo of her husband and children, along with
other personal items on display, provided a window into aspects of her
life that we hadn't seen before during our nine-year relationship.

As Bruce described his symptoms, she did a quick physical exam
and didn't detect anything.

"I'm going to order a CAT scan, followed by an endoscopy, if warranted." I had expected this would be the next step. At least we could
be confident that they wouldn't make the same mistake they had with
the first one, falsely raising our hopes by not using the required contrast
material.

"If the scan is clear, it could be an ulcer. In the meantime, here's a
prescription for Prevacid that you can take if it helps with acid reflux."

We didn't talk on the ride home, or at any point during the weekend,
about what was going on, but neither of us thought it was an ulcer or
stomach acid, or anything other than that the cancer had returned. Bruce
always preferred not to worry about something until he had a reason to.
I, on the other hand, liked to anticipate the five possible outcomes and
what I might do in response, so that I'm prepared for anything. I
couldn't totally turn off the "what if" demon churning up my mind, but
I tried. It was his body, so I deferred to how he wanted to handle the
uncertainty. I believe Bruce's outer self was true to his inner self, and
that he was content to wait for the results. We managed to enjoy each
other and a low-key weekend.

***

On the last day of March, we met with Dr. Nerenstone in Avon. As soon
as I saw her face, I knew. Forgoing the usual small talk, she pulled a
chair to face us and sat down.

"I have the test results and it's what I feared. The cancer has returned." My stomach tightened. Focusing on Bruce and speaking in a

quiet voice, she continued, "All the original affected areas are impacted and there are some new tumors in your liver."

Even though I had expected it, I was shaken when I heard the words out loud. Bruce sat dazed as she talked about options for more treatment. We knew he could never get Cisplatin again because of the kidney damage, but she told us there was a single drug, Taxol, he could try. Given that we'd already thrown the big guns at it, it was hard to believe there was any chance this drug would work.

"What would you do if it were you?" Bruce asked.

"I would probably try one or two treatments to see if the cancer responded."

I understood that it was difficult for her, an oncologist who wants to save patients and who'd had a long, and so far successful relationship with us, to give up. But as empathetic as she wanted to be, she wasn't the one with cancer. She wouldn't be the one tethered to home by drip lines of poison and the risk of infection from low blood counts. I didn't doubt she believed what she said, but wondered whether, if the question were not hypothetical and she really were in Bruce's situation, she would try Taxol.

We sat quietly for a few minutes, all three of us in our own thoughts.

"How long am I likely to live if I don't have more chemo?" I was stunned by the directness and bravery of Bruce's question.

"Three to six months. You could have a feeding tube inserted that would keep you alive longer." I could feel Bruce recoil at the very mention of this. Dr. Nerenstone sensed it too.

"Think it over and come back in a few days to tell me your decision."

I expect some number of patients, possibly most of them, wouldn't even see this as a decision. Of course, they would try everything, grasping at the smallest chance to stay alive, no matter how short the extended time or what the quality of life.

On the way out, we ran into Helen, our nurse, in the hallway. It was clear she already knew the results of the CAT scan and the prognosis.

"What would you do, Helen, if you were me?" Bruce asked.

"I'd try one more cycle to see if it helped." I wasn't surprised that none of our caretakers wanted to pull the plug.

Bruce acknowledged her reply with a muted, somewhat bittersweet smile and we continued to the front desk to schedule an appointment with Dr. Nerenstone on Friday.

When we got in the car, Bruce paused before starting the engine and turned to face me. I looked at him and gently put my hand on his arm.

He spoke softly and deliberately. "I started with the strongest drugs they had, and they didn't work. If I try more chemo, I know my quality of life will deteriorate every day, and for what? A few days, a few weeks? Maybe nothing?"

I squeezed his arm, tears welling up. I gave him time and space to continue his thoughts. Some birds flew out of the meditation garden and over the car.

"I wish I weren't in this situation, but given that I am, I can't do more chemo. It's not how I want to spend my last days."

I could see his struggle was not with the logic of the decision but with the inevitability of facing his mortality, the realization that what remained of his life was short. I knew it was time for Bruce, and for me, to accept that the battle was lost. He was dying.

I pulled myself closer and gave him a kiss. "What do you think about all of us going to the beach for a week? I could find someplace warm, maybe Florida."

His expression softened as he nodded approval. Bruce started the car, backed out of the parking space, and we began the next stage of our journey.

***

Bruce's decision had been made before we walked out, probably before we walked in. But as close as we were, knowing each other's innermost thoughts, and feeling each other's fears, choosing to die is the most personal decision one can make, and he had not explicitly told me until now. So long as the return of the cancer hadn't been confirmed, we had been able to avoid taking that first step onto the tightrope with no balancing pole, from which it would not be possible to step back. But now it was time.

Bruce transitioned from being someone who was sick to someone who was dying. The breakpoint of when to switch from fighting for time to fighting for other things—family, traveling, chocolate, and wine—had been reached. It felt as though we'd been preparing for this our whole lives, learning each day how to do a better job of living, not aware it would serve us well when we got to this final stage of living— the letting go.

As we drove home I thought back to my mother's death one month shy of her ninety-first birthday. She was still living alone in her own home, gardening and delivering Meals on Wheels to "the old people." While working in her garden, she coughed into her white handkerchief and blood appeared. It wasn't the first time, but I was there to see it this time. Alarmed, I asked if she had been to see Dr. Abraham. Her answer confirmed my fears. I strongly encouraged her to get checked, and with her agreement scheduled an appointment for the next day.

When a needle biopsy of a suspicious looking spot on one lung did not find cancerous cells, Dr. Abraham referred her to a surgeon. Although the surgeon said he would not normally operate on someone who was ninety, after consulting with Dr. Abraham, he was convinced that Mom was strong enough to survive the surgery and had the potential to live many more years.

Unfortunately, when the surgeon operated he found that the tumor was cancerous. I had always considered my mother strong and healthy, but in reality, she had just graciously dealt with chronic, long-term health issues. She was stoic or perhaps, more accurately, appreciative of life and content to deal with whatever fate threw her way. So, I should not have expected anything less when, facing cancer for the second time, she survived the surgery in good spirits.

After a week in the hospital and a few weeks at McLean Health Center for rehabilitation, she was sent home. She stayed alone in her house for several days but was getting worse rather than better. When difficulty breathing made her anxious, we moved her into Sasha's room. Our bedroom was on the second floor and she was in the opposite corner on the first floor, so Bruce rigged a series of ropes and pulleys that ended with a cowbell ringing near our room when she pulled the rope by her bed.

After a test of the Rube Goldberg alarm, we went to bed only to be awakened several hours later by a loud metallic clank. We rushed downstairs to find Mom in distress. After sitting with her briefly in the living room, we called the local volunteer ambulance who transported her to the hospital. By the time we arrived, she had been given a bed in the ER and was resting more comfortably. She was stabilized within a few days, but there was no diagnosis of why she had suddenly deteriorated. Bruce and I were visiting her when Dr. Abraham checked in on her during his daily rounds.

"How are you feeling, Minnie?"

"I'm OK. But if anyone needs my organs, I'm ready to go."

I smiled, not the least bit surprised.

Dr. Abraham laughed. "You're not ready to give up those organs yet!"

"I just want you to know that I am at peace and I'm ready to go."

"I understand, Minnie," he said and knowingly smiled.

Mom had watched her parents and my father die a slow painful death, and she made it clear to us and Dr. Abraham she was not going to repeat the process.

When she took a turn for the worse, her words became my guiding beacon. When she was transferred to hospice at McLean Health Center, I rode with her in the ambulance. She couldn't talk but her eyes were open. I held her hand and chattered about how everything was going to be OK. I did not try to tell her that she was going to get better, which she wasn't, but I needed her to know that I had heard her wishes and would do everything in my power to make it OK.

She was calm. I knew her faith was of great strength and comfort to her. I envied her certainty of an everlasting life, and though I had not been able to buy into formal religion, all that mattered was that she believed she would be joining God, and she was ready to go.

Less than six hours later, Bruce and I were awakened by the phone. Mom had died. I was strangely grateful, certain she willed it. When we arrived, she was still in the bed, in the position and the clothes she was in when she died. What struck me most forcefully was that her face was completely devoid of wrinkles. She was truly at peace. Our tears had been shed when it had become clear she would die, that she would leave our lives forever. There were no tears now as she got her wish for a peaceful death on her terms.

CHAPTER TWENTY

ENOUGH IS ENOUGH

Tuesday, March 31, 2009

We had continued to talk with Justin regularly, about what they were up to, how school was going, if he and Kylie liked their new place, and of course, Ruby, but had decided not to share the probable recurrence of cancer until we knew for sure.

"Hello," Justin's deep voice answered, as though he were in the middle of something important. Even with caller ID, it was not his habit to acknowledge the caller identity with a *Hi Mom* or *Hi Dad.*

"Hi, Just," we responded in unison, taking advantage of speaker phone.

"What's up?"

Bruce and I looked at each other and he took the lead.

"I've been having a loss of appetite and nausea the last couple weeks, so I went for a CAT scan yesterday." We had learned to slow down the sentences and insert a pause to let difficult news be digested in small bites. "I'm afraid it's not good news." Bruce paused again, for himself as much as for Justin. "The cancer is back and worse than before."

We heard the echo of a long deep inhale and a slow exhale as Justin composed himself. "I'm so sorry."

"Me, too," Bruce sighed then went on with more detail on the prognosis, the options presented and his decision to stop treatment.

"I understand." We both felt relief when he didn't try to persuade Bruce to try more treatment. Frank discussions and sharing our living wills had set the stage for this conversation.

I took the lead next. "I'd like to take all of us to the beach for a week where we can be together and do all the things Dad loves, hopefully in the next few weeks, ideally over your spring break. Would that work for you?"

"We already booked a trip to Jamaica that week, kind of a delayed honeymoon, but we'll make it work somehow."

"Thanks, Just. I'm going to start working on it now, so I'll be in touch soon. Love you."

"Love you, Just," Bruce shouted from next to me.

"Love you too, Dad," Justin responded with his full heart and soul.

I pushed end on the phone and hugged Bruce tightly.

Sasha and John had witnessed Bruce's declining appetite and his attempt to minimize it. She was probably not surprised when we called her with the scan outcome and Bruce's decision, but learning that her father had only months to live was still devastating. They signed on immediately to the beach trip, determined to do whatever they could to make these next few months the best they could be.

I called George, and Bruce called his siblings, telling them of the cancer recurrence and explaining his decision to stop treatment. Everyone had been getting our medical updates, so it wasn't totally unexpected if they'd been following the survival statistics.

The next day I sent out a gut-wrenching update to my book club. Although we had been together at Beth's a few days earlier, I hadn't mentioned anything about Bruce's appetite. As I expected, but still appreciated, their responses overflowed with warm thoughts, big hugs, wishes for wine and chocolate, honor at being included in Bruce's journey, admiration of our strength, confirmation of our priorities, and lots of love to us both.

CHAPTER TWENTY-ONE

LIFE IS SHORT

Friday, April 3, 2009

We were back in Hartford to talk with Dr. Nerenstone. Sitting side by side, my hand resting on his thigh, his hand atop mine, tears in our eyes, Bruce told her, "I'm done. I don't want to die with chemo in my veins or a tube in my stomach." He would not spend his last days tethered to an IV for treatments that would sap his body and addle his brain, choosing instead to live his life as fully as possible.

"I understand." She wasn't surprised.

"I want to die at home," Bruce emphatically told her.

"I don't see any reason why you can't. Hospice can come to you on an outpatient basis."

"You said last time that I'd probably have three to six months. Do you think it will be closer to three or six?" Bruce was already pivoting to planning the rest of his life.

"It's impossible to tell," she replied, not comfortable going beyond citing a range.

Bruce didn't let her off the hook. "If I made you guess, what would you say?"

"I'd say it would be closer to three months."

As it turned out she was right on the money: Bruce would live another two months and twelve days.

Bruce's decision to stop treatment was not as hard as one might expect. We had been talking about it in the abstract for months, even years. We had living wills and health care directives, had reaffirmed them when I'd had open-heart surgery, and then again when Bruce was diagnosed, and now, when the abstract became real, did not agonize over whether it was still what we wanted. Our end-of-life wishes had been formed over a lifetime of watching people die and, just as importantly, watching people live.

It was strangely calming to have a more certain future and to be in position to better plan. The path became so clear, the priorities lit in neon. How Bruce wanted to live and to die was his choice, and my role was to make it happen. Our family had a single goal that everyone could devote themselves to—Bruce living the rest of his life as fully as possible. Little did we know that by focusing on easing his transition we would also be easing ours.

Society often characterizes stopping the battle against terminal illness as giving up hope. Bruce hadn't given up hope; he had simply changed what he hoped for. He had always hoped to celebrate life up to his last breath. Now he hoped that his last breath would be taken at home, surrounded by his family.

***

Dr. Abraham saw us as soon as we arrived. As always, he was very clear about what would happen over the next few months. As the tumor grew, it would completely close off Bruce's stomach. In the meantime, so long as it was comfortable he should eat whatever he wanted. When necessary, he would need to supplement with liquid nourishment, such as Carnation Breakfast, for as long as he could.

"Since you don't want a feeding tube, at some point you won't be able to ingest anything. When that happens, you'll die of dehydration."

I flinched on hearing this matter-of-fact pronouncement of death even though Dr. Abraham was being exceptionally kind and gentle.

"It's not a bad way to go. You'll just sleep more and more each day until finally you don't wake up. The body has a very orderly and undramatic process for shutting down. There should be no medical emergencies and nothing that requires invasive intervention."

It was comforting to envision a gradual and peaceful end.

"There should be no reason to go to the hospital. Hospice can handle anything at home, even pneumonia."

"Let me know when you want to start. Medicare will cover either curative or hospice care, but not both at the same time, so once you start hospice you won't be able to get hydration or other treatments. Of course, you can choose to go off hospice at any time."

"That's good to know, but I won't be changing my mind." Bruce was not just at peace with his decision; he was certain it was the only option affording the quality of life that was essential to him.

"Here's my home, cell, and beeper number," Dr. Abraham told us as he wrote them down on a pad. "Call me if there's *any* change. We're going on vacation to the Grand Canyon, so there may be periods when I don't have cell coverage. But keep trying."

Dr. Abraham's presence became one of our greatest sources of comfort. Always a source of clarification, no matter when, no matter where he was, his honesty and compassion helped us on a day-to-day basis.

That night we called Mike, Aimée, John, and Jane to invite them down for cocktails. The next night, we went forward with our plans to have pizza at our house with the Kidders and Christophers. We were all avid, some would say rabid, fans of the UConn Women's basketball team. We loudly cheered as they beat Louisville 76–54 for their sixth national championship and third perfect season. Two hours of pure joy and inspiration.

We were discovering the value of knowing that Bruce's time was short. There would be no delays in reaching out to friends, saying meaningful goodbyes, or living each day to the max. Bruce was giving himself the chance to shape this last chapter of his life. We would continue to celebrate life and friends every day.

CHAPTER TWENTY-TWO

A BITE OF THE BIG APPLE

Monday, April 6, 2009

The conductor repeated his announcement. "Next stop. Penn Station. Five minutes."

"Time to pack up, Ruby." I took our roller bags down from the overhead compartment as Ruby stashed her books, pads, and pencils in her backpack. "Hold on to the seatbacks," I cautioned her, the train jerking side to side as we moved toward the exit.

Three days after telling Bruce's doctors that he was declining further treatment, we were on the road again. Once it was clear the cancer had returned, I hastily arranged to steal Ruby away from her parents, so she could join us for a few days in New York. Luckily it was her spring break.

Although Southwest allowed children as young as five to fly alone, her parents were not comfortable letting Ruby take the one-hour nonstop to Connecticut solo, so I flew down to pick her up. Justin and Kylie met me at the airport and took us to the Amtrak station at Baltimore-Washington International Airport. To mark the beginning of our grand adventure, Ruby and I posed for a photo outside the shiny silver Amtrak Coach Class car, me in my white turtleneck, thigh-length wrap cardigan sweater and red slicker, Ruby in her leopard print fleece and dark pink knit poncho, both ready for the chilly wet weather we were heading into. Beaming with confidence, she kissed her parents good-bye, and boarded the train without looking back.

We initially had trouble finding a seat together, having to ask several people if they would mind moving before someone said yes. Settling into our seats, I put our roller bags overhead as Ruby took her books, activities, and snacks out of her backpack. The three hours flew by as we talked and laughed, read and played, and visited the Café Car. In those days, before children had their own personal electronic devices, it was easy to converse and share time together.

"Stay with me, sweetie," I cautioned her as we left the train and walked along the track to find an escalator. "Don't let go of my hand." Emerging into the main arrival hall, we joined the throngs of people exiting other tracks and merging into the crowds of passengers who were waiting for their outbound trains. Bruce had driven down from Connecticut and was to meet us at the train station.

"I don't see Pa. I'll give him a call."

"We're here," I chirped, smiling down at Ruby, "right by the status board in front of Track 12. Where are you?"

"I'm on the other side. Stay put and I'll find you."

I scanned the crowds until I saw his familiar weathered blue New York City ball cap coming our way. I put both arms up and waved.

"There's Pa." I turned to Ruby and pointed at Bruce. She grabbed my jacket and looked up at me nervously. I wondered if the noisy crowd, or someone in the crowd, had scared her. As Bruce came closer, she moved behind me and clung more tightly, studying him intently. Then I realized it was, indeed, someone in the crowd—Bruce—who had frightened her.

I squatted down to her eye level and put my arms on her shoulders. "Pa has grown a beard, sweetie." She looked at me and then at Bruce. "Did you not recognize him?"

She slowly shook her head, still eyeing him warily.

"I'm sorry!" I said. "I didn't think to warn you." She was beginning to ease her grasp on my coat. "I'm so used to it now that I forget he looks different."

Bruce smiled, and she ran to him, locking her arms around his neck as he picked her up. He took her pink monogrammed roller bag, and we navigated our way to the Seventh Avenue escalator and up to the street. After a harrowing taxi ride, accelerating and braking, weaving and dodging through city streets rife with vehicles and pedestrians, we arrived safely at 200 West Fifty-Sixth Street. Before we could gather our belongings, a bellman was opening the cab door.

"Welcome back." His smiling greeting was sincere and personal. Ruby had been coming to the Manhattan Club since she was a toddler, so the bell staff knew her and had enjoyed watching her grow. Even when we came alone, they always asked how she was.

We bought our timeshare at the Manhattan Club in 2001, the year after my cancer and heart surgery, as part of our celebration of life. We had always loved New York, the sights, the tastes, the sounds, even the smells. When our kids were little we came for weekends, staying in various hotels and seeing Broadway shows. Now, with a timeshare that gave us seven nights a year that could be used all at once or in any combination, for the last eight years we had been coming three to four times a year, each time branching out to explore new and unfamiliar neighborhoods.

Our suite had a bedroom with private bath, a living room where Ruby slept on a sofa bed and a second full bath. When we arrived, she unpacked her toiletries into "her" bathroom, arranging them neatly on the marble countertop. I hadn't seen her do this before, and smiled at the realization that she was not only maturing, but also that she was a well-traveled five-year-old.

We loved everything about Ruby's company, and on this trip, were excited to see New York through her child's eyes and go to places we otherwise wouldn't. We had a long list of things to do. I wanted her to have fun and to remember her time with Bruce, in a way that created lasting memories so that after Bruce was gone she would hold dear her time here with him.

We grabbed a quick lunch at Serafina, a nearby favorite restaurant, and then continued down Broadway to the first thing on Ruby's list, the flagship's Toys 'R' Us store on Times Square. We waited in line for a half hour to ride the sixty-foot-high indoor Ferris wheel. As the colorful cabs slowly spun past—Mr. Potato Head, a fire truck, Sherriff Woody and Buzz Lightyear, a boat, Barbie, a yellow taxi—Ruby kept changing her mind about which one she hoped to ride in. I'm not a fan of heights but this Ferris wheel was slow and as we climbed and descended through multiple stories, the store's displays distracted me. It was a little girl's dream—most importantly, our little girl's dream. We spent another half hour walking through the store, seeing the twenty-foot animatronic T-rex and life-size Barbie dollhouse, and repeating a polite but firm "no" to the seemingly hundreds of things Ruby wanted us to buy.

Her disappointment was short lived, swept away as soon as we exited to the sights and sounds of Times Square. Brightly adorned billboards and advertisements flashed and beckoned to the thousands of people passing through Times Square. Cars, buses, taxis, and bicycles franticly jockeyed for position as Seventh Avenue and Broadway merged. Street performers mimed, danced, sang, lip-synched, and hustled. Steam and smoke carried the aromas from food trucks selling hot dogs and sausages, roasted chestnuts, pretzels, pizza, empanadas, biryani, gyros, kebobs, and tacos. The sights were exhilarating; the energy was palpable.

Back in our hotel suite, still buzzing from Times Square, we relaxed for a while before getting ready for dinner. Confidently declining offers to help, Ruby went into her bathroom and emerged fifteen minutes later wearing a long-sleeved dress in an abstract print of pinks and blacks, her hair in a fashionable side ponytail. Bruce and I looked at each other. *How did she get so big?* I was thrilled Bruce had gotten to see her grow into this lovely young girl but saddened there would be many ages and accomplishments that he wouldn't be part of.

The rest of the trip was a whirlwind. When Ruby was younger we spent most of our time at parks, either uptown in Central Park or downtown in Battery Park, but now she was at an age where we could enjoy more things together. We did a combination of old favorites and new adventures, a good prescription for life.

At the Museum of Natural History, we started with a disappointing film about dinosaurs. The large screen 2D technology was at least twenty years old and the story was far from riveting. Ruby was not fully engaged but didn't complain or ask to leave. The dinosaur exhibit was more exciting, especially when Ruby posed for a photo under the massive brontosaurus skeleton.

When the dinosaurs overwhelmed her, we moved on, stumbling upon the Butterfly Conservancy where 500 fluttering, iridescent butterflies flitted among blooming tropical flowers and lush green vegetation in 80-degree temperatures. Ruby and I quietly gasped with delight when an exquisite butterfly, with wing bands of orange, brown, and black, landed on top of Bruce's hat. The universe, or at least this butterfly, had chosen to bestow this honor on him. Later, I wondered if it was perhaps a message from this tiny life form that had so recently passed through its transformation. Everyone around us moved closer to catch a glimpse as I captured the moment in a photo. Bruce then very carefully removed the hat (with butterfly still attached) and put it on Ruby's head where it rested only long enough for me to snap her picture.

Monsters vs. Aliens, a computer-animated science fiction action-comedy film created in stereoscopic 3D, was a highlight of the trip. Going for the full effect, we opted to pay more to see it on the seventy-foot-wide three-story-high screen of the IMAX Theater near Lincoln Center. After riding the four soaring escalators to the top floor, we bought popcorn, found our reserved seats, settled in the plush red rocking chairs, and put on our 3D glasses. The quality of the animation, the size of the screen, and the 3D effect blew me away. We kept gasping as objects flew out from the screen and seemed to come within inches of our face, miming to each other *Can you believe that?* The pure delight and awe made going to the movies feel like a big event. But just then, being alive and together was a big event.

At the Children's Museum of Manhattan, we explored all five floors. Some of the exhibits were a bit young for Ruby but she enjoyed them anyway. She climbed into a giant wooden Trojan horse, tried on Roman clothing, and donned a kid-sized fireman's uniform to "drive" a fire truck with five other kids. Our last stop was the ground floor where we sat around a blond wood table in kid-sized chairs and played with blocks for an hour. As befitted a planner, Bruce's eight-story tower was well-designed and executed. Ruby and I collaborated on tall and complicated structures that were eclectic and varied. We all had fun, seeing who could go the highest without the blocks toppling down. I confess to enjoying it much more than I expected.

As good-natured as Bruce was, I could see he was getting tired, not just the temporary fatigue at the end of a hard day, something that can be remedied by a good night's sleep, but a weariness from which it was increasingly difficult for him to bounce back. His physical decline was accelerating and there was a limit to how far Ruby's energy could carry him.

Macy's Flower Show was a first for Ruby and an annual event for Bruce and me. This year's theme was *Dream in Color*. The main floor of their flagship store was transformed with vibrant colors and extravagant floral designs. The intricate garden displays had more than one million bulbs and over 30,000 varieties of flowering plants and trees from six continents. The view was simply breathtaking, and the fragrant freesia, hyacinth, and lilac blooms perfumed the entire area.

I took a picture of Bruce and Ruby, both glowing with excitement, in front of one of the three pairs of ten-foot-tall flamingo topiaries constructed with hundreds of pink kalanchoe. As we neared the end of the exhibit, Ruby grabbed my sleeve and, pointing to a replica of the Statue of David, said in a stage whisper, "That man doesn't have any pants on." Everyone within earshot joined in our laughter.

On our last morning, with the weather finally warm and sunny enough that we didn't need coats, we went downtown to Battery Park to visit some of Ruby's favorite playgrounds. We would have normally walked everywhere, but Bruce didn't have the stamina he used to, so we took the subway for all but short distances. Ruby was fine with that, proudly swiping her own metro card, then standing and holding a pole while Bruce and I sat.

It had been a delight to be with Ruby at an age where she could enjoy adult activities with us and we could happily participate in kid things with her. This was her best yet bite of the Big Apple.

It hadn't hit me at the start that this was the beginning of a farewell tour of the places and experiences that had given us joy and helped write the history of our life together. Bruce's farewell was obvious; he would never visit New York again, but mine was profound knowing I would never again experience New York with Bruce. As his impending death ran its course from abstract to concrete, my mind sometimes wandered to thoughts of what my future would be like without him.

After lunch, we left New York behind and I drove the four hours to Silver Spring, letting Bruce nap. Justin's apartment was a welcome refuge away from crowded elevators, sirens at all hours and rooms where sunlight squinted through adjacent high-rises.

Friday began as every morning did when we were with Ruby. She got into bed between us, and Bruce began the familiar call and response that had been going on since she was a baby. His playful love for her was a constant and he never stopped calling her sweetheart.

"It's going to be sunny and warm. Let's go to D.C. and see the cherry blossoms," I enthusiastically proposed.

"Yay," Ruby replied, turning to Bruce to see what he thought. He smiled in agreement.

Normally we would have eschewed the crowds, even to see the cherry blossoms at their peak, but we had reached a time where it was worth working a little harder for a special experience. Getting off the metro at the Smithsonian stop, it was a short walk to the Tidal Basin Boathouse. We rented a paddle boat for an hour-long spin around the Tidal Basin, admiring the thousands of spectacular pink cherry trees that lined it. Bruce and I did most of the pedaling, but happily gave Ruby a short turn.

Leaving the Tidal Basin, we walked up the National Mall toward the Capitol, looking much different than the last time we had seen it during the inaugural concert in January. As we waited for the walk light to cross Third Street and enter the Capitol Park, I noticed a man and woman, both obese and unhealthy by any measure, waiting in line to buy ice cream from a street vendor. They were neither engaged with each other nor the beauty that surrounded them. My heart pounded, and I felt a rush of heat as my body tensed. This physical reaction was quickly followed by strident thoughts that came out of nowhere. *Why is my fit, funny, loving husband dying, a man who has done everything right, and these people who seem to have done nothing "right" are boringly waiting to have ice cream?* I was not proud of what I was feeling, but there it was nevertheless. *It's not fair!*

Of course, rationally I knew the universe wasn't fair and was never going to be—there are no rules or standards for who wins and who loses. Life isn't fair even when we ostensibly have some degree of control. Life and death just are. Fair has nothing to do with it. Still, there they were, those feelings. I tried to shake them off as the light turned and we joined the crowd crossing the street.

At the park, Bruce found a bench to rest on while Ruby and I sat on the steps that led from ground level down to the Capitol Reflecting Pool. She walked along the edge of the pool, occasionally disturbing the ducks and seagulls that were swimming there, while I enjoyed the reflections of the Capitol, the surrounding sights and the spectacular blue sky. But I had trouble getting that couple, and the shame I felt, out of my mind.

On Saturday, I helped Ruby make our traditional Easter cake. When Sasha and Justin were little, I saw an ad in a magazine that showed how to make a bunny's head and ears from two round cake layers. Once pieced together, frosted, sprinkled with shredded coconut for fur and embellished with candies or colored frosting for eyes, nose and mouth—voila! The Easter Bunny! We exchanged pictures of our cake with Mae who was making her own masterpiece in Nashville. The details of the bunnies would change every year, but their existence kept us united across distance and generations. We continued all our traditions, enjoying them, as we always had—in this case, a cake that reflected the artistic vision and capabilities of Ruby and Mae. But I was aware of the finality for Bruce of our traditions and hoped the joy of experiencing them outweighed any feeling of sadness.

With the cake ready for Easter brunch, I suggested to Ruby that we make an album of our New York trip. She had brought her own camera to take pictures and I had methodically taken more pictures than usual, making sure I had plenty with Bruce and Ruby. I had gotten prints made from both our cameras, and had brought an album to put them in, so that she could conjure up this memory when she was older.

We spent Easter with Gerry and Leigh, Kylie's father and stepmother, and their family. The following morning, we headed back to Connecticut after a joyous visit with Ruby. Years later, her memory of what we had done together that week would fade, but one image was apparently imprinted in her mind, something that she had talked to her dad about the day we came back from New York.

"I was scared of Pa when I saw him at the train station," she had confessed to Justin, confused about feeling afraid of her beloved grandfather.

"How come?" Justin calmly asked as he put his arm around her.

"I didn't recognize him. He had a beard and he didn't have any hair." Ruby snuggled closer.

"But he was still Pa, right?" Justin reassured her. Ruby nodded in agreement as he continued. "He's just sick."

"What do you mean 'sick'?" Ruby quietly waited for his answer.

"He has something called cancer. He lost his hair because of the medicine he's been taking."

Ruby sat still, questions silently forming in her head.

"It's not something you need to worry about getting," Justin assured her. "You can't get cancer in the same way that you catch colds."

"Is he going to get better?" Each answer led to a new question.

"I don't know." Justin paused. "His cancer is very serious."

"Does that mean he might not live?" Her voice softened.

"I hope he'll be OK, but he might not." Ruby was trying to understand what she was hearing, but had no frame of reference for serious illness or death.

After a long moment she asked, "What happens when you die?"

"Your body stops working. You can't walk or run, or eat or sleep, or see anymore, and you don't feel any pain." Justin was watching for her reactions.

"Where do you go?"

"No one knows for sure. People believe different things. Some believe you go to heaven. Some believe in reincarnation, that you come back in another form. Some people think nothing happens."

When Ruby didn't respond, he asked her, "What do you think happens?"

"I think Pa is going to come back as an eagle," her sadness now lightened with the excitement of possibility. Bruce often told Ruby, "You make my heart soar like a hawk." Eagles. Hawks. Close enough.

CHAPTER TWENTY-THREE

A WALK DOWN MEMORY LANE

Tuesday, April 14, 2009

"Here's where I got hit by the car," Bruce said.

I'd heard this story many times—it was one of the granddaughters' favorites—but, even though we lived only forty-five minutes from Bruce's hometown, in all our years together I had never been to the scene of the crime.

"I was so excited to get my first library card that I ran into the street without looking," Bruce continued.

The library was quite grand, a one-story neoclassical revival made of pink granite. Buff terracotta panels, carved with the names of Dante, Shakespeare, Goethe, and Tennyson ran above the windows. Now I could visualize Bruce, the enthusiastic young boy I never knew, toothy smile and eyes almost shut with delight, racing down the six wide steps from the library door, along the sidewalk, and out to the street, book firmly in hand.

"Good thing you weren't seriously hurt. It certainly would have changed my life, and not for the better." I gave him a smile and a quick hug as we strolled arm in arm down the sidewalk.

Bruce had recently bought *Legacy: A Step-by-Step Guide to Writing Personal History*. His sister Barbara and her husband, Rick, had traveled the eastern United States, searching records to piece together a genealogy that began in the 1830s in Pennsylvania with his great-grandfather Patrick Hoben who was possibly murdered by the Molly Maguires. To start filling in the detail of his branch of the family tree, Bruce had drafted four single-spaced pages of his earliest recollections. We were now on a walk down memory lane, really a walk down Church Street in Naugatuck, Connecticut, to photograph the places of Bruce's childhood.

Although most of Bruce's early years were spent in Naugatuck, it had all started on Grandview Avenue in the neighboring city of Waterbury. The first picture he took for his legacy project was of his family's two-story house and the three-story three-family house next door where his maternal grandparents, his grandmother's mother, and his uncle's family lived.

We already had plenty of photos of the nine-bedroom house where Bruce moved when he was five, but his legacy tour would not be complete without at least a brief stop. I recalled my first time there, entering a reception hall that was as big as my family's combined living room, dining room, and kitchen, and seeing the massive open staircase to the upper stories. Oriental carpets covered every floor, compared with the plain, thin carpets in our single-story ranch house.

Our next stop was the train station, from which Bruce and his preteen friends took the train to the much larger city of Waterbury. He took a picture of the station, a long, low Spanish colonial revival made of stucco with brownstone and brick blocks at the corner and a grand arch over the entrance.

"We always visited Grandpa Butler's print shop," he said fondly. "I loved watching the linotype machines turn molten lead into words."

Perhaps this was the beginning of his reverence for words and language. It was a memory repeated often that I never tired of hearing. Bruce took two pictures of the tracks, one looking in each direction. I guessed the tracks, and the memories of where they took him, were more important than the building. While he had been riding trains to the city, I was playing in the woods and meadows of my parent's twenty-five acres with one of my two friends who lived within walking distance.

A short block west from the train station on Church Street was Bruce's grammar school, an imposing three-story building made of brick with granite lintels and sills. Above the main door, a large panel marked the entrance: *St. Francis of Assisi School - Family of Faith*. Bruce talked about his elementary school days and how terrified he was of the nuns with their black outfits and strange headgear, and how, on his first day in kindergarten, he had cried and cried and cried.

"There wasn't any affection shown by those ladies, and it didn't improve with time. God was a very tough taskmaster," he emoted. I laughed, seeing that young boy in the family photos come to life.

"My favorite part of school was recess. We often played bounce the tennis ball off the wall. One day the ball landed on the roof of a garage next to the schoolyard. I climbed up a tree to the roof and got it, but I managed to fall out of the tree and knock myself out." I'd also heard this story before but had to laugh along with him. "All my friends thought I was dead! The doctor prescribed bed rest and with only a couple of weeks remaining in the school year, I had an extralong summer vacation."

Bruce tried to convince me he had been a good student and generally well behaved for most of grammar school, but that a significant change had come after an incident in seventh grade.

"It was a sunny winter day with a fresh six inches of snow. My friends and I were walking back to school after lunch at home when we bombarded a car with snowballs. The lady driving was furious and to escape her wrath we ran into the woods and took a shortcut back to school. Settled down in the classroom, we soon became unsettled when the lady came into the room with the principal. She identified us as the culprits and we were marched into the hallway where we had to get on our knees and listen to the Sister tell us how badly we had behaved, that, in fact, we were communists!" Bruce dramatically imitated the angry nun. "Calling us communists was really over the top, even for a thirteen-year-old. The Sisters of Mercy's stock plummeted in my eyes that day and really never recovered."

Right next to the school was St. Francis Church, a brick Gothic revival with three pointed-arch doorways, a large Gothic window, gabled roofs, a buttressed clerestory, and a tapered octagonal spire. What beautiful buildings Bruce had spent his time in.

"I was attracted to the rituals of the Catholic mass, so I tried out to be an altar boy, successfully joining the holy team. Weddings and funerals were good duty because usually someone tipped me one or two dollars, an amount that could buy a lot of candy." His fondness for candy had carried forward into adulthood.

He often served early morning masses with his best friend, Tommy. "In those days, the mass was said in Latin, so we had to memorize all of the responses. We used to race each other with some of the trickier passages. Even more exciting, Tommy was subject to fainting spells. If the priest was going slowly and Tommy had to stay still for a prolonged period while kneeling, he would topple over and cause a bit of pandemonium," Bruce gleefully recounted.

I was tickled to hear the funny tales of his early Catholic experience, a faith that he would turn away from as a young man, despite going on to attend a Catholic prep school and university to please his parents.

On the other side of the school was the YMCA. Most days Bruce and his friends went there after school, and when he was a bit older, to dances. He reminisced about one dance that, no matter how much he pleaded, his mother would not let him go to. So, he stuffed pillows under his sheets in the shape of a sleeping boy and went out the window of his second-floor bedroom, using the downspout to reach ground level. When he tried to sneak back in, he was busted.

I had heard stories of these places before but hadn't realized they were in such proximity, all within a block of each other. I could see that the whole of his childhood experience was much more than the sum of his stories. It was a real-life, action-packed video game, like the make-believe world of Jim Carrey in *The Truman Show*. What fun to be able to walk or take a train to everywhere you wanted to go. At each stop, I continued to be struck by how opposite our lives had been before we met. He had grown up in a small but vibrant city while I had been playing in woods and streams, pretending to be a cowgirl as I rode my horse through our fields.

We drove a short distance past the YMCA to the site of the old movie theater. It had most recently housed the Lighthouse Christian Church. The marquee was intact, but instead of movie titles it now alerted passersby that it was for sale.

"When I was young, Saturday afternoon was matinee time with cartoons galore and an episode of an ongoing series such as *The Rocket Man*. Fifty cents was more than enough to get into the movie, get a soda, popcorn, and two or three candy bars. It's unlikely anybody's parents had any idea of how much sugar their kids consumed at a typical matinee," Bruce bragged.

He then went on to recount seeing the science fiction movie *The Thing* when he was about ten years old, walking home alone in the dark, terrified, and praying every step of the way. I remembered a similar experience at the beach when I was about the same age. The movie was *Creature from the Black Lagoon*.

Our last stop was a three-minute drive away. From the top of a small hill, we looked down on the Little League baseball field as Bruce told the story of when he played against his older brother Richard, a natural athlete like their father.

"I was all thumbs and elbows, but in the last inning, with bases loaded and two outs, I took a wild swing at the first pitch. It looked like it was going to be a clean hit down the right field line when suddenly Richard, reaching high above his head, snagged that hit and saved the game for his team," he wistfully recalled.

I knew how deeply Bruce had been hurt by a father who never went to any of his Little League games but attended every one of Richard's. It was tough enough getting his father's attention being one of seven children in a chaotic Irish Catholic household, and proved impossible when an older brother seemingly fulfilled all their father's aspirations. I was glad to know that since Richard was playing, his father must have also seen Bruce play at least once.

I believed I understood what Bruce was feeling as we revisited the scenes of his childhood memories. When I drive by my elementary school, I still see myself at the playground, pushing the roundabout as fast I can before hopping on. Every time I go to Hammonasset Beach, I see my young self, diving off my father's shoulders into the ocean, or a preteen me lying with my friends on beach blankets, radio playing, or a teenage me bringing food to Bruce on his dinner break from lifeguarding.

I didn't anticipate how I would feel being a part of Bruce's walk down memory lane. I had heard almost all the stories before, but now, with a clear mental image, his childhood came to life as it never had before. I absorbed Bruce's animated energy as he relived and retold his story. When we had started the legacy road trip it had been just for him, but I walked away with an emotional and physical connection to Bruce, the boy, that I would hold onto long after he was gone.

Our magic carpet ride through Bruce's childhood made stark the contrast in our early experiences and I marveled that we were able to meld into what I had always thought was the "perfect couple." Not to say we were that imaginary unattainable couple who never has a bad day, a jealous thought or a selfish act, but the couple whose love, compassion, care, and tolerance nourished an enduring love until the end.

CHAPTER TWENTY-FOUR

AN IRISH WAKE

Saturday, April 18, 2009
With legacy uppermost in his mind, and many more stories to share, Bruce had decided to have a family party. We sandwiched it into the few days between our Easter trip with Ruby and a planned family beach vacation in Florida. I had suggested we ask John and Jane to host so that we wouldn't have to do anything, but Bruce felt strongly that he wanted to have it at our house.

It was a beautiful April day in Connecticut, sunny and 75 degrees. The forsythias and daffodils were in full bloom. I jumped the gun on summer, breaking out a long black and gold spaghetti strap sundress and my chunky black and gold jewelry, but keeping a black shawl draped over my arms just in case. Bruce wore what seemed to be his new daily uniform, his New York City ball cap, a long-sleeved thermal tee under a heavy, long-sleeved navy shirt, and faded jeans held up by the same worn belt, cinched a little tighter. It was unusual for him to be more warmly dressed than me, but I remembered the constant bone-chilling cold I felt during my bout with cancer.

The food was easy: a potluck with everyone contributing their specialty. I put beverages on the kitchen counter and arranged the casseroles and platters on the center island. Some ate inside, and some ate outside. Bruce and I had brought the table and six chairs from the screened porch to the deck, so our guests could be warmed by the spring

165

sun. A bouquet of daffodils graced the table. An oval pot of purple and white pansies cheered those who sat at the nearby patio table. After dessert and coffee, and refilling our wine glasses, we gathered the chairs in a circle and began reminiscing. The nieces and nephews spoke fondly of crazy Uncle Brucie, Aimée perfectly capturing a young child's view of his joie de vivre.

"Brucie made everything fun when we were kids—even driving to the grocery store. He had an ongoing game where he would coast his car down East Hill with the goal being to get up enough speed to make it through the flat spot and up the next rise, which as you know is followed by another downhill stretch. It was our very own roller coaster, and endlessly exciting as we all knocked around in the back of the VW bug."

Bruce's siblings had much edgier tales to tell.

"Remember when Richard flunked out of college and lived on the third floor for three months before Dad discovered him?" Marion asked in mock disbelief.

All the siblings gently nodded and chuckled.

"Remember Nanny Murphy?" Sandra quizzed her siblings. Their great-grandmother, who had a fondness for whiskey and snuff, had lived with them. "I remember one morning when someone must have left a bottle of whiskey on the kitchen counter. We came down for breakfast and she was sitting in a kitchen chair ten sheets to the wind. We carried her to her room in the chair and put her to bed."

"I often served as her dealer," Bruce confessed, "taking her fifteen cents and purchasing a tin of Red Top Snuff at the drug store."

We briefly paused as Beth's daughter, Serena, playing Pied Piper to the younger children, ran onto the deck then circled back out to the lawn, blowing iridescent bubbles that were lifted high by spring breezes.

"I remember when you banged my head against a window pane and shattered the glass," his sister Barbara scowled, shaking an accusing finger.

"I was imitating a scene from a western movie where the bad guy bangs the good guy's head against the wall," Bruce defended himself.

"Lucky for you, nobody got hurt," Barbara shot back with her sly *dare you* attitude.

Jane smiled in amusement at these tales while Aimée listened with false shock, mouth agape.

"I remember the Breach of Peace charge brought against me and Boncal." In Bruce's teenage years, he had turned to cars, girls, and beer, and Billy Boncal was the coconspirator in many of his exploits. "Officer whatever-his-name-was was driving a Studebaker Lark. The Studebaker was a dog and we would almost let it catch up with us and then stomp on the gas. I was driving Dad's 1957 Ford Fairlane 500. It was a V8 with a four-barrel carburetor—the car flew! But the cops outsmarted us. They waited at Boncal's house for me to drop him off and nailed us. Mother had to come to court with me to pay a ten-dollar fine. She was mortified."

There was a theme to the stories: falling off roofs, crashing cars, evading police. Goings on at the Hoben House, or "56 Rockwell Avenue," as Bruce and his siblings referred to it, were always on the edge of chaos. It's a wonder they all survived.

Along with the tales of bad judgment and mischief, there were also warm remembrances of gathering around the radio to listen to Saturday morning serials, Bruce riding the bus to Waterbury with Marion and her friends, laughing so hard his stomach and jaw hurt, rescuing a very young Sandra from an angry nest of yellow jackets by scooping her up and running to safety.

Bruce's sister Marion then brought us back to where it all began in 1941.

"I remember when Mother brought you home from the hospital. You were so tiny."

I looked from Marion to Bruce, knowing what was coming next.

"I was sooo tiny that I came home in a Kleenex box," Bruce interjected, mischief in his smile and eyes.

"No, you didn't," his brother John wryly corrected for the umpteenth time. "It was Snoopy who was brought home in a Kleenex box." Snoopy was the family dog.

Barbara dismissed everyone. "I don't remember anything about Kleenex boxes, only that Bruce was really premature."

"He wasn't premature," Sandra piped in. "He was a blue baby."

By now everyone was laughing. This story had been told, including the corrections, for as many years as I'd known Bruce, but the urban legend of Bruce and the Kleenex box endured. All the sibling remembrances were murky and/or partially disputed, a kernel of truth in all of them but needing to be consumed with a shaker full of salt. What was important was that the experience of telling and hearing stories, conjuring up a time and place and stirring up thoughts and emotions, preserved a strong family narrative and testified to their lifelong bonds.

Before the sun faded and the party ended, we took group photos in front of the tall graceful hedge of golden yellow forsythia. Aimée's husband Mike, our photographer for the day, took separate group pictures of the eight of us in Bruce's generation, Bruce with his four siblings, the thirteen nieces and nephews of the next generation, and the nineteen members of the next two generations. The last pictures were of just Bruce and me.

Before Bruce's Aunt Rosemary had moved from her big house with its expansive lawns, she used to hold large family reunions. I enjoyed looking back at the candid shots, but it was the group photos that had the most lasting impact, positioning us in the continuum of time and ancestry, and creating a lasting record for future generations. On this afternoon we had contributed to the family historical record. I envisioned our children and grandchildren, and their children, looking at these photos after we'd gone and hearing stories about us that have been handed down over generations. I had never been more aware of being part of a large family that will continue to extend across time and distance and cultures.

As people were saying goodbye, I was struck by how similar this party had been to what I imagined as an Irish wake. The glorious send-off of a departed loved one. Laughter and tears as people recalled stories about the deceased. Food and drink flowing freely. A life remembered and treasured. Following our philosophy of celebrating life, we had created our own Irish wake with a new spin. We weren't grieving Bruce's death but the impending loss of his presence in our lives, and our "guest of honor" was still alive to hear the stories and feel the love that would remain fresh in his heart and mind over the next weeks, and would stay with us, his survivors, for the rest of our lives. How fortunate for him—and for us.

Before going to bed that night, I looked through the photos from the afternoon, stopping at the one of Bruce and me. I wasn't sure if the clouds had suddenly cleared away or the close-up shot framed us with vibrant yellow forsythia, or maybe it was our radiant love, but our photo was much brighter than the others.

CHAPTER TWENTY-FIVE

LIFE'S A BEACH

Sunday, April 19, 2009

We made our way through Orlando International Airport with luggage carts overflowing with two Pack 'n Plays, three car seats, two strollers (one of them a double stroller), one Boppy nursing pillow, and assorted luggage. Sasha nursed Bette, a baby blanket discreetly draped over her shoulder, while I fed Harper a bottle of expressed breast milk and John pushed the luggage cart. Justin was right behind us, pushing another cart brimming with luggage. Ignoring the stares of fellow travelers, we hailed the Hertz bus. As the door opened, the driver raised an eyebrow, pushed himself out of his seat and began clearing space on the luggage rack. Unsuspecting passengers looked at each other, then moved closer together, shoulder to shoulder, to make room for us. Some, who looked of an age that they might have young children, smiled knowingly. I felt I should be wearing a sign: *Sorry. We're on a mission of mercy.*

On April 1, the day after Dr. Nerenstone had confirmed Bruce's cancer was back, I had begun scheduling a trip for our family to be together one last time. My requirements were that it had to be warm, on or near a beach where we could swim, with a house big enough to accommodate us in one unit, and easily accessible by air for all of us. I quickly zeroed in on Florida. I spent most of the day researching houses, when the perfect rental appeared: a luxurious 6000-square-foot beach house at the southern end of New Smyrna Beach. The goddess of travel had

171

smiled upon us. The price for a week was more than I had wanted to spend, but this was, literally, the trip of a lifetime and it was a spectacular house right on the ocean.

Ordinarily, it would have been very difficult, probably impossible, to get the whole crew together with two weeks' notice, but these were not ordinary times. Sasha and John were relatively easy schedule-wise, since Sasha was still on maternity leave and John's job was flexible enough to handle any necessary work remotely while we were gone. But I was well aware that traveling with seven-week-old twins and a two-year-old was not a trivial pursuit, and one they would not have otherwise undertaken.

We knew that Justin and Kylie had already booked their trip to Jamaica the week of April 25. Adding on the Florida trip, they would be away from home, work, and school for two weeks. For Ruby, missing two weeks of school in first grade was not insurmountable, but for Justin, who was substitute teaching while taking courses for his master's degree, this would mean losing class and study time, as well as paid teaching time. As a hair stylist, Kylie would also lose two weeks of income. The financial impact on them would be significant.

Profoundly grateful for what Sasha, Justin, and their spouses were willing to do to make this last trip together possible, we paid all expenses.

One beach house: $3,790.63

Ten flights: $3,754.52

Two cars: $751.39

Time together: priceless

Knowing we'd arrive at the house too late to get groceries or go out to dinner, I had asked the owner to recommend a place that had good pizza and would deliver. As we neared our destination, I called Justin, who was following us, to see what his family wanted to eat.

I leaned forward and touched Bruce's left arm. "Would you like some minestrone soup?" He had been eating very little regular food.

Most meals were now canned soup, usually minestrone or chicken noodle, with the solids cooked to the point of borderline mush, or yogurt, or Carnation Instant Breakfast, preferably chocolate.

"I'll have a Genoa grinder." I felt my breath catch in my chest.

"Are you sure?" I didn't want to deny him a food that had been a lifelong favorite, but I knew a grinder, thick with salami and cheese, would not be easy to swallow, even if he chewed for a long time.

"I'll be fine," he assured me.

I feared he was being overly optimistic but didn't push back.

We arrived at the house at 8:00 PM. The trip from the airport had taken us one and a quarter hours, but with two infants, it felt like an eternity, especially after our vanload fell apart the last fifteen minutes when Harper tired of trying to get milk out of my knuckle and Bette would not be consoled by anything. Much as I loved those babies, with their screams ricocheting off the van's interior, I was wondering if teeth could ache from tension. The moment we were parked in the driveway, I propelled myself out of the van and took a few long deep breaths, lips pursed on the audible exhale.

The house was gorgeous! Marketing photos are often not accurate representations, but in this case the photos didn't do the house justice. All our bedrooms were on the third floor. I put our luggage and a Pack 'n Play in one of the two oceanfront master suites and assigned the other suite to Sasha and John who would need the extra space for all the baby paraphernalia. Both suites opened on to a covered balcony that connected them and wrapped around the sides of the house. Ruby had her own room, the only one with twin beds. Justin and Kylie took the room next to Ruby. Their rooms also opened on to a shared covered balcony that ran the length of the house and overlooked an estuary of the Intercoastal Waterway one block away. Every room had a ceiling fan, and the rooms were laid out to maximize cross ventilation from the sea breezes.

While the others explored the house, unpacked and changed and fed the babies, I set the dining room table, so we'd be ready to eat as soon as the food arrived. When the pizza arrived, I called everyone to eat. Justin got out beers and opened the wine, while Sasha cut up Mae's pizza. By the time we were all at the table, Ruby was already half way through her first piece. We were famished, happy to be at our destination after a long stressful trip, and grateful the twins were asleep, nose-to-nose, in the Pack 'n Play in Sasha's room.

Sitting next to Bruce, I watched with heightened awareness as he lifted the grinder from his plate, one hand in front of the other grasping the Italian bread, head tilted slightly over the plate in case some lettuce, tomato, hot peppers, or oil oozed out, and took a bite. Time slowed as he started to chew. I didn't take my eyes off him, imagining worst-case scenarios. Unable to swallow, agitated, he left the table, darting toward the bathroom in the adjoining office.

Conversation ceased as we shifted our glances, one to the other, with unvoiced understanding of what had happened. I gave Bruce a few minutes and then went to check on him, feeling everyone's eyes on my back.

"You OK, sweetie? Can I heat you up some soup?"

"No thanks." His voice was almost a whisper, sounding defeated, like he wished he could flee. "I'm not hungry." The pain in his voice seared my heart. A few minutes later he emerged, face ashen, eyes damp, beads of sweat on his forehead. "I'm going to go up to bed."

"OK. I'll be up soon." I gently took his hand. "I love you." I let him go, respecting his need for some time alone to process the dinner experience and what it meant for his future.

Returning to the table, the mood had turned somber.

"Is Dad OK?" Justin said, voicing what everyone felt.

"Yes, he's tired. He'll see us in the morning."

Ruby and Mae were still chattering away, eating their dinner, oblivious to the drama they had just witnessed. I cleared away Bruce's plate, came back to the table, and tried to eat my pizza.

We had reached a milestone on Bruce's journey. I had known it was coming, as did he, but it still hurt. From now on, consuming food would be a chore required to keep his body functioning, not a pleasure to be savored. It was clear that the time when the growing tumor would completely close off passage to the stomach was not far away. We didn't talk about it. Other than "I'm sorry" there was nothing to say.

From our east-facing suite the dawn light woke me, softly illuminating the seafoam green walls. Bruce and Mae were still sleeping soundly, so I quietly slipped out of bed and went out on our balcony to greet the day. In the morning light, I could see the beautiful panoramic views that had been promised online. Across the dunes I heard the waves crashing on the shore and felt a pleasant breeze carrying moist warm air and a clean salty smell. I watched the sun climb, starting in a rosy gold funnel of light that was so broad and bright at the horizon it completely obscured the water. Then, like an hourglass, with the sun at the top and the ocean at bottom, sunbeams flowed, scattering diamond sparkles over the water. I could feel the ocean's energy working its magic, just as I hoped it would, putting me in a mildly meditative state of calm.

Downstairs in the kitchen, while my cup of tea steeped, I checked out the view from the second-floor balcony. The squawking bark of seagulls was music to my ears. Tea in hand, I went back up to our bedroom balcony, where I listened for signs of life from Sasha's suite. Hearing no baby noises, I tiptoed across our shared balcony to their open slider. Still nothing. I was sure Sasha had been awake every few hours during the night to nurse the twins. At home she had a double Boppy nursing pillow, specifically made for two babies in tandem, but it had been too big to bring. She resigned herself to feeding them one at a time, meaning she would be constantly nursing babies.

I settled into the cushioned teak lounger on our balcony, my mug of tea on the wide wooden armrest, until I heard Mae begin to stir. Bruce was awake too, so I lifted Mae onto our bed where she snuggled between Bruce and me.

When Justin, Kylie, and Ruby got up, we all went downstairs where they made coffee and took Ruby and Mae to check out the beach while I stayed with Bruce. After the girls had breakfast, Justin, Kylie, and

Ruby investigated the bottom floor of the house, finding surfboards, boogie boards, pails and shovels, kites, beach chairs, beach towels, a tarp to provide shade, and a pop-up tent we could use to shade the babies as they napped. They also found a full laundry room with a Bosch large-capacity washer and dryer that were perfectly designed for our multi-generational group of ten.

Continuing their explorations on the second floor, while searching the office for games, videos, toys, and books, Ruby came across a tote bag full of what appeared to be doggie bags, each one addressed to one of us.

"Can we open them?" she asked me.

"I don't know." I had never seen them before.

I turned to Justin. "Did you bring them?"

"No." He shook his head, as puzzled as I was.

"Please . . .," Ruby pleaded.

"I don't know what they are, sweetie, or where they came from."

"Please. It has my name on it," she pressed, wearing me down.

"Oh, OK." I was curious to see what they were too and not in the mood for a fight.

She opened the doggie bag addressed to her, and retrieved a napkin, a bag of chips, and what looked like a grinder, wrapped in butcher paper, decorated with stickers—*Mild Italian* in bright red, *Chicago Style* in bright green, and a blue sticker with a six-pointed Star of David and *Kosher* in white lettering.

Ruby tore open the "grinder" to reveal a rolled up black tee-shirt with yellow lettering across the front. I did a double take when I read it. F#CK CANCER. Mae was already opening hers—a bright green tee-shirt with white letters. I saw Justin's uneasy smile build as the surprise sank in and he reached for his own bag. His was light tan with black gothic print. Kylie grinned as she held hers up—gray with red lettering—and we glanced at one another. I giddily opened mine—soft lilac with hot pink letters. Bruce's was the pièce de résistance—a white tee, with navy bands at the collar and sleeves, and the message spelled correctly.

Sasha must have heard the laughter because she and John soon came downstairs.

"Morning, Sweetie. Do we have you to thank for these delicious doggie bags?"

Since no one else was taking credit, I figured it had to be her. I wished I hadn't let Ruby open them, sure that Sasha would have wanted to open the tee-shirts as a family, so she could see Bruce's face. Unfortunately, she hadn't hidden them well enough.

"You do," she smiled. "They're from Stacy."

I guess the *Chicago Style* sticker should have been a clue. Sasha's good friend from childhood, Stacy, who now lived in Chicago, had become our "adopted" daughter. She had organized Sasha's bachelorette party and participated in our Celebration of Life parties and skits.

After pouring a cup of coffee, Sasha opened her doggy bag—peach with hot pink lettering. John's was medium gray with black letters. Not to be left out just because they were only seven weeks old, there was a pink onesie with white lettering for Bette and a blue onesie with black lettering for Harper.

After a marathon record-breaking grocery shopping trip and a quick lunch, Bruce and Mae went upstairs to nap. As Bruce's appetite waned and cancer continued its march through his organs, his fatigue deepened. He generally slept late, took a nap in the afternoon and went to bed early—right up Mae's alley. She always had company—and Pa's stories—for her nap and bedtime.

Before arriving in Florida, we had learned that the reason New Smyrna Beach had once been chosen for a family reunion was that our nephew Patrick, the youngest of Suzanne's six children, lived there.

I vividly remember first meeting him on Thanksgiving in 1970 when he was a toddler. We had just moved to Atlanta for Bruce's master's program at Georgia Tech and could not afford to fly home to Connecticut for the holiday. Suzanne, who lived just a two-hour drive away in

Dalton, Georgia, had invited us to spend the long holiday weekend with them. When we pulled in their driveway, Suzanne was getting Patrick out of the car. Entering the house, we crossed the threshold into a foreign land. Six children and a barking dog raced through the house, oblivious to the football game on the TV in the living room and the other football games playing on various radios. Suzanne took my homemade cheesecake and put it next to her Sara Lee pumpkin pie on the dessert table. We had planned to stay for the weekend, but left the next day, the chaos being too much. I remember reevaluating our naïve thought that we might want a large family, ratcheting the number down to something well south of six.

We had seen Patrick a few times in the intervening years, when his family drove to Connecticut to visit relatives or when we attended his siblings' weddings. When we called to let him know we were in town, he asked if it would be OK for him to stop over that evening, just to say a quick hello. He arrived with a big mesh bag of grapefruits and oranges slung over his shoulder, a Florida Santa Claus.

"What a great house," Patrick said. "Super location."

"We're loving it." I replied.

"And you're far enough south that you're on a no-driving stretch of beach."

Noticing that I was too puzzled even to ask what that meant, he told us that in this part of Florida cars were allowed to drive on the beach! I'd never heard of such a thing.

"Have you seen any sharks yet?"

Another possibility I hadn't considered.

"New Smyrna Beach is the shark bite capital of the world," he proudly told us. "We account for fifteen percent of all bites worldwide."

I was speechless, but not Ruby. "They won't bite us. My legs are too muscly, and my dad's legs are too hairy."

Patrick smiled. "Most of the bites are on the northern part of the beach anyway, where the ocean meets an inlet."

I wasn't convinced. Sasha even less so.

Our days were dedicated to helping Bruce do what he loved most—fly kites, play Frisbee, bodysurf, swim, walk the beach, and savor time with his grandchildren.

Bruce always kept a kite at the ready, in the trunk of his car and stashed above the washer and dryer at home. New Smyrna Beach offered a broad, flat expanse of sand with endless possibilities. Bruce gave Ruby the string to the kite she had found amongst the beach toys, then, holding the kite, backed away from her in the direction the wind was blowing. "Run Ruby," he yelled as he released the bright red biplane with black crosses on the wings. It took a few tries to get the kite launched, but when it sailed up into the sky Ruby was ecstatic.

After giving Bruce a bit of a rest, holding the Frisbee in my right hand, I turned to him with a smile, cocked my head to the left, and raised my eyebrows in a silent invitation to play. When Bruce nodded yes, I extended my hand to help him out of his beach chair. Walking far enough from the cluster of chairs to not endanger anyone with the soon-to-be-flying disc, we passed Sasha who had just finished checking on the babies asleep in the popup tent.

"Wanna join us?" I asked.

"Sure!"

Bruce and I spread out across from each other while she moved to complete the triangle.

I curled my hand backward and released the Frisbee with a slow steady snap. Not wanting to make Bruce run or jump, I had positioned myself a little closer to him than usual to increase my accuracy. He caught it easily, swiveled, and released it forward to Sasha. We continued at that pace until Ruby, who had just dug her way out of being buried in sand and decorated as a mermaid by her parents, noticed what we were doing. She made it a foursome and we ratcheted the torque down one more notch. I made sure she was on Bruce's right so that he would throw to her, but her potentially wild or short throws would be chased by Sasha, not Bruce.

Before long, Mae wandered over.

Bruce positioned her about ten feet away from him and propelled the Frisbee in a way that was somewhere between a snap and a gentle lob. The trick was to give it enough speed that it didn't crash to the ground and not so much that it would hurt Mae if she wasn't able to catch it. We switched to a freeform order and direction of play, making Mae feel included and engaging all the adults with each child.

Walking back to our chairs, Bruce held the Frisbee high as he turned to Justin. They walked down to the shoreline and started tossing the Frisbee back and forth, parallel to the water. They were farther apart than we had been and throwing with a greater velocity, though not as strongly as they had in earlier times. Whether by accident or design, Bruce's throws tended to curve high and towards the water, causing Justin to run into the water where he jumped and successfully caught the Frisbee, then, carried forward by momentum, crashed into the waves. When it happened a few more times, I guessed it was more likely by design than accident. Justin's throws were precise, requiring no theatrical catches on Bruce's part. I smiled, remembering the many happy times on the beach at Napa Tree in Rhode Island when Justin was a boy and they both ended up in the ocean, laughing and whooping. My heart was filled by the sights and sounds, past and present.

Bruce loved bodysurfing. He and the kids never tired of getting tumbled and smashed onto the beach. There had been times that I felt the waves were too intimidating, but Bruce would still take Sasha and Justin in. On one occasion, the three of them were caught in a riptide. I trusted that he would keep them safe—he was a lifeguard and knew what to do—but I was still anxious as I watched from the beach. He held both of them, one in each arm, and swam parallel to the beach until they were free of the tide.

Now, it was a grown Justin who watched over his father. They slowly walked out to where the waves were breaking. As the mounds of water moved towards him, Bruce watched how the waves were rolling, waiting patiently for the best one. At exactly the right moment, he turned around and pushed off the ocean floor towards the shore, swimming to give himself enough forward momentum. As he extended his arm out in front, continuing quick short kicks, I could see on his face the exhilarating rush of the wave pushing him forward. Unlike his pre-cancer days, he stood up before getting pummeled into the sand.

Bruce had not been able to indulge his passion for biking and running for the last several months, but on this trip, with Justin by his side, he managed a very short run. When they got back, and Bruce was comfortably resting, Justin came to find me.

"Hey, Mom. I noticed on our walk that Dad seems a bit strange. Is he on drugs?" Justin asked.

"He isn't," I answered, taken aback at first. "But now that you mention it, he does seem a bit different. I'll give Dr. Abraham a call."

I didn't remember being warned about mental changes, but before saying anything to Bruce I wanted to talk to Dr. Abraham, who had made it clear we could call or page him anytime. After some discussion of symptoms, Dr. Abraham concluded that Bruce was probably suffering from dehydration. Not aware of the side effects to watch for, and consumed with our busy household, I had not tracked his fluid intake as carefully as I should have. At home, and when he was having chemo, I monitored it closely and encouraged him to drink often, but down here, with none of our usual routine, I had paid less attention. Saying nothing about it to Bruce, I began watching his water intake more carefully, and made an appointment to see Dr. Abraham for when we returned home. I had Bruce back to normal—at least the new normal—within a day. Lesson learned. I needed to be vigilant. His life depended on it. My role in helping him live the remainder of his life as fully as possible was critical.

Every afternoon we had cocktails and snacks on the beach, gathered together on the long wide stretch of white sand, the late-day sun on the water, no one else around. Bruce's taste and appetite allowed for, at most, just a small glass of white wine, but the rest of us had the cocktail du jour, and the children toasted with juice boxes. Seagulls, which had been walking along the shoreline, flew above and around us when they realized we had food. The girls chased them away, laughing and waving their arms. Bruce sat in his beach chair, wrapped head to toe in a warm towel as the sun dipped low in the western sky.

I am always happy at the beach, but I especially loved these late afternoons, spent from the day's activities, reflecting on joyous moments of the day, recalling memories and emotions from many happy times spent near the ocean. The magnificence of where we were and everything that was around us left me feeling deeply relaxed and revitalized. I was hopeful it was doing the same for Bruce.

Most of the time, we just relaxed at the house or on the beach, but as arranged, Patrick returned one evening with his girlfriend, Katherine. After some drinks and conversation, Patrick got out his newly acquired guitar and strummed some tunes with Justin.

As far as I knew, there was no other musical talent in our family, on either side. Justin and Sasha had both subjected our household to the stress of band participation in middle school, Sasha playing the flute and Justin the saxophone. Virtually every student took band, making recitals in the gym, sitting on hard bleachers, long and tortuous. Rehearsals at home were almost as bad, the difference being the seating options and the duration. With neither child showing much interest or promise, music was replaced by sports in junior high and high school.

Then, after college, Justin took up guitar. As with skateboarding and virtually everything else at which he excelled, he was self-taught. We first saw him perform at a small dive in D.C. when he was twenty-nine. I was impressed by his talent, though less enamored with his rock and roll songs. Nonetheless, we were proud parents.

He began writing songs with clever meaningful lyrics, the genre softened, and his skill increased. He wrote an album's worth of songs and was signed with a small D.C. label. When we attended his record release show, we were blown away.

"I am in awe of you," Bruce had told Justin, standing to embrace him. From that day forward, Bruce, still in awe of his son, cried at every performance, including the one today.

Justin generally did not like to perform, but he was happy to take our requests. I asked for my favorite, "Miss Amputee West Culver County," a haunting ballad about a beauty pageant winner and her forlorn lover.

Mae requested her favorite, "The Ballad of Big Snake and Mister Frog," about a snake, a frog, talking trash, and shots of rye, gin, and mash, that does not end well for the frog. Justin calls it a drinking song for kids, but an adult hearing the lyrics will appreciate a completely different level of humor. Ruby and Mae, inspired by the catchy lyrics and beat, danced their little hearts out.

Justin also debuted the start of a song that, unbeknownst to me, he and Bruce had been working on during the week. Justin cleared his throat, strummed a few chords, then, confident that he remembered this work in progress, started again and added the lyrics about someone who's only happy when he's unhappy, rhyming gin with Ramada Inn.

Bruce and I had begun writing the story of Ramona at the Ramada Inn years earlier in Cinque Terre on the Italian Riviera. Each day, as we lounged at the beach, we took turns improvising and developing aspects of the plot and characters. Bruce recorded the emerging story in a notebook he carried with him, presumably the basis for their collaboration. Perhaps he hoped that this story, or our story, would live on through Justin's song. I hoped they wouldn't run out of time before their collaboration was complete.

One afternoon we walked, very slowly, a little over a block away to a popular local restaurant billed as "Southern seafood with an attitude." We started with drinks at a table outside. It felt awkward at first when Bruce didn't even order water, but we were soon all talking and laughing. As his ability to eat deteriorated, he helped us renegotiate how we would adapt. Bruce set the tone, as he had from the beginning, putting us at ease. As the adults laughed and joked, Mae and Ruby made friends with a snowy egret who they named Whitey. The mood was light. Bruce, who hadn't wanted any food, walked around the restaurant with a restless Mae while we ate our fish sandwiches.

I reflected on how much Bruce had loved to eat—not in gluttonous consumption but in celebration of flavor and pleasure. As his ability to enjoy food continued to slip away, I realized how central food was to our lives. As much as I grieved that Bruce could no longer enjoy eating, I also mourned my loss of being able to cook for him, one of the loving gestures that enriched our relationship.

I envisioned that when we got home from this trip, mealtimes would begin changing for us, as we would lose the pleasure of breaking bread together. From the time we married, our agreement was that when one of us cooked, the other cleaned up, though in reality we were usually both in the kitchen from start to finish, assisting the other with chores or just visiting. I could see a time, in the not too distant future, when I would prepare a simple dinner for myself and eat at the kitchen counter, giving Bruce the option to sit with me or not. I knew at some point I would have to create my own solitary rituals, but I just wasn't ready yet.

Wanting to have an album of our time together here, I had asked John to take a lot of pictures with his digital camera and telephoto lens. It would be especially valuable for Mae, whose toddler memories would surely fade, and for Harper and Bette, who were too young to develop any memory of Bruce, let alone their trip to Florida.

Of the hundreds of photos chronicling our time together that week, I have a few favorites: Bruce and Justin bodysurfing, Ruby leaning back as she looks up at her soaring kite, Mae proudly standing on the boogie board as Sasha holds the lead, Bruce and Justin sitting shoulder to shoulder laughing at something they are watching on the beach. But one picture stands out. With the camera on a tripod and timer, we all stand together on the beach, the surf in the background, in our special F#CK CANCER tee-shirts (and onesies), with expressions of smiling defiance. John holds a screaming Bette, Sasha holds a sleeping Harper, and I have a smiling Mae. Bruce is in the middle of the frame with his right arm around me and his left arm around Justin. Justin's other arm is around Kylie's shoulder, whose hand rests on Ruby's shoulder.

For our family there is no such thing as a bad day at the beach, but this entire week had been beyond perfect. Our time together was everything I could have hoped for, for Bruce and for the rest of us. We were surrounded by beauty and in control of our days, in an environment both physical and spiritual that stirred fond memories while we created new ones: memories that would bring us joy as well as comfort and security in a time of grief.

Even though we all knew the end was near, it didn't feel like the end. Because of his decision to stop treatment, Bruce was not tethered to an IV or worrying about blood counts, infections, or side effects. He was physically, mentally, and emotionally free to savor the joy of each moment.

Much of our time is spent in the past or the future, rather than the present. We end up passing through a moment on the way to somewhere else, and in so doing we miss the moment we are in. The past can't be changed. The future we can't control. On this trip, our family was in the present moment and our time together was some of the most meaningful that we had ever spent.

I was thankful that Bruce's end of life was going as he had hoped. Not the old hope for a cure, but the new hope to celebrate life fully in the moment, to do what he loved for as long as he could. I was keenly aware, as was Bruce, that this trip had many "lasts" —the beach, the ocean, bodysurfing, playing Frisbee, flying kites, running—but Bruce was reveling in each and every experience, not sorrowfully regretting that there wouldn't be more. The decision to stop treatment had made each accomplishment sweet for its existence rather than for its loss.

Although I mourned for Bruce, I was not yet grieving for myself and the inevitable new reality of being alone. I was right there with him, not yet worrying about having to do these things, like walk the beach alone at some point in the future. There would be plenty of time to adjust to that later. For now, enjoying the here and now together was enough.

Bruce didn't want us to stop living just because he was dying, any more than he wanted us to stop eating just because he couldn't. He wanted us to continue to have fun. That's who he was, and continued to be, even in dying, and it was his small (and large) acts of generosity and compassion that made that possible.

We didn't have to leave for the airport until 3 PM on Monday. When I called the owner to see if we could stay later than noon on the last day he said no problem, the house had sold. We would be its first and last renters. Kismet. After packing up the van and before heading out, we walked over the dunes to say goodbye to New Smyrna Beach.

We stood together.

On the coast of Florida.

At the edge of a continent.

On the verge of a great unknown.

Like explorers of old.

CHAPTER TWENTY-SIX

ON THE ROAD AGAIN

Thursday, April 30, 2009

Good news. The blood work all looked pretty good and the liver was still processing everything the way it should. The bad news was that there was nothing Dr. Abraham could give Bruce to reduce the strange new sensations in his body. He thought they were probably a combination of the constitutional effect of the tumors and the lingering effects of the cranial radiation. Bruce's anti-nausea medicine had a side effect of impacting his muscles, so Bruce stopped taking it to see if that would help him feel better. I regularly reminded him to sip fruit juices, more vigilant than ever about hydration. This was probably the new normal, at least until we moved to the next new normal.

I was not adjusting well to the chilly rain and wind. The day after returning home, we enjoyed Florida-like temperatures, but as is common in a New England spring, the temperature had plummeted twenty-five degrees overnight. I had just returned from my morning Body Bar class at the gym when I got Sasha's email. She wanted to know if there was any word on whether we'd be coming to visit.

Hi Sweetie,

We have talked about coming. As of now, Dad is saying no, but I'm still hoping he'll feel better and change his mind. He's

187

been spending his time sitting on the couch and reading magazines. Very frustrating! He says he's totally consumed with how his body is feeling.

You know I'm a big believer in mind over matter, and I'm trying to get him to "get his head in the game" so he can keep "alive" as long as possible. It may be unfair since I don't know exactly what's going on in his body, but based on my experience with major surgery (and I expect yours) I know it takes some mental determination to overcome the physical and get on with life.

Anyway, I'm trying to get him to talk to me about how he's feeling and if he has anything he wants to do while he still has time left. Maybe the good blood test results and the hydration (and my counseling) will put him in a better frame of mind. I think being around you and the girls will make him happier, and I'm touting your comfortable recliner as a great place to relax.

He's never been a particularly good patient and hasn't had much experience with major illness/discomfort. He also didn't come from my strong line of Yankees. We know what Mom would do. Anyway, I'm not canceling our flights until the very last minute.

Love you,
Mom

Hi Mom,

I'm hoping he'll change his mind, too—especially since the liver test came back good. I could understand it a little bit more if the test came back bad, but it didn't, so part of me (selfishly) feels like there's no excuse. But like you said, we don't know how he's feeling.

*We can (and will) come up there, but it would be a lot eas-
ier, at least for us, and more comfortable (for me, asthma wise)
if you guys came here. I know you know all of this and I hope
I'm not being insensitive, but I really want to spend more time
with him and would like him to feel the same, which I know he
does. I was thinking about our recliner and how it would be a
good spot for him.*

*It must be really frustrating for you. I appreciate that
you're trying. Should I say anything to him? He has sounded
better to me over the last day or two.*

*Hang in there—keep working on him and I'll keep my fin-
gers crossed.*

Love you!
Sasha

I tried to walk a fine line between focusing only on supporting what
Bruce wanted to do and satisfying our family's desire to spend as much
time with him as they could. I was grateful Sasha and I had each other
to vent our frustrations. I knew Bruce had enough of his own feelings
to deal with and it wasn't appropriate or helpful to vent at him. At the
same time, if I held in my frustration I felt guilty that I couldn't be the
perfect matriarch, calmly solving everyone's problems. Never a big
talker, Bruce seemed to be drawing within himself even more. Based
on past experience, I was confident he'd be happy once he got to
Sasha's, but I had to acknowledge that I was not in his shoes. In fact,
these were new shoes for him, too.

Bruce had told everyone about his journey except Rosemary, his
ninety-two-year-old aunt and godmother. I didn't understand why he
wasn't able to tell her, but since his diagnosis he had been unwilling to
see her, even with prompting from Sasha and me. As with most in-
stances of delaying the delivery of bad news, I feared the longer it went
on, the harder it would get.

With Bruce's consent, his sisters Sandra and Marion had broken the news to Rosemary when they were in town for our "Irish wake," but it still took continued, dare I say relentless, gentle prodding before Bruce finally agreed to visit her. As we pulled into the parking lot of the assisted-living facility where she had resided for several years, Bruce got very quiet. I took his arm as we entered the building and rode the elevator to the second floor. Feeling him tense as we neared her door, I gave his arm a squeeze and gently pulled my body against his. Once over the threshold and seeing her tearful smile, he moved naturally to her open arms. Over time, she had become increasingly confined to a chair, but Bruce didn't let that stop him from giving her a very long close hug.

Her body may have been failing but her mind was sharp. She was a remarkable woman who had led a full, rich life and remembered more details of it than could be expected of someone in her fifties, let alone her nineties.

It was rarely said out loud, but acknowledged by Bruce's siblings, that he was Rosemary's favorite, and the affection and admiration was reciprocated. Perhaps it had been so difficult for Bruce to call or visit her because he feared it would be too painful for him, or perhaps he thought it would be too painful for her, but once reunited with his beloved aunt, the love and respect they had always felt for each other took over.

Rosemary's son, Chip, happened to be visiting at the same time. As the four of us reminisced, we pointed to photos that spanned generations that covered the walls of her room. It was a nostalgic display of smiling children and joyous celebrations.

When it was time to leave, Rosemary held her arms out again and Bruce moved close.

"Goodbye, dear."

'Goodbye, Rosemary," Bruce told her as they looked into each other's souls.

"I love you," he told her as they held their tearful warm embrace for what seemed like minutes, not wanting this time to end. I could feel Rosemary's angst, outliving another loved one, and this one far too young.

Emotionally exhausted, I took his arm again and we walked to the car, still crying. For Bruce, this was one more step on this journey, each one more difficult, more emotionally laden, signaling he was drawing closer to the final destination. We sat in the parking lot for a few moments before I started the car and slowly pulled out onto the main road.

Driving through the quaint scenery of northwestern Connecticut occupied our senses until I noticed we were entering the town where my brother lived, and suggested we stop for a visit. George lives half of the year in Florida and half of the year at Lone Oaks, a 250-acre campground in the Berkshire foothills. Although George's trailer home can hardly be considered camping. He has a large corner lot, abutting the expansive fields of a neighboring farm and offering stunning views of the mountains.

We sat in George's compact but comfortable living room, chatting about our respective children and grandchildren, and it didn't feel like small talk. There was no discussion of Bruce's illness, but since George knew everything there was none of the awkwardness of consciously avoiding the topic. Bruce's impending death was never out of our subconscious, but we didn't dwell on it. Amid dying, life went on and Bruce continued to take great pleasure in the little things that made it worth living.

***

On Thursday, May 6, we flew to Nashville to visit Sasha for a week. With the stress of seeing Rosemary behind him, and rested after a week at home, Bruce was feeling better about making the trip. Because Sasha was still on maternity leave we got to spend a lot of time with her and the girls. With culinary feasts no longer an option, we enjoyed the simple pleasures of reading, playing with Mae, sitting on the deck or the patio, and napping.

Often, while we ate dinner at the table, Bruce sat in the nearby recliner, graciously holding a baby if required. He enjoyed the cuddle time, more so when they were not fussing, but his absence at the table amplified how life had changed, and how sorely he was missed during these simplest of pleasures. He was still able to eat soups and Carnation Instant Breakfast, but to the extent that Bruce continued to participate in mealtimes it would now be purely for the social interaction.

Bruce's sister Suzanne, who lived in Georgia, was the only sibling who hadn't been able to come to his Irish wake in April. She'd recently had breast cancer and then negative reactions to the drugs being used for her treatment. Now she was feeling better and wanted to see Bruce while we were in Nashville. She and her husband, Dick, made the two-and-a-half-hour trip, chauffeured by their son, Jimmy. We hadn't seen this nephew in fifteen years, so we were doubly glad they were all coming.

Sasha and I set her dining table with yellow and blue Provence linens befitting a spring luncheon. Suzanne, Dick, and Jimmy chose their seats while I put the quiches, mushroom pie, and salad on the table. I then took my place next to Bruce, the sun streaming through the tall window, warming my back. I served everyone, discreetly giving Bruce smaller portions, while Dick, the consummate storytelling salesman, kept us entertained throughout the meal. Not wanting to make his eating a topic of conversation, Bruce sat with us for lunch, taking a few baby bites of quiche, but mainly moving bits of food around the plate to give the appearance of eating. Fortunately, the ruse worked. Suzanne and Dick didn't seem to notice his lack of appetite.

After lunch, we sat outside on the deck, alternating between watching Mae play and holding the babies, who had cooperated by sleeping through the meal and then getting up in time to provide entertainment. I was enjoying the company as well as the perfect 70-degree weather, and the backyard full of trees and flowers, blooming a full month ahead of Connecticut.

I wasn't surprised that Suzanne was upbeat throughout the visit, not mentioning anything about her recent medical challenges or Bruce's. Of the seven siblings, she had always been one who was more private and less apt to pry. She was also the only family member who had not supported Bruce's decision to stop treatment. Thankfully the topic didn't come up during this visit. She had either changed her mind or realized there was no benefit to pursuing it.

The rest of our visit was quiet, which was perfectly OK with everyone.

***

We flew home on the fourteenth. The next day, Bruce had blood work and a routine visit with Dr. Abraham, if it's possible to say that visits during the last stages of life can be considered routine. Normally, we visit doctors in hopes they will cure a specific complaint, but these visits were to keep us updated on what was coming next, and to help Bruce achieve his end-of-life goals. Dr. Abraham was upfront with us about the process of dying. Bruce and I wanted information in all its gory, but helpful detail and Dr. Abraham was at ease giving it to us.

I knew there had to be a lot of change going on inside Bruce's body. In yoga, I had experienced how profoundly internal changes can be perceived. When I lie on my back and lift one leg straight up, stretching it for several minutes, and then place that leg back on the mat next to the other one, the stretched leg feels flatter to the ground and slimmer by an inch or more. Even though I am sure there is no discernable difference on the outside, the internal sensation is dramatic. I couldn't imagine what it would feel like to have my organs undergoing the kind of transformation that Bruce was surely experiencing. Other than telling me he was consumed by how his body felt when we were debating whether to visit Sasha, we didn't discuss it. I doubt that he could have even described these totally new and foreign sensations.

***

We had never missed Ruby's birthday. She would be turning six on May 23, and Bruce was determined to celebrate with her. Even though I would have to do all the driving, it was much easier on Bruce to travel by car rather than to fly. He was able to recline the seat and rest or sleep along the way, stopping every couple of hours for a stretch and bio break.

Ruby's celebrations had gotten grander each year. The Saturday afternoon party was held in a private room at Jackie's, a neighborhood restaurant they frequented. Housed in a converted auto parts garage in an industrial section of Silver Spring, the 1970's retro design had a vibrant pink, yellow, and orange color scheme, exposed brick walls, and twenty-foot ceilings with exposed rafters. We knew many of the guests—Justin's musician friends, Kylie's relatives and friends, and families of Ruby's friends. There was updated comfort food and an open bar. Justin and other musicians played while the party goers danced. Ruby wore a hot pink, sleeveless minidress with flapper-like horizontal layers of fabric.

Usually we would have been mingling, partaking in small talk as necessary. "What's new?" from acquaintances. "What do you do?" from strangers. But Bruce didn't have the stamina to stand for any length of time and I didn't want to leave him. I sought out a few people I knew when I got up briefly to get something to eat or drink, or to dance a little with Ruby and her friends, or to gather and sing as she blew out her candles, but most of the time I stayed with Bruce. People stopped over to say hello—mainly close friends of Justin who had a connection to our family and a fondness for Bruce.

Stationary and seated, I felt conspicuous and isolated, even amid the celebratory noise and motion around me. For the past months, I had become accustomed to either being with small groups of family and close friends or in the quiet restorative calm of being alone with Bruce. The energy of this large and noisy crowd felt different and jarring.

Observing the partygoers absorbed in the festivities, my selfish and irrational internal dialogue alternated between *How can they be so oblivious when Bruce is dying* and *We're only an insignificant cog in this party wheel.*

I felt outside of my body, observing us from a distance. I floated in limbo, not the Christian region of afterlife between heaven and hell, but some indefinite state, a transitional step. I realized how much I relied on the warm cocoon of friendship to keep me feeling safe and supported. I was thankful that, knowing Bruce would probably not want to stay for the whole party, we had driven our own car. Saying our goodbyes to Ruby and Justin, we headed back to the comforting embrace of their apartment and each other.

Except for the birthday party, our time with Justin was very quiet. The day after Memorial Day, I took the wheel again for our drive back to Connecticut while Bruce slept. It was our last trip to Silver Spring.

CHAPTER TWENTY-SEVEN

SELLING THE CAR

Tuesday, May 26, 2009

Bruce had not driven for some time. Mindful of how hard it would be, we reluctantly agreed it was time to sell one of our two cars. I was driving a 1995 Acura Legend with an automatic transmission and 140,000 miles on it. Bruce had recently bought a 2005 Acura Legend with modern amenities, low mileage, and a manual transmission. Bruce loved a stick shift, so much so that when he drove my car he still shifted! I, on the other hand, had not driven a manual transmission in years and had no intention of using a stick shift ever again. Although financially it made sense for me to sell my car, we came to the decision that we would sell Bruce's.

For me, a car is something to get me from point A to point B. For Bruce, it was much more. When he got out of the army he bought a black MGB with red leather interior. It was completely impractical transportation—no back seat, miniscule trunk space, and a fabric top that, no matter how tightly you rolled up the windows, did not protect occupants from the forces of nature. I have vivid (and frigid) memories of stuffing newspapers between the top of the windows and the convertible top in a futile effort to keep warm as we drove through upstate New York on snowy winter nights. I have an equally vivid memory of driving from Waterbury to Hammonasset after buying my engagement ring, the top down, my long, blond hair blowing, the front held in place by a monogrammed blue scarf folded in a triangle and tied at the nape of my neck. The scarf was one of many presents that Bruce bestowed on me while I was in college and he was deployed in the Dominican Republic. In route to Hammonasset, we had stopped at a little package store to buy a bottle of champagne, so our family could toast our engagement. It had all felt surreal. Was I truly old enough, adult enough to be getting married? And yet it was the best thing that ever happened to me.

As impractical as the MGB was, I must confess that when we were first married, and Bruce was relegated to the big Ford Fairlane provided by his employer, I had enjoyed driving a hot little sports car. When I graduated from college and we moved back to Connecticut, my mother gave me her old green VW Beetle and Bruce enthusiastically reclaimed his MGB.

I would not characterize Bruce as a stereotypical male who was defined by what he drove, but he did take pride in his cars, keeping them clean, polished, and running smoothly. He did most routine maintenance on both our cars himself, which was good because I would have paid no attention to putting water in radiators, refilling washer tanks, replenishing the oil, or putting air in tires, let alone following up on little things like a "check engine" light. But most important to him was the sense of freedom and adventure he felt when driving, the pure exhilaration of speed and agility, especially on winding country roads. I enjoyed it too, except for the occasional moments of terror. I was less enamored by his refusal to turn around or ask for directions when we were lost.

For most of our time together, my indulgence of his affair with cars was a small price to pay for something that brought him such joy. One of our rare serious disagreements, though, was over his purchase of an Alfa Romeo (the second of two) from his friend Tom. I contended they were uncomfortable and expensive to maintain. It might have been acceptable if he were the only one using it, but his car was the family car, so anytime we went somewhere together, I was an unwilling and unhappy passenger. I tolerated the first Alfa Romeo but vetoed the second. He bought it anyway, the first and last time we disagreed on a major expenditure.

I knew how hard it was for him to give up his car, another milestone on this forced march to the end, but I much preferred handling the sale with him by my side. I checked prices, took photos, got a CARFAX report, and drafted a Craig's List posting that Bruce, John, and Sasha reviewed. Several people responded right away, and two young guys came for a test drive. The second one asked Bruce why he was selling it. His simple reply, "I'm retired now, and we only need one car." I could hear the loss in Bruce's voice, though the young car enthusiast was oblivious. Two days after posting it online, Bruce sold his beloved Acura. The young man was excited to have found the car and Bruce knew it would have a good home.

CHAPTER TWENTY-EIGHT

YOU'VE GOT A FRIEND

Wednesday, May 27, 2009

Although the story of our lives is punctuated by the big events, it is family and friendships that are the basis of our everyday memories, the shared experiences that are part of our story. Bruce had been reveling in time spent with friends and family, and as impossible as it seemed, the pace of visits continued to ramp up, cradling both of us in love and friendship.

I had considered not going to our May book club meeting at Susie's, trying to balance time with Bruce against time with my friends and supporters, but I had decided that I needed some time with this warm, wonderful, inspiring group of women.

I walked into Susie's kitchen, already abuzz with conversation, and put my potluck lunch contribution of salad on the counter. I was instantly surrounded with hugs and words of support. It was an unexpected treat to see Lisa. She was the only one who knew Bruce since she and her husband had sailed with us and we often had dinner at each other's house.

"I thought you were too busy to come." I gave her a special squeeze.

When the embrace ended, she smiled at me. "If you can make the time for book club, then I can definitely make the time!"

For the next several hours we did what we always did, share stories and laughter, complement each other's cooking, and bask in the warmth of friendship.

***

Visits continued, with friends we saw often and those with whom we had lost touch. As with library cards, active membership in a friendship can lapse, but if it has been real and deep at one point, it can sometimes be reactivated. For Bruce, even lapsed relationships took on increased importance as his life drew to a close.

The next morning, Gary called to see if he and their mutual friend Paul could stop by. Gary and Bruce had been close friends for many years, first meeting when Bruce was the Town Planner for Avon and Gary was developing subdivisions in town. We had socialized since the 1970s, initially with Gary and his wife, later with a string of girlfriends, and finally with a long-term girlfriend who became his second wife. Over the years, from the time our children were young, our families had spent many good times together at the beach and each other's homes.

Although I was sure Gary knew Bruce was sick, he had not reached out. A few years earlier, Gary's closest friend had died after a short illness. Perhaps he wasn't prepared to face the loss of another close friend. Whatever the reason, when Gary called, Bruce was delighted.

We sat in the living room, sharing what had been going on in our respective families and reliving old times. He and Bruce had been wild and crazy partners in crime—well, maybe just mischief. The two of them had been known to take a bottle of wine in the middle of a work day, to go pick strawberries, and sit on the bank of a stream. During one of our dinners out together, in the middle of laughing over some funny story, Bruce had abruptly fallen off his chair, mimicking a move that Justin had perfected as a young boy. Whereas Justin's frequent chair episodes were accidental, Bruce's were for comic effect and, egged on by Gary, he repeated the move several more times that evening. My fears that we were being too loud were proved unfounded when diners at a neighboring table stopped by on their way out to thank us for the entertainment.

It was a joy to laugh again with the Gary I remembered from days gone by, the perennial life of the party, and to experience his rapid-fire storytelling. But I sensed an undercurrent of disquiet, like being with Kylie's family at Easter. Some people don't know what to say or how to act around a person who is dying, and their discomfort is palpable. Gary's love for Bruce was unquestionable, but there was no doubt he was not as comfortable as others who had been on this journey with Bruce since the beginning. I wondered if he brought Paul to act as a buffer. When he got up to leave, wrapping up another laughter-filled hour, Bruce and I got bear hugs that conveyed the significance of this last goodbye, lingering much longer than the gesture that we Americans have coopted as the new handshake.

My brother George had arranged to stop by with his eldest child, Bissy. Justin had been the ring bearer at her wedding; a cute but devilish seven-year-old in his light blue tux. We'd seen Bissy rarely after she moved to California, but she put a lot of importance on family and managed to keep in touch with letters and emails.

I brought a chaise lounge down from the pool for Bruce, and chairs for our visitors, placing them in a circle on the deck. It was a perfect day to welcome the month of June, sunny and in the low 70s. White bleeding hearts, yellow and purple irises and purple PJM rhododendrons in full bloom reminded us that spring comes every year, no matter what the winter has thrown at us.

We were expecting George, his wife Patty, and Bissy, but were glad to see that Heather and Monique, George's daughters from his second marriage, were also with him. I'd always enjoyed Heather and Monique, but until now hadn't appreciated how funny and lively they were. They must have gotten it from my brother, whose wry wit and jovial sarcasm I had come to appreciate over the years. They recounted hilarious stories involving family members in a way that made it easy for us to laugh at ourselves. It truly was the best medicine; my stomach ached from almost nonstop laughter.

A short time later, I was puzzled to see two women, who had been walking along the road, turn into our driveway. As they got nearer I saw it was my cousin Joyce, also from the West Coast, and a friend of hers. In town for her brother-in-law's funeral, Joyce had just visited her mother's grave at the Canton Center Congregational Church and decided to walk up East Mountain to see if we were home. She was delighted to have happened upon this unexpected gathering of her cousins.

We saw Joyce rarely, but through the wonders of technology, were in communication by email. Even before Bruce was sick, she had been exceptionally good about sending us electronic cards and updates on family events. There is usually at least one person in a family who takes on that mantle. It has never been me, despite all my good intentions. For our extended family on my mother's side, it was Joyce and I told her how grateful I was.

When Bruce started looking tired, I urged him to rest and our guests said their goodbyes. This day had been a whirlwind of visits, lifting his spirits and far outweighing the toll it was taking on his increasingly weakened body. Were we doing too much? I didn't think so. This was not a time to ration visits. It was exactly the right time for family, friends, and love.

In the last two months, we had spent half our time with our children and grandchildren. Even when we were home, I could count on one hand the days we were not physically surrounded by love and friendship, and on those rare days there were cards and letters waiting in the mailbox, emails and calls, CDs, books, inspirational tokens, and deliveries of homemade food, all valued for themselves and for the gesture of care that they embodied. The value to Bruce of the compassion, comfort, and laughter of friends was obvious.

A reward of illness is discovering how much people care for you. In the warm glow of good will it was easy for me to forget why we were being blessed with so much affection. Even Bruce's invisible internal reminders did not seem to diminish his joy. I wondered if this feeling of exhilaration would be sustainable over a long period of time or if it would become so routine that our appreciation of it would decline. For Bruce, it was a moot point. I took comfort in knowing that he would not have to answer that question. For him, it would last for the rest of his life.

Bruce was well along the path of saying goodbye to family and friends. Now it was time to say goodbye to his colleagues. He had learned early on in this journey that it was he who set the tone for how people would react, first to his cancer diagnosis and now to his impending death. He drafted a note to send to his colleagues, asked me to review it for suggested edits, and then posted it on the electronic bulletin board of the Connecticut Chapter of the American Planning Association.

Dear Colleagues,

As some of you may know, I retired from Planimetrics earlier this year. I did so because I have been diagnosed with cancer of the esophagus and liver in September of '08. I underwent chemo and radiation therapy and for a short period of time, the cancer was in remission. However, it has returned, and the prognosis is not at all good. Some additional chemotherapy is possible, but I don't think it is an alternative because the possibility of positive effects is very low and the deterioration of quality of life is high.

So, there you have it! I am in the third act of a play called life. The good news is that I get to say goodbye and have

experienced an outpouring of love and concern and care.
Please feel free to call me, email me, or visit me.

Bruce

The responses started flooding in, from planners who knew him and had worked with him in Connecticut, planners who knew him through his many years of active involvement in the national American Planning Association, serving on the Connecticut Chapter's Executive Committee for twenty-three years, five of them as the chapter president, and from people who barely knew him or had never met him in person but had benefited from his experience and knowledge.

Everyone expressed admiration for his generosity and professionalism, his sense of decency and calm demeanor no matter what the situation, his friendship. Many lauded his honesty and breathtaking courage in sharing this journey with them, facing the end, and not backing away from life or crawling in a hole, but instead choosing to savor all he could; taking a cleareyed approach to an unimaginably difficult decision and charting his own course surrounded by loved ones. They thanked him for reaching out and giving them the opportunity to say goodbye; for taking advantage of the many friends and colleagues who supported, admired, and loved him from all corners of the United States. They told him he would be sorely missed. That he was truly loved by so many. That he would be remembered.

I knew Bruce enjoyed what he did and was proud of his accomplishments, but until I read the scores of emails I didn't have a full understanding of his professional life and the people and communities he had directly impacted. The affection and admiration were overwhelming.

Many people near death achieve clarity about what is important, and Bruce was no different. His priorities were beyond simply prolonging his life. He wanted a sense that his life was complete, that his life had meaning and that he would be remembered. The responses to his simple

Dear Colleagues email left no doubt. For Bruce, whose reputation was well known within the planning community, the words of love and respect were probably not a surprise, though the passion and magnitude of the response may have been.

The unforeseen value was to me. I knew that Tom, Glenn, and other colleagues I had met held him in the highest regard. I had listened for years to his stories of accomplishment, sharing a slice of pie late at night after he had come home from a successful meeting. But before these emails, I hadn't fully grasped how broad and deep his tangible and intangible impact had been. It was a gift for me, and for Sasha and Justin, to see Bruce through the lens of his colleagues and for Bruce to be present for these testaments of admiration and affection that would have otherwise lived on only in condolences sent to me.

THE BOY SCOUT MOTTO

Thursday, May 28, 2009

My sister stopped by on the way home from her job at the library. She had checked out a few books on death and dying that she thought might be of interest. After reading the dust jackets and scanning the tables of contents, I decided *Jane Brody's Guide to the Great Beyond: A Practical Primer to Help You and Your Loved Ones Prepare Medically, Legally, and Emotionally for the End of Life* was the most far ranging and potentially most informative. Although death is a natural order of things, we had seen people who had known for some time that their condition was terminal, yet they and their families were unprepared for the final stage. I wanted to be prepared and since we only die once, and have no direct experience to draw on, I wanted to see what I could learn.

While Bruce napped on the couch, I sat across from him and perused the book in more detail. I somewhat smugly had assumed we were totally prepared. We had shared our views and experiences over the years, drawing on what we had learned from watching others die. Bruce knew what he did not want: aggressive treatments such as intubation and mechanical ventilation, tube or intravenous feeding, or resuscitation if his heart stopped. His living will and health-care directives were up to date, filed, and communicated to our children and medical team. We had a supportive medical team and had engaged hospice.

After finishing reading Chapter 1, I was still feeling prepared but not quite as smug. We had done a great job so far, working towards Bruce's goal of living life fully to the end, but as I now looked ahead to the end, I realized I was not fully prepared for this next stage, the dying at home surrounded by family. We were prepared for death in the abstract, as some future event, but knew little of the realities of the final days and weeks. This book would be of immense help with that. Dr. Abraham had been straightforward and honest with us, but until then I didn't know how much I didn't know.

On a more philosophical level, I read about the need to confront and prepare for death, to achieve a sense of control, to make meaning of one's life and death—tying up loose ends, resolving conflicts, saying goodbye, knowing that survivors will be OK, that things you are responsible for will be handled, that all will be forgiven, and that you will be remembered. Seeing it spelled out, I realized that this was exactly what Bruce had been doing intuitively. The week in Florida, the visits with friends and family, the legacy tour of his hometown, the Irish wake, the *Dear Colleagues* letter, were all part of his making meaning of life and death. None of which would have been possible if he had not openly confronted his death.

I had one of those Aha! moments where something you read or hear provides context, connecting the dots, reaffirming a feeling, revealing a dimension you hadn't considered. I was enjoying each of the things I had helped Bruce do, but had been viewing them as individual acts of love rather than parts of a whole, a whole that was a sacred rite of passage. I was wishing I had read this book earlier. I had done lots of research at the time of diagnosis and throughout treatment, but virtually nothing when we had transitioned from working on a cure to preparing for death.

Bruce stirred, looked around in a fog of sleep and sat up, drawing my attention back to the present. As I went over to give him a kiss, I told him about Jane dropping off the books and put the pile on the coffee table in front of him, suggesting he start with Jane Brody. I then went to the kitchen to make dinner. When I came back out to the living room after eating and cleaning up, I walked over to give him another kiss and then went to "my" couch to settle in for the evening.

"I was scared about not being able to breathe," Bruce announced, looking up from the open book. His words were matter of fact, the emotion anything but.

I was dumbstruck. Of course, he was thinking about dying, the actual process of it. While I was intellectually understanding and preparing for my caretaker role, Bruce was imagining and anticipating how it would *feel* to die. I would be terrified of not being able to breathe. Whenever I had involuntarily imagined my death, I got so scared that I had forced myself to stop thinking about it. His bravery was stunning. I hoped that when my time came I would be as brave as he.

"Pulmonary congestion, another common symptom when death is near, can cause breathing problems and prompt patients to gasp for air," he continued, calmly reading from the book. "However, supplying oxygen is not the way to relieve this 'air hunger' because the dying person usually cannot benefit from it . . . A more effective way to relieve breathlessness is to open windows, use a fan, allow space around the patient's bed, and administer morphine or a related drug, which can reduce both breathing difficulties and the anxiety that typically accompanies them." I could see the profound and soothing value of understanding the process of dying and how proper care would be able to ease the anxiety.

When, after a while, Bruce had grown tired of reading and put the book down, I picked it up to read the section he had referenced, the one that was most critical to his peace of mind. I learned that active dying, the process of total body system failure, usually occurs over a period of ten to fourteen days. The patient becomes dehydrated, swallowing becomes difficult, peripheral circulation decreases, the skin feels clammy and cold to the touch, and pulmonary congestion may make it difficult to breathe. Without fluids or nutrition, the patient experiences a euphoria from the buildup of ketones and as the body gradually shuts down the patient spends more time sleeping and focuses on inner contemplation as he leaves the outer world behind. Hearing is the last sense to leave the body. The absence of fluids and nutrition is nature's way of bringing gentle closure as the body gradually shuts down. The key word here for me was *gentle*.

This was what would happen to Bruce, I realized, when his tumor completely closed off the opening to his stomach. Reading about the many internal physical changes, I could see that Bruce's strange bodily sensations over the last month, while not yet active dying, were the precursor of organs and systems succumbing to the invading cancer cells. I wished I had known this earlier, too, although it's hard to say if it would have had meaning to me until this point.

CHAPTER THIRTY

TIME IS OF THE ESSENCE

Friday, May 29, 2009

I was in the front yard, watering the potted plants that I had moved outside a few days earlier from their winter home in the greenhouse. At 10:30 AM, it was only in the 50s, a bit cool for late May, but the forecast for the next day was more seasonal. The geraniums were greening up and sprouting more flower buds. I had hoped that Mother Nature would have done the watering for me, but we'd only had dribs and drabs over the last few days. My ficus tree, notoriously unhappy about being moved from the interior microclimate to the exterior one, seemed still to be holding on to most of its leaves.

I looked up to see Glenn's car turning into the driveway, punctual as always. He honked the horn when he saw me, and I waved in return. I set down the gallon jug of water, went in the kitchen slider door, and walked into the living room where I found Bruce reclining on the couch, dozing over a magazine open on his lap. He was spending more time stretched out, if not quite sleeping. I gently touched his shoulder and kissed his forehead. "Time to wake up, sweetie. Glenn is coming up the driveway."

We had scheduled this visit a few days earlier. Glenn wanted to get Bruce's input on criteria to be used for a new award that the Connecticut Chapter of the American Planning Association planned to create in Bruce's name. Since then, prompted by Bruce's *Dear Colleagues*

213

email, Glenn had gotten a call from one of the chapter leaders suggesting, almost demanding, that the chapter find a way to have a get-together for Bruce. When Glenn contacted me about it, I had told him I thought it was doable, and I was sure Bruce would love it, but advised him the sooner, the better. There was no telling when the tumor might obstruct his esophagus or stomach enough to make things very difficult. Glenn was hoping to flesh out the details of the party this morning, so he could arrange a location and get the invitation out ASAP.

I met Glenn at the door with a hug. "How's he doing?" Glenn asked sotto voce.

"He's doing OK—a bit tired, but we did go for a ride yesterday to look at a few subdivisions. He wanted to see how Tom's new subdivision in Avon looked." Glenn had been concerned that pain or fatigue might prevent Bruce from being comfortable traveling and sitting for a party, but I had assured him Bruce would rise to the occasion for a few hours.

Glenn cheerily walked into the living room. "Hey Bruce." Bruce got up to hug him then they sat on the couch while I took a seat facing them.

After the preliminary talk about family, Glenn got down to business. I had to smile at Bruce's allusion to one of his heroes, Mr. Rogers, when, with tears welling up, he told Glenn, how "special" the proposed chapter award had made him feel, and that he had nothing to add to the criteria.

Moving on, Glenn switched subjects. "Susie tells me you're up for a party." Bruce smiled his assent. "I'm leaning toward a roast." I was pleased that Glenn felt comfortable enough to discuss this openly. From an earlier email, I knew Glenn had been worried that roasting Bruce might make it seem his colleagues were ignoring or minimizing the reality of his situation.

"I think a roast would be right up your alley," I said, looking to Bruce for his reaction.

"Sounds great." Bruce smiled at Glenn. "The sooner the better."

Noticing Glenn's surprise, I interjected. "I know you and I had talked about two weeks, but I've been thinking about it and I think we need to do it sooner." We didn't know exactly how much time Bruce had left but we knew it was short. *Time is of the essence* had become our mantra since his diagnosis.

When Glenn continued to look uneasy about being able to pull it off in less than two weeks, I offered my insight from recent experiences. "We've found that people really respond and free up their calendars when they understand the situation."

We agreed the following Friday, June 5, would be ideal, even though it would be very short notice to try to get everyone together.

"I don't know if Sasha or Justin will be home, but I assume that family members are invited, too," I confirmed with Glenn.

"Of course. Feel free to invite whomever you'd like."

Glenn drafted an invitation to the party to Celebrate Bruce Hoben, sent it for our review and shared it with Bruce's APA colleagues.

***

On Wednesday, June 3, we had another routine visit with Dr. Abraham. They were becoming more frequent as the end neared. We had known for some time that Bruce would slowly succumb to dehydration, that he would get more and more sleepy, until one day he would simply not wake up. Now, as the time grew near, we were fleshing out more detail.

Both Dr. Nerenstone and Dr. Abraham had made it clear that dying from dehydration would not be painful, but Bruce was beginning to experience pain from the tumor, so Dr. Abraham wrote out a prescription for Fentanyl transdermal patches to provide a continuous dosage of pain medication.

After a short pause, Dr. Abraham solemnly told Bruce, "This would be a good time to start hospice."

Another milestone. They were coming faster now.

"As we discussed earlier, I don't foresee any need for hospitalization. You should be able to die peacefully at home." He was compassionate and truthful. We were silent. "I'll call McLean and they'll contact you to arrange the first visit, probably tomorrow."

Another pause. This is really happening. I had a feeling throughout my body that was reminiscent of the times I'd had surgery. There is a level of fear when I learn I need surgery, then a lull until it gets close to the date, and then terror when I am on my way to pre-op. We had just arrived in pre-op.

"How are Sasha and Justin doing?" Dr. Abraham was truly a physician who treated the whole patient, including the family who would be left behind.

"They're doing OK. Sasha and John are with his family in North Carolina for their annual visit. They're planning to come here the twelfth to the twenty-first. Justin will come on the nineteenth after school gets out."

"I strongly suggest you see if they can come earlier."

I was taken aback. It's really happening, and soon. When Bruce had stopped treatment, Dr. Nerenstone had told us Bruce would likely live three months, so I should have been expecting that, as we approached the three-month anniversary, it would not be much longer. Now based on Dr. Abraham's telling us to gather the family, the time left would probably be counted in days. The switch had flipped from logically knowing death would come at some point to knowing in my bones that death would be soon.

"I'll give them a call," I said, trying not to sound as shaky as I felt. "Sasha had wanted to be here for Bruce's roast on Friday so maybe it'll work out."

In response to his curious look, I gave Dr. Abraham a quick overview of the planned festivities. He smiled and looked at Bruce. "Perhaps you should consider getting hydrated. It would make you feel better for the party."

He had respected and supported Bruce's decision to eschew a feeding tube or IV hydration, but part of palliative care role was supporting Bruce's quality of life, helping him retain enough function for engagement in the world. That meant helping Bruce enjoy his party as fully as possible. Bruce and I looked at each other, mirror images of raised eyebrows, cocked heads and smiles. Neither of us had thought of that. Seeing our positive response, Dr. Abraham continued. "I can arrange to have you go to the UConn emergency room."

"Can we just go to Dr. Nerenstone's office?" I asked. "It's closer, with a nicer atmosphere, and it would be good to see Helen."

"Of course. You can set that up yourself. But you'll have to wait to start hospice until after your hydration. Medicare won't pay for both curative and palliative care at the same time." I could see the government needed rules to prevent abuses, but it didn't seem reasonable to have to put off hospice just to get a single IV infusion.

When we got home, I called Justin and Sasha. Justin couldn't leave until after school and work on Friday, so I bought them tickets arriving late Friday and returning to Maryland on Monday morning. Sasha had considered coming home on the fifth, but she decided to fly home the next day when I told her about the roast.

I then called Dr. Nerenstone and arranged Bruce's hydration appointment for that afternoon. It was great to see Helen again. She threw in some cortisone to pep him up. The mood was celebratory, everyone happy to see Bruce's smiling face again and to be contributing to making his roast the best it could be.

That evening, as I stood at the sink preparing vegetables to sauté for dinner, Bruce came up behind me, put his arms around me, and gently swiveled his hips against my bottom as his hands found their way to my breasts, a move he had perfected during years of "applying sunscreen," ostensibly to my back, while I was wearing my bikini. Before the interruption of children had consumed more of our time, we made love every day and twice on Sunday, the first time being after a leisurely breakfast and perusal of the Sunday paper. We couldn't change clothes in the walk-in closet at the same time without ending up in bed. Time and age had tempered the physical ardor, but never the pleasure and connection of making love. Even now, in these waning days, his body pressed against mine brought a smile to my face as I turned my head to the left and met his lips reaching down over my left shoulder. He moved back to let me carry the veggies to the pan that was heating on the front burner. I turned down the flame, dropped in the veggies, added salt and pepper, and gave them a stir.

Out of the corner of my eye, or maybe the corner of my brain, I sensed Bruce standing nearby and turned to face him.

"I want you to find someone who will love you as much as I do." His words were carefully chosen and deliberately spoken with all the love he had in his heart.

"That's not possible," I told him, crying as I looked deep into his eyes in one of the most intimate moments of our life together. I was devastated, that he had been thinking of me and my life after he was gone, and that he loved me enough to sincerely have that wish.

After an embrace that lasted minutes, I don't know how long because time really did stand still, we looked at each other, crying. There was nothing more to say. We both knew that what had been said was heartfelt and true. It wasn't just that he wanted me to marry, or to find someone. That might have been possible. But no one could ever know me as well or love me as much as Bruce did. It was an impossible conundrum. I wasn't just losing Bruce, the person, I was losing being loved.

The next day, while Bruce rested, I drove to the airport to pick up Sasha and her family. After dropping me at home, they took my car to Aimée's house, where they would be sleeping. Sasha had developed asthma as an adult and spending too much time inside our house caused flare-ups. As a teenager, I too had developed allergies. Mine were to cats, dust, and mold, all of which were present in my family's home to at least some degree. I eventually outgrew it, but for a period of several years I suffered asthma attacks whenever I spent any significant time in my childhood home. I remembered sometimes being awake all night, edgy from the inhaler medication, not able to breathe, and yet having to wait to take another dose. In tears, I was frantic that I wouldn't be able to breathe and, of course, the fear just aggravated the asthma.

Sasha had been able to control her symptoms using an inhaler, but the medication also made her shaky and the relief was short term. The solution was to spend as little time as possible at our house, even though her father was dying. It helped that it was June and she could spend lots of time outside or on the screened porch, but her primary base had to be at Aimée's. Mae stayed with us, sleeping where she usually did when she visited, on the floor near my side of our bed. Bruce got a huge boost from having them near and even though dinner on the screened porch with the babies was less than peaceful, I was reminded of how nice it was to cook for people I loved.

CHAPTER THIRTY-ONE

THE ROAST

Friday afternoon, June 5, 2009

I pulled in to the roundabout at Avon Old Farms Hotel, skirting the center island of thirty-foot trees with pink begonias planted in the shade of their branches, and stopped at the entrance to the conference wing of the hotel. Glenn was waiting at the curb under the elegant dark green canopy that protected arriving guests as they walked from curbside to the entrance. No canopy needed today—it was only in the low 60s, the light showers in the morning had cleared away and the sun was brilliant. Glenn opened the front passenger door and helped Bruce get out while Sasha got out of the back seat. I went to park the car in the nearest lot of many that surrounded the sprawling hotel complex.

As I passed the dense plantings of pink begonias lining the brick walkways, the chirping birds seemed to be playing processional music. I hoped Bruce had noticed them. He loved birds. Opening the doors to the main conference entrance, I was immediately transported back to Sasha's wedding reception, which we had held here nine years earlier. I could almost see myself greeting guests in the Atrium Lobby with its brilliant chandeliers, marble foyer with antique furnishings, and curving, three-story open staircase. This had been the location for her predinner cocktails and hors d'oeuvres. I could hear the laughter, see the smiling faces of family and friends, and feel the energy of that joyous celebration. Straight ahead, as I crossed the lobby, was the Towpath

221

Ballroom, with its adjoining glass four-season terrace, where guests had gathered for dinner and dancing. I would not have been surprised to hear the thumping beat of Gloria Gaynor's *I Will Survive,* Bruce's favorite dance number. I wondered if Sasha, who had not been back here since her wedding, had the same sensations of flashback when she walked through the lobby.

I heard jazz playing over the speaker as I passed through the pub and taproom to get to the restaurant where Bruce's party was being held. I looked to the left at the bar where Sasha and her wedding entourage, including Bruce and me, had gone for nightcaps after the band stopped playing. It had been such a joyous time, right up there with our wedding and the birth of our children. Today would be a different type of celebration.

The riffs of jazz gave way to a buzz of muted party voices as I entered the Seasons Restaurant, a twenty-five-foot by fifty-foot half-moon shaped room. On my left I saw a photo board that Glenn must have put together. There was an enlarged photo of Bruce conferring with his Planning Assistant, Betty, from a 1970's newspaper article on him as Avon's first town planner. I smiled, remembering the mutual admiration and affection that had continued until her death from cancer many years later. Several smaller photos seemed to have been taken at various planning functions, some of them showing Bruce in goofy headgear, including one in which he appeared to be wearing red devil ears. I would have to ask Glenn for the backstories.

The room was flooded with light, thanks to massive windows that covered the curved exterior wall, and cheery, thanks to the thirty to forty celebrants, talking in small groups. I walked across the red and tan patterned carpeting and the dark wood floors to where Bruce was standing near a couch, Sasha on one side of him and Tom, with his wife LeLee, on the opposite side. Others had taken note of his entry, but hadn't rushed over, giving him a chance to settle in. Glenn got Sasha and me a glass of white wine from the artful spread of light hors d'oeuvres and drinks on the marble counter across the room. Bruce had chosen to wear a black cashmere sweater over an old familiar pair of khaki pants that swallowed his slight frame. He had lost over twenty pounds from an already lean body, and although I had gone shopping the day before to pick out some new, smaller-sized "party" clothes, after trying on a few pairs of pants, he ending up wearing the too-big khakis.

I urged Bruce to sit on the couch or one of the chairs I had asked Glenn to provide, but he chose to stand, with a physical toll that I was aware of, although others probably didn't notice. I had to admit it did make him appear more approachable and likely contributed to people feeling more comfortable. It's unlikely that anyone had been to a roast for someone who was known to be near death and they were probably not quite sure what to do at first. In time, some of Bruce's closest colleagues started coming over to see him, breaking the ice.

When it was time to kick off the roast part of the gathering, Glenn got everyone's attention. "I'm sure most of you know this story, but just in case there is someone who doesn't, several years ago the CCAPA Executive Committee, of which Bruce was a member, put together a presentation for the Chapter Presidents Council to get their vote to come to Rhode Island for the Fall Leadership Meeting. But the laptop that had the presentation on it was left behind. Everybody was panicked and trying to figure out what to do. Bruce just shifted his thinking into another gear and decided to 'paint the picture' and make it memorable.

"While other chapters gave out little basketballs (Indiana) or aprons (Louisiana) to entice people to come to their state, the New England bunch simply put on a slide show with no projector, no slides, no nothing, and asked everyone to use their imaginations about what they were hearing about: the clam bake, the great amenities, the wonderful location, the fantastic beer . . . you name it. It took a lot of nerve and confidence to pull that off and he did it!

"Imagine being outside that room. Bruce says, 'Don't worry, I've got this,' and you want to believe him because you don't have any other choice, but doubt is in your mind. *What? Do a PowerPoint without a*

PowerPoint? What are you talking about? Finally, you conclude that you just have to follow his lead, and he does it. He parts the waters!

"The recipients probably can't believe this guy doesn't have a PowerPoint. But Bruce makes them believe. They can see the sights, they can hear the sounds, they can smell it. I mean, who else could have done that?! The Council voted for Newport and came our way."

Glenn read emails from friends and colleagues who hadn't been able to attend, and then turned the floor over to Dwight Merriam, another longtime friend and colleague of Bruce's, who delivered a tongue-in-cheek acknowledgment and admiration of Bruce's easily identifiable style of writing land use plans and regulations. Bruce and everyone laughed out loud as Dwight presented Bruce with the framed American Planning Association's first ever, and only, Groundhog Day Award, complete with a prominent groundhog photo. It was such a joy to see the big smile on Bruce's face as his colleagues applauded.

Then Dwight, who was a director on the national leadership team of the 40,000-member American Planning Association, and a past president of the American Institute of Certified Planners, turned more serious as he read a letter of commendation from Paul Inghram, the president of AICP.

The final announcement, met with resounding applause, was of the Bruce Hoben Distinguished Service Award, "to be given in memory of Bruce Hoben, whose selfless involvement with and longtime leadership in the chapter, along with his many contributions to the practice of planning in Connecticut, truly exemplify the spirit of distinguished service."

Standing to the very end, we left right at 5:00 PM, after Bruce had had a chance to talk with everyone who came to celebrate him. I brought the car around to the entrance where I had dropped him off and Glenn helped Bruce into the car.

I rested my hand on Bruce's thigh. "That was really nice."

He responded with an exhausted but warm smile. Sasha beamed with pride. I was so happy she had been able to be part of this event.

At home, after getting Bruce tucked in, I looked at the pictures Sasha had taken. In some Bruce looked weary, but most were smiling shots where the real Bruce shone through. He was collecting highlight reels to use in the story of his life. If he was looking for proof that his life had meaning, here it was. He had made an impact on individuals and communities. He would not be forgotten.

CHAPTER THIRTY-TWO

HOSPICE

Friday morning, June 5, 2009

As it turned out, Bruce started hospice the morning of his roast party. Sasha was in the living room with Bruce, whom I'd had to wake up "early" for our 9:00 AM appointment with McLean Hospice Care, who arrived right on time. When I opened the door, I found two women dressed casually but professionally. I guessed they were both in their late thirties, maybe early forties. The older I got, the harder it was to assess the age of people younger than me. Linda, wearing pants and comfortable shoes and carrying a medical bag, introduced herself, and then she introduced Bonnie, who was dressed in a modest skirt and blouse.

Taking a seat on the couches, Linda began by thanking us for the privilege of assisting with Bruce's care, and asked how familiar we were with hospice. I briefly told them about my mother's very short stay at McLean after leaving the hospital, and that Bruce hoped hospice would allow him to avoid hospitalization and die peacefully.

"Our focus is on comfort. There will be no extraordinary treatment undertaken and hospitalization will only occur if comfort can't be achieved at home," Linda reassured us.

"That's exactly what I want." Bruce was clear in his determination to die at home, a decision the kids and I fully supported. It felt right to now be putting in place the mechanisms and resources to make this happen.

"We're here to serve you, as the patient," she told Bruce and then, looking at Sasha and me, she added, "and the family."

"Well, you've met Sasha." I nodded my head in Sasha's direction, cueing her to tell Linda and Bonnie about John and the girls. I then proudly told them about Justin and his family who were scheduled to arrive later that day.

"We work as an interdisciplinary team," Linda looked to each of us in turn. As your hospice nurse, I'll be monitoring Bruce's vital signs, helping with medications, and ordering equipment as needed. You'll see me often, probably a couple of times a week."

"I'm your social worker," Bonnie told us. "I'll provide individual and family counseling and support as needed." Turning to Sasha, she continued, "If you'd like, I can give you ideas and materials for helping Mae cope with Bruce's death."

"That would be really helpful," Sasha replied, relief in her voice.

"The third member of our team, Amy, will be your spiritual counselor. She had a previous commitment and will be joining us as soon as she can." I was a bit skeptical about our need for a spiritual counselor but cautioned myself to reserve judgment until we talked to her.

"We also have an emergency twenty-four-hour line," Linda continued. "Susan will be your on-call nurse for any questions that arise when I'm not available. And of course, our extended team includes Dr. Abraham." He was the constant. With the hospice team in place, I doubted Bruce would be having any more office visits, but it was comforting to know our trusted GP would still be in the loop.

"Do you have advance directives," Linda asked Bruce.

"I do," he replied, "up to date and on file with Dr. Abraham."

"I'll get you copies of them for your next visit," I offered, proudly smiling when she commented how well prepared we were.

"Where is your bedroom?" she asked Bruce.

"Upstairs." I took Linda to the next room, so she could look at the stairs.

"Is he having any difficulty?"

"He goes slowly, one step at a time, and I'm behind him for support," I answered quietly.

"If at some point, you don't feel comfortable, I can order a hospital bed for downstairs."

I hadn't thought ahead to that possibility. Although I should have known logically it could happen, I subconsciously didn't want to make it real by planning for it. Now that Linda had brought it up, I had to admit it was probably inevitable. I had wished we could sleep together until the end, but I could see there were safety and logistical reasons for a hospital bed. I just didn't want to take away any of Bruce's independence until he made the decision it was time.

Back in the living room, Linda reached into her bag and handed me a box of rescue medications that she called a Comfort Pak, along with an eight and a half by eleven-inch buff colored reference card with a table of symptoms, what drug to use for each symptom, and dosage. As Linda explained the details of how hospice would work, I realized how little I had known. Each new responsibility felt daunting, but I was still confident that once I got familiar with the demands, I'd be fine.

"Bruce is also using a Fentanyl patch," I told her, worried about interactions.

"You'll need to be very careful about using Fentanyl with morphine." For me, the very mention of morphine conjured up addiction, despair, spiraling into oblivion. But then I remembered that morphine would calm Bruce's air hunger and it became a savior rather than a reason for fear. Still, it was a powerful drug that had to be administered precisely.

She handed me another reference sheet, this one for pain assessment in advanced dementia. It would be my guide for how to determine pain medication and dosage if, probably when, Bruce couldn't tell me. Its table of pain ratings was based on observations of breathing, negative vocalization—that is, speech with a negative or disapproving quality—facial expression, and body language. I was already anxious about morphine. Now I had to worry about him not being able to communicate with me.

I convinced myself that I was still feeling confident, but never had I had Bruce literally dependent on my ability to provide his medical care. Granted, I would be part of a team, but most of the time I would be alone with him. It wasn't life or death, after all. We knew it was death, but at the same time I knew this last leg of his journey could be peaceful or dramatic, and I wanted the former. If I felt out of my depth, Linda and the on-call nurse would walk me through medication questions and any other concerns, but the care of the love of my life was solely in my hands. I had to trust that I could rise to the occasion, that the hospice team would help me overcome my dread that I wouldn't know what to do.

My mind was swimming with the complexity and responsibility of my new job. Up until then, my caregiving demands had been minimal, mainly tender loving care, doing what came naturally, and learning as I went along. I didn't expect the medical and physical care would become overwhelming, given that Bruce wouldn't live long, and dehydration would be peaceful. I was grateful, for all of us, that Bruce's march towards death would not be a long, painful one, that he had chosen to not prolong his life. My heart went out to patients, and their caregivers, whose final stages lasted much longer.

When Amy, our spiritual counselor, arrived, she described her role as providing counseling related to sense of purpose, meaning, and connectedness.

"We're not religious," I immediately informed her, trying not to sound too abrupt or dismissive but wanting to make myself clear. I did not want any sermons or proselytizing. Bruce told Amy of his experiences, from altar boy to his break with the Catholic Church. She listened without judgment. I told her of my experience, being brought up in a much more forgiving faith.

"That's fine. I'm a spiritual, not just religious counselor." Perhaps I had overreacted.

"My mother was religious." I told Amy. "She was certain she was going to heaven and it was of great comfort to her." I sometimes wished I could make myself believe, but it just didn't speak to me. I considered myself to be a humanist, having no religious affiliation but believing a moral life is desirable, in itself. I followed my heart and did what I felt was right, resulting in a close match with what would be considered Christian values. I recognized I didn't know the answer to life, but there were too many aspects of adherence to the dogma and rules of organized religion that I couldn't accept.

"Dying is probably much easier for people who are religious," I commented. It was a question as much as a statement.

"Actually, that's not always the case," Amy answered, to my surprise. "Some people are worried they won't be going to heaven and it's frightening for them."

Bruce told Amy about his "Einsteinian view" of what happens after death. Just like the conservation of mass there must be conservation of energy. Therefore, his soul, his energy, would continue to exist somewhere, somehow, although he didn't know the form.

I had learned much more about death and dying, but the afterlife was still unsettling. I couldn't comprehend how, at some point, I would no longer exist. The Sunday school teachings of heaven and hell were not comforting. What if I wasn't good enough? How would I know? Even when I was feeling righteous, I wondered about the logistics. Where exactly was heaven? Was hell inside the core of the earth? How would everybody fit? How can everybody be with their family when their parents' families will be in two different places? These were troubling thoughts for a child, and when my friend Karen told me one day on the bus that I was going to hell because I wasn't Catholic, my world was shattered. Learning more science as I grew older only made things worse.

I thought back to a few nights earlier when we were lying in bed, propped up by extra pillows, reading. Bruce was well into a Jack Reacher novel while I was reading *Sum: Forty Tales from the Afterlife,* a clever little book, written by a neuroscientist, of funny, wistful, and sometimes unsettling vignettes about what may await us in the afterlife. I'd heard about it in an NPR interview and thought it might offer comedic relief, the perfect counterbalance to all the serious books about death that we'd been reading.

"Listen to this." After chuckling every five or ten minutes I finally had to share with Bruce how funny it was. "Here's an afterlife in which you're consigned to replay a lifetime's worth of accumulated acts, spending six days clipping your nails, six weeks waiting for a green light, sitting five months on the toilet, spending two hundred days in the shower, sleeping thirty years straight. Wouldn't that be awful?"

Bruce barely acknowledged me.

"Or what about an afterlife in which we exist on an earth peopled only by those we knew in life? Makes me think we should have been expanding our social circle," I said facetiously. "Or where we work as a background character in other people's dreams," I could hardly contain myself, "or we're forced to live out our afterlife with annoying versions of who we could have been if we'd taken the path we didn't take, or worked a little harder, or pursued that girl a little more forcefully."

Since Bruce wasn't laughing I decided not to tell him about the afterlife where God is the size of a microbe, battling good and evil on the battlefield of surface proteins, and thus unaware of humans, who are merely the nutritional substrate, or another version where we download our consciousness into a computer to live in a virtual world, where God exists after all and has gone through great trouble and expense to construct an afterlife for us.

For me, it was just a fun, fast read, albeit with some lessons and concepts to ponder, the implied conclusion being that the wider mysteries of life cannot be solved, but that civilization has come too far to believe verbatim the testaments and preaching of a long-ago age. It would have been comforting to have some sense of what was coming afterward, but unfortunately there was no clear answer.

I had been surprised that Bruce, always one to respond to absurdity, didn't see to the humor. He loved *Catch 22*. I was suddenly ashamed at my insensitivity. This was cathartic comedic relief for me, but not for him. His contemplation of the afterlife was not abstract.

Before the hospice team left, I discreetly pulled Bonnie aside, out of Bruce's earshot, to bring up something that had been bothering me.

"Bruce seems to be spending a lot time reading magazines or just sitting on the couch. I don't understand how he can do such mundane things when he's dying, and we have so little time left together." She could hear the frustration in my implied question. I felt selfish complaining about anything he did, and guilty for feeling that way.

"It's not unusual for someone who's dying to turn inward and be less communicative. It just reflects his need to focus on inner contemplation. The spirit, as well as the body, goes through an orderly shutdown. Emotionally letting go and drawing within is normal and natural."

It made a huge difference for me to understand what had been happening within. After talking with Bonnie, I had a very different and much more supportive reaction to Bruce's moments of self-absorption.

Linda ordered a commode and urinal for delivery that day to be sure they were on hand when Bruce needed them. I would keep them in the garage until required. I thought back to my Grandpa Johnson who had slowly succumbed to stomach cancer, and the medical equipment my mother had kept on hand for his visits from the nursing home.

The last thing Linda did was get out a bright orange DNR bracelet and put it on Bruce's wrist.

"Do not call 911," she emphatically told us. "EMTs are legally required to take extreme measures, even if you're wearing the bracelet."

Another chilling milestone. There had been many opportunities for Bruce to change his mind, even Medicare lets you opt out and opt back in, but Bruce's certainty and our unwavering support prevented him from ever second guessing his decision.

When Linda had first showed up at my door, I'd had only a vague notion of hospice. My mother's stay in hospice had only lasted a few hours and I hadn't stayed with her. My father had been in McLean as a rehab patient and he had bounced back and forth between McLean and Hartford Hospital before ultimately dying in the hospital. But that was before palliative care was a formally acknowledged medical specialty. Grandpa Johnson died in the nursing home, but the other three grandparents died at home with a family caregiver. I supposed that was still hospice, just not formalized and lacking outside support. In fact, it seemed to me that Bruce had been "in hospice," albeit a DIY version, since he had decided to stop treatment. Linda and her team were the third leg of a stool that included Dr. Abraham and a better informed us. All I knew, or hoped, was that we now had everything in place for Bruce to die peacefully at home.

As soon as Linda and her team left, I immediately created a spreadsheet to track the delivery of medications as well as the date and time of other events such as bowel movements and dry heaves. After three days of use, I had to rework it to handle unforeseen complexities. I had appreciated Linda's encouraging words, telling us we were a "model family" and had been doing everything right, but the coming responsibilities were staggering.

I could see why Linda said hospice was a privilege. I would be witness and aide to a sacred rite of passage, one of the two most consequential ones in our lives. We do so much preparation for the rite of passage that is birth and the role of parent, but very little for the rite of passage that is death, and the role of dying.

CHAPTER THIRTY-THREE

THE FINAL DAYS

Saturday morning, June 6, 2009

Sasha and Justin joined Bruce and me at the patio table. The canopy of maples that we had planted in 1982 was now extending well over the patio. Temperatures had been warming, in the 70s and on the way up to low 80s, but Sasha, a confirmed Southerner now, was dressed warmly in a sweatshirt and socks, as was Bruce. The sun was shining—a beautiful day to be alive. I saw a flash of red out of the corner of my eye and then heard the cardinal calling to his mate, both flitting between the maple trees and the verbenas on the berm. This pair had lived with us for years, providing a welcome burst of color when I looked out my kitchen window on a snowy winter's day. Briefly watching their aeronautics, my gaze dropped to the cat statue under the lilac, marking the grave of Muffin, the best cat in the world.

Kylie and Ruby, who with Justin had flown in the night before, were getting ready to go up to the pool with John and Mae. The twins were asleep in their Pack 'n Play, with a baby monitor on call to report any noises.

Mark Diters, the closest thing we had to a spiritual advisor, was meeting with our family to plan Bruce's memorial service. Mark, Bruce, and I had last sat together at this table in September 2001. A week after the infamous 9/11 terrorist attack, Bruce was still feeling the trauma and his fear for our safety that day when I was in New York and

Justin had been in Washington. I could still hear Mark's calming words, even as I felt the angst and the tears that welled up every time a plane flew high overhead on its approach to Bradley Airport.

Now, on this lovely June day eight years later, Mark asked, "How's everyone doing?" His serious and thoughtful tone required a serious and thoughtful answer.

"I'm doing pretty well," Bruce responded. He was tired from his roast the day before but had been able to get a good night's sleep. Fatigue was now a permanent condition to which he had adjusted as best he could.

"We started hospice yesterday," I added. I knew Mark was a hospice chaplain and would be glad to know we had taken this next step. "If I'd known the scope of what they did, I would have started earlier." He smiled knowingly.

"So, tell me what you're thinking in terms of the memorial service."

"We're planning to have it on a Saturday and we'd like to have it at the Canton Center Congregational Church," I said, knowing it wasn't a sure bet. The location was important to us because that's where we had been married, where my mother's second wedding and memorial service had been celebrated, and where Mark had officiated at Sasha's and John's wedding nine years earlier. My mother had been an active member for over seventy-five years, but we had never been members, and Mark, whose congregation was elsewhere, had no current affiliation with them.

"Let me see what I can do. They have a temporary interim minister. I'll contact her and see if I can arrange it."

"I don't want a religious service," Bruce told Mark, "but I know religion is important to some of the people who will be coming, so we need to have a little." This was Bruce at his compassionate best.

Mark chuckled. "Well, Bruce, you can take religion out of the service but you can't take religion out of the minister." We all laughed.

How many ministers could you ask to perform a ceremony in a church that wasn't theirs and tell them you didn't want it to be religious?

"A prayer would be fine," Bruce countered with a smile.

"Will you need an organist?"

"No. We're going to use music from a CD by Eva Cassidy." Bruce had planned the heart of the service, but I was choosing the music, and since we weren't having any hymns we had no need for an organ.

Sasha and I had begun talking about Bruce's memorial service in April when we were in Florida. I had fallen in love with Eva Cassidy's pure, expressive voice, the emotional depth of each song, her gift for phrasing that at times was heart-stoppingly eloquent, and the depths of longing and regret, as well as hope and love. Her interpretation of "Somewhere Over the Rainbow" never failed to bring me to tears. The fact that she died of melanoma at the age of thirty-three made her performances all that more powerful and fitting.

"Will anyone be speaking?"

Bruce took this question. "I've asked Tom Francoline, Glenn Chalder, and my brother, John, to speak."

"Do you have any guidance for them?" I asked Mark.

"They should keep it short, ideally no more than five minutes, and make sure they write it down." I made a note to pass this on to them, putting a big star next to *Write it down.*

"How about the family? Will any of you speak?"

"I plan to," I told Mark. I wanted and needed to eulogize the love of my life.

"You should write it down too—and give me a copy so I can read it for you if you find, at the last minute, that you can't." I was already having my doubts. I'd wait and see but be prepared.

Bruce then turned to Justin. "I'd like you to sing 'If Not for You' and dedicate it to Susie."

Dylan's raspy voice flooded my memory, calling forth a boundless love that took hold of my heart and caught in my throat. I couldn't breathe. I started to cry, a common occurrence of late, so filled with the bitter and sweet, I didn't think I could contain it.

"Of course," Justin tenderly replied, without hesitation but barely on the edge of composure. He didn't tell Bruce he would have to learn to play it on his guitar and memorize the lyrics, but whatever his father needed, Justin was going to deliver.

No one spoke for several minutes, the silence filled by birdsong. *How am I ever going to get through this service? I can't even listen to Eva Cassidy without crying.*

With the mechanics settled and "to dos" documented, the rest of the family joined us on the patio as we reminisced with Mark about the many memories forged during the long arc of our lives together, starting when teen-aged Sasha had become the first-ever babysitter for his three-year-old twin girls and infant son. When Mark and Sue arrived home from an evening out, Sasha would often stay and talk with them for hours. They soon became Sasha's *de facto* second set of parents.

"You probably don't realize what a profound effect you had on me," Mark turned to Bruce. "When I was still working as a dry cleaner, leaving the house at five AM, I was rarely able to do much of anything other than bath and bedtime with the children. Sasha's delight at your lunch creations was so enthusiastic and unmitigated that I unconsciously promised myself that if I ever could, I would love to play that role. When I left the working world, and returned to divinity school, the first thing I did that fall was buy lunch bags."

Bruce tenderly smiled. What an exquisite yet simple tribute to Bruce as a father and as a man.

That evening, we celebrated Sasha's thirty-seventh birthday with an impromptu family dinner. Sasha's actual birthday wasn't for another three days, but Justin, Kylie, and Ruby needed to fly back to Maryland on Monday. We were all committed to spending as much time together as we possibly could, living life fully to the end, and what better way than by celebrating a birthday. John, Jane, Mike, Aimée, and their toddler son, Beckett, joined us, completing our menu with a salad and hors d'oeuvres.

**

On Monday, I called Suzanne of Pastels, who always catered our annual Celebration of Life parties. She was stunned when I told her why we would not be doing our Celebration of Life party that year, but said I wanted her to cater the party after Bruce's memorial service. I let her know the date wasn't certain yet, but that it would be on a Saturday, probably in the next week or two. Within an hour she was at our door, unannounced, with delicious food that Sasha and I enjoyed over several lunches.

Other people had also begun delivering food. A few days earlier, my book club friends, Susie and Donna, brought homemade soup and bread, the first of many food deliveries to nourish my body and soul. I gained a new appreciation for how important, practical, and loving a gesture it was.

On June 9, Sasha's actual birthday, I took John to the airport. This side trip from North Carolina to Connecticut had been unplanned and he had to go back to his office for a few days. Later that afternoon, with the rain keeping Sasha and the girls inside at Aimée's, Bruce and I wrote his obituary. We sat beside one another on the living room couch as he carefully chose every word, every person and accomplishment to include, and the opening sentence that would describe how he died.

I had started with a draft of the basics—his siblings, parents, children, and grandchildren, work history extracted from his resume, and service on Canton town commissions. I printed it out and sat down next to him to review it.

"I hope the way I described myself is OK," I grinned, the implied question rhetorical. I had taken the liberty of writing that *Bruce lived most of his life in Canton with his best friend, love of his life, and wife of 42 years.*

"I love it," he beamed.

"I've listed a few options for the lead." I had included *died* and *passed away*, with qualifiers of *peacefully, suddenly, unexpectedly, after a long illness.* I had not included *after a courageous battle with cancer*, though no one would ever doubt his courage, in life or in death. If courage is the ability to do something that frightens you, to confront the reality of death, and then act on the truth you find, facing death on your own terms, rather than continuing a futile battle with treatments that were almost certain to fail, then Bruce was certainly courageous. He had made a very deliberate decision not to battle to the end.

"I like *peacefully surrounded by his loving family*," he told me, "and I think of myself as *departing this world.*" What a perfect expression of his exit from this life. He had always been a thoughtful master of language.

I read the first paragraph of his obituary back to him.

Bruce Hoben, 67, peacefully departed this world at home on June xx, 2009, surrounded by his loving family. Born in Naugatuck, he lived most of his life in Canton with his best friend, love of his life, and wife of 42 years, Susan Ducharme Hoben.

As I read it aloud, the day we first met, and all the intervening years of love and friendship, flashed before me in an instant, lingering blissfully.

Reading further, he approved the language, excerpted from testimonials at his roast, that I had included as an introduction to his professional accomplishments.

During Bruce's long and distinguished career as a leader and cheerleader for planning in Connecticut, he influenced the development, conservation, and character of many towns across the state. His impact will be felt for many years to come.

I watched his gaze work its way down the page.

"I included Mom and Dad along with your parents." I believed that, for a variety of reasons, Bruce had felt closer to my parents than he had to his own. "You really were their *beloved son-in-law*, you know."

"I do," he responded, with a fond and wistful smile of remembrance.

When his gaze made it all the way to the bottom, he put down the page and looked up.

"You left out my military experience."

"You're right." I hadn't even thought of it. "It wasn't on purpose." I knew that Colonel Costa, whose adjutant he had been for two years, had been a powerful role model and mentor, but that had been over forty years ago. I added a sentence.

Bruce saw service as a 1st Lieutenant in the 82nd Airborne Division from 1964–1966 during which time he was stationed in the Dominican Republic.

"Any other changes?"

"I'd like to add Tom and Rosemary." It seemed he had already been thinking about how to tell this very abbreviated version of his life, who and what had meant the most to him. It was liberating to feel there were no constraints on what he wanted to include, no protocols of who could or could not be honored.

"How would you like to describe Tom?"

"My beloved friend." What a simple yet meaningful tribute to a long and special friendship.

After asking him where he wanted donations sent, I updated the draft and printed it out for his final review. The last paragraph contained the details of his memorial service, the date of which, like the date of his death, I had left as June xx, 2009.

At 7:30 PM that night, I got a call from Becky. She and Marty were leaving the next morning on a two-week trip to visit friends in Seattle. They wanted to see Bruce before they left, but at the same time were cognizant of how tired he was and were reluctant to intrude. Bruce had already had a pretty busy day but when I gently woke him to ask about the Kidders stopping by, he had a straightforward answer. "If I don't see them tonight, I'll never see them again."

Once I recovered from being stunned by his calm response, I was filled with admiration for Bruce's composure. I called Becky back and they were at the front door in minutes, Becky in her PJs, totally comfortable given that we'd spent many PJ-clad mornings with them on our boat. It was a short and sweetly emotional visit. We all knew the end was just days away, that we'd never be together again. I believe it was harder on Marty and Becky than it was on Bruce. Unfortunately, he'd been getting a lot of practice with last goodbyes. Those who visited Bruce, though he was clearly on his deathbed, knew they were with someone who did not fear death and was comfortable saying goodbye. Knowing Bruce was at peace put them at peace.

The next day, with book club scheduled for that evening, I sent my regrets. I would miss them, and their discussion of the poignantly titled *Hotel on the Corner of Bitter and Sweet*.

On Wednesday, Kay called. She worked from home and most days, weather permitting, we walked for an hour or more, keeping up an energetic and far-ranging dialogue. In addition to topics of the day, she shared with me her frustrations with work and family, and was a sympathetic listener when I felt the occasional need to complain. Our walks had helped me stay balanced.

"I'm scheduled to be on a business trip next week." She sounded distraught. "I'll probably be gone for the memorial service. . . . Is it OK if I stop down now?"

"Of course. He's awake and we'd love to see you."

As I hung up, one of our recent walks thrust itself, uninvited, into my consciousness. When Bruce no longer had the energy to run, he had started to walk with us. It was assumed that when I got dressed for the daily walk, he would too.

"I'd like to go alone today," I had told him when, seeing me put on my walking shoes, he got up from the couch to get his. I felt awful as soon as I said it. Seeing his hurt and confusion, I felt the need to say something to justify myself.

"You have lunch with Tom all the time, without me." I knew that wasn't equivalent, but my need to vent about the unfairness of Bruce's situation was stronger than the compassion I should have had for him. Bruce's presence would allow no complaints about life's fairness, or lack thereof. It was important that I respect his wishes, but I still needed to rail against the universe on occasion, even if I knew life wasn't fair and my protestations would make no difference.

"I'm sorry," I meekly apologized, and I was sorry, but I still didn't ask him to join us.

I'm sure he quickly forgave me, and although at the time my actions felt imperative, the feeling that I had let him down would always haunt me.

Now, Kay sat next to Bruce on the couch and turned to face him. Not knowing if she'd be able to see Bruce one last time, she had written him a letter which she read aloud to him, wiping away tears with the back of her hand every few seconds.

Dear Bruce,

I love you. I have wanted to see you and yet have been respectful of all the chaos surrounding the last week or two.

In case we don't get a chance to talk I want to share a few things with you. First—I can't imagine where you are now. I can only hope and believe that you have spent your time between diagnosis and now living. You will always be full of life and joy in my heart and my mind. I love you and wanted to thank you for the time we did share. You have taught me so much about love, living, communication and just joy.

Going forward, I want you to know a few things.
- *I will brush, pet, talk with, and love Spenser, Kinsey, and Jake—reminding them of how you loved them*

- *I will see your smile every time I look across the ocean*
- *I will think of you each time I see ANY FORM OF CHOCOLATE*
- *My world is richer for knowing you*
- *I will be there for Sue, for whatever she needs*
- *When feeling down, I'll pull out the photos of the BVI and laugh my silly contagious laugh to get grounded*
- *I will miss you*
- *You will live on in my heart and my memories*

I hope that you are not in pain and that when it's time to leave this world that you leave peacefully knowing that your light will continue to shine as the brightest star in the night sky.

I love you,
Kay O

That evening Mike and Aimée came by, one of their many and frequent visits. Bruce had expressed an interest in having Mike, an audio engineer with an Emmy Award to his credit, interview Bruce about his life to record his legacy. But Mike had been on the road a lot, and unfortunately, by the time he was able to bring his equipment down, there was very little time and not enough energy left to record more than a few minutes.

There were so many people wanting to say goodbye. On Thursday, Bruce's siblings had begun gathering. They were all up the street at John and Jane's and had determined among themselves to come in groups of two or three to say goodbye. Sandy and Jane came first, then Suzanne, Barbara, and Marion after a short break. Bruce napped on the couch after each visit. He was now only awake a total of two to three hours a day, generally getting up after noon.

That night, as I helped Bruce very slowly navigate the stairs, I feared it was time to order the hospital bed. I helped him get ready for bed and

then joined him for what would probably be our last night sleeping together. Both of us too tired to read, I turned out the light on my
nightstand.

"I'm not afraid," he calmly told me. It required no explanation and
no verbal response. I moved across the king-sized bed reaching out to
put my arm around him as he turned on his side. As I wiggled and nestled into a comfortable position, still a perfect fit, our heartbeats and
breathing slowed and synchronized. From that moment I have not been
afraid of dying.

THIRTY-FOUR

THE FINAL HOURS

Friday, June 12, 2009

Linda arrived for our third hospice visit of the week and ordered a hospital bed for delivery that afternoon. On Wednesday, when I told her I had been nervous about Bruce showering, staying in the bathroom with him and helping him dry off, but stopping short of actually getting in the shower with him, she had ordered a shower chair. I was impressed with how quickly requests for equipment were fulfilled. Now Bruce would have everything he needed in one place.

Bonnie also came and, as promised, brought materials with information on how children of various age groups understand the concept of death, what their grief response might be, signs of distress, and possible interventions. Sasha and I went to my office with Bonnie where she coached us with specific wording on how to talk to Mae about Pa's death.

Mae was too young to grasp concepts, so it was important to be specific.

"You should tell her that Bruce had a disease, called cancer. Don't use a generic phrase like 'Pa was sick.' You don't want her to think that anytime she or a loved one gets 'sick' that they are going to die."

She would likely see Pa's death as abandonment, but reversible, not permanent.

"Tell her that he died, not that he has gone away. You don't want her to think that he is coming back. Reassure her you will still have wonderful memories of him and she can see him in pictures."

Sasha and I practiced the short but meaningful speech. We used that speech often with Mae in the days, weeks, and months to come. So often, in fact, that she could recite the answer herself when she asked the question "Where's Pa?"

Before Linda left that day, she reminded us that hearing remains until the end, that we should say whatever we need to that would help Bruce let go, but leave the room to say anything we don't want him to hear. I didn't question Linda when she left without scheduling the next appointment, but to me it was an unspoken signal that she did not expect him to make it through the weekend.

While I was busy with the hospice team, Kay went to the airport to pick up Justin and John. The hospital bed arrived and was set up that afternoon. John had helped me rearrange the living room furniture so the hospital bed was at an angle, letting Bruce look out the windows onto the estate he loved, or watch TV if he wanted. That night, Bruce spent his first night in the hospital bed. At Linda's suggestion, I had bought an egg crate mattress pad, some nice sheets, and a light blanket to make him comfortable. At the same time, I had bought a good twin-size blowup bed and linens for myself. I slept on the floor next to him. From that time forward, at least one of us kept him company at all times.

I had been working on the schedule for the memorial service, finalizing the selection of Eva Cassidy songs as I listened once more, in tears, to the entire CD, determining the order of the prayers and eulogies, thoughtfully choosing the music that would precede each speaker. Satisfied with the estimated duration, assuming everyone stuck close to their time limit, I emailed a draft to Mark for his comments, incorporated his suggestions, and sent him the final version. He inquired about how we were holding up, particularly Sasha.

Mark,

Sasha had a terrible night but mine was pretty good. She has lots of help today and is going to see Dr. Abraham as we "speak" to see if he can give her something stronger for her asthma.

When Bruce woke up this morning he had deteriorated/weakened quite a bit. The hospice nurse thinks he only has a couple of days left. Based on that, we'll plan the service for June 20.

I'm doing OK. Mae is not staying with me anymore which makes it easier on me but harder on Sasha. Sasha and I are having some good cries. Justin arrived early this afternoon which made Bruce very happy.

Sasha knew from experience that her asthma would be a problem, and she also knew that she would likely be in Canton for a while. I called Dr. Abraham hoping he would see Sasha, even though she wasn't an established patient. He fit her in that day. She came home with a prescription for Advair, an inhaler that she would use daily to prevent her asthma attacks, a sample to tide her over, and a stern admonishment that asthma was a very serious condition and should not be ignored.

When we had met with Mark to plan Bruce's service, he had given us a prescription, one that he sometimes actually wrote on a prescription pad, for the rest of our time together. He told us to use these words liberally: *I forgive you. Please forgive me for any ways we may have hurt each other. Thank you for your presence in my life. I love you.*

Bruce had taken it to heart. He looked at Justin, who was sitting next to him at the head of Bruce's hospital bed.

"Remember that time I pushed you into the swimming pool in Puerto Rico?"

Justin didn't, but rather than contradict Bruce or stop where the conversation was headed, he answered "Yeah."

"That was a bully thing to do," Bruce continued, his tone serious.

"I had forgotten all about it," Justin replied. It had been twenty years earlier.

"Anyway, I'm sorry."

"That's OK," Justin lovingly responded.

After a moment of silence, during which Bruce continued to look at Justin with anticipation, Bruce spoke again. "Your turn!" They both laughed, after which Justin assured his father that he had no regrets.

Sasha had already taken an opportunity in Florida to tell Bruce she had no regrets.

"I don't have any regrets either," Bruce had told her. "Regrets are no way to live."

As I kept my vigil Saturday night, still nervous about what was now Bruce's ongoing need for morphine, I heard him stir. It was late, but I had not yet retired to my makeshift bed. Anything short of exhaustion and I wouldn't be able to sleep. Bruce was still able to communicate, though sometimes his words were halting and slurred. I moved closer to hear what he wanted. He was barely lucid, definitely not rational.

"Coke." I moved close, leaning in to put my ear closer to his mouth. "Can I have a Coke?" He had been used to having this coffee alternative every morning but hadn't wanted anything at all for days and there was no way for the food to reach his stomach. Before I had a chance to answer, he whispered again.

"Ice cream."

What do I do? Tell him he can't eat? Hope he forgets? He kept asking, pleading. I visualized the coke and ice cream traveling down his esophagus only to be met with a barrier. What would happen then? Would he choke to death? I was alone in the house.

I dialed Susan, my on-call nurse, and explained the dilemma, my heart breaking for him and for me.

"Let him try a little," she calmly instructed. With her still on the phone, I searched for the leftover cans of Coke I had stashed away, and poured a tiny amount into one the plastic cups I kept on hand for Mae.

I scooped out less than a teaspoon of chocolate ice cream that was left in the freezer from when he had been able to eat.

"Here you go, sweetie," I said, trembling as I put the glass to his lips. He weakly took a baby sip. Next, I rested the teaspoon of ice cream on his lower lip and he gently closed his mouth, taking the smallest amount onto his tongue. I held my breath and waited.

"He's OK," I told Susan, my relief flying through the air waves. "Thank you so much."

The tiny sip of Coke and little dab of ice cream had soothed him and hadn't caused any problems. Before going to bed, I wiped his teeth and the inside of his mouth, dry from breathing with his mouth open, with glycerin swabs, as I had been doing regularly.

When Tom and LeLee stopped by the next day, the house was chaos. With the end near, Sasha felt she needed to stay by Bruce's side. Since she was still nursing the babies, her presence always included the twins, and their screaming, combined with Bruce's heightened reaction to noise, increased his agitation. I was trying to keep things as calm and quiet as I could, and even though LeLee had gone into the other room to help with the babies, there didn't seem to be enough hands to accomplish the goal.

Prefacing my plea with "I'm sorry to bother you, but . . . ," I finally took Kay up on her many offers of help. Why did I feel the need to apologize for reaching out, especially to a good friend whose offer I knew was sincere? She was there in minutes, as grateful to be called on as I was to have her there. Why was it so hard for me to ask for help? If there was ever a time to ask, it was now. I needed to learn to ask for, and accept, help more comfortably. It was easy with a spouse or child, often happening without anything said. Maybe that's the secret, not having to explicitly ask.

As we sat on chairs that surrounded his bed, his favorite music playing softly in the background, we silently sent him our love, taking turns holding his hand. He said very little except "Are you OK?" to which we each responded, "Yes, we're fine. It's OK for you to go." I lamented the pressure Sasha was under trying to care for two infants, her two-year-old and yet spend Bruce's last hours with him. Though her use of Advair was helping, her asthma, combined with stress, continued to take a toll on her health.

Linda had told us that in addition to reconciling close relationships and receiving permission to let go from family members, a part of the process we go through when getting ready to leave this world is resolving unfinished business of a practical nature, and Bruce was no different. We'd had problems recently with our clothes washer and Bruce, who was only semi lucid, wanted to make sure it was fixed. John and I managed to convince him it was. But then a particularly disturbing problem for him had to do with IBM and a land use issue. I couldn't understand what he was saying but I assumed IBM was part of it because I had worked for them. Luckily, Mike and Aimée happened to be visiting at the time. Aimée is a lawyer specializing in land use, so she was able to hold his hand, look him in the eye and assure him that she would handle it. His specific concerns were not logical but representative of his need to leave us cared for. We could easily conspire to give him those loving assurances.

Mark continued to call often, seeing how we were holding up and encouraging us to tell Bruce it was alright to go, that we would be OK. Justin sat by his side, his chair pulled very close, tenderly touching and talking to him. Even the cats jumped up on his bed, snuggling in the curves of his body and falling asleep.

We had always said "I love you" every day, always with meaning and always true, never just the perfunctory phrase. When it had become clear our time together was limited, it had seemed important to add the word *forever*. The next evening, with death looming ever closer, and Bruce unable to talk, when I told him, "love you forever," he responded with a thumbs up and a smile. Although his body was well on its way to an orderly shutdown, his eyes revealed the abiding love that would always hold me near.

When Linda left on Friday, she had told us Bruce could have vision-like experiences as he began to detach from life and that we should be prepared for bursts of strength at the end. With Bruce getting harder to manage at night, it was too much for me to handle, and I didn't want to leave him alone, without someone awake to watch. Justin, John, and I took shifts. Justin took the first one, sitting with Bruce while John slept in Sasha's room. At 2:00 AM, part way into John's shift, I was awakened by him calling me. I rushed down to find Bruce trying to get out of bed with a determination and a strength that amazed me. John, a very strong and fit man, was physically unable to hold Bruce down. I helped some with the physical restraint, more with the emotional calming. He was not coherent enough for us to understand where he needed to go or why, but that did not diminish the urgency or forcefulness that he felt. When we finally got him calmed down and laying back down in bed, I took over for the final shift but did not sleep.

In the morning, I emailed Pastels with the final menu and the time for the service.

When Linda came on Monday, Sasha, Justin, and I were in the living room with Bruce. We'd been taking turns sitting with him. While giving Bruce a sponge bath, she asked me if I had turned him and I replied no. I felt awful that it hadn't even occurred to me. I knew that people who were in bed for periods of time needed to be turned to prevent bed sores, but I thought Bruce had very little chance of living long enough for that to be a problem. Still, there was dignity to be maintained. She began showing me how to turn him, pulling the sheets and repositioning his body.

Mark called again to see how we were doing and remind us to let Bruce know he could leave. We had been telling him regularly, but I immediately told him again. Sasha brought Mae, who had just woken up from her nap, to the living room to see Bruce. She took Pa's hand and told him she loved him.

Linda was just turning him on his right side when she said, "He's gone." His color had changed and there was a stillness that was not possible in a living body. It was 3:00 PM on Monday, June 15. Bruce's physical death—his body completing its natural process of shutting down—was almost anticlimactic. His death had been a process, a journey. The physical end—the clinical death when the heart stops due to the cascading failure of interdependent systems, and the subsequent biological death four to six minutes later when the brain sustains irreversible damage from lack of blood—was just the final step.

We had been saying goodbye and easing his path for months, knowing what was coming. I can't say there wasn't a stab of loss and grief, but I was grateful that he had not died suddenly, that we had all had time to celebrate life and prepare for the end. Death had come exactly as he had wanted, peaceful for Bruce and for the loving family that surrounded him.

CHAPTER THIRTY-FIVE

SAYING GOODBYE

Monday, June 15, 2009

Justin had gone to a nearby Borders book store to study. At Linda's suggestion, when I called him I said that Bruce had taken a turn for the worse and that Justin should come immediately. My voice sounded unreal as I tried to disguise that Bruce had just died.

I saw our car coming up the driveway, fast. Justin must have broken every speed limit to get home. I opened the door as he ran towards the house. "He's gone," I said as I moved into his arms. I felt Bruce was indeed finally gone. Justin knowing was the last thing that had to happen. Justin sat by his father, stroking Bruce's body and nourishing his soul.

When Justin had finished saying goodbye, at Linda's behest, we left the room while she rolled him onto his back and did what she needed to do to prepare his body.

"Would you like him to be buried with his wedding ring?"

"I'd like to keep it." I wasn't sure what I'd do with it, if anything, but it would be a tangible reminder of our love.

"I'm sorry I couldn't get his mouth closed," she apologized.

"That's OK," I laughed. "That's exactly what he looks like when he falls asleep on the couch. His head bobs and rolls back with his mouth wide open. I'm always afraid he's going to get whiplash."

Although Mae had been with Bruce when he died, she was too young to understand what had happened. Sasha called John who took Mae to Aimée's while Sasha, Justin, and I sat quietly with Bruce.

I called Bruce's brother, John. He and Jane immediately came to say goodbye. I gladly accepted his offer to call the rest of the family. Since none of Bruce's other siblings lived close enough to get here quickly, I didn't feel I needed to let them know right away.

I called Tom who was there in minutes. "I'm so sorry." Tom held me close.

"I am too." I was sorry for Bruce, that his life had been cut short. I was sorry for myself, that I had lost the love of my life. I was sorry for Tom, that he had lost his dear friend.

As Tom sat with Bruce, I could see he was looking at what Bruce was wearing. "He's got his Fuck Cancer tee-shirt under your Avonridge sweatshirt," I told him. "That's what he'll be cremated in." We smiled at each other.

Sitting with Bruce's body was strangely peaceful and reverent. I'd had a similar feeling when I privately sat with my parents' bodies. But when I have attended calling hours for others, I have always felt uncomfortable, an intruder at a most intimate time. When possible, I discreetly avoid the viewing. The body rarely looks like the person had in life and no matter how skilled the mortician, there is no way to capture the personality, the essence of the deceased.

Linda filled out Bruce's death certificate. She must have also notified Dr. Abraham and Dr. Nerenstone because, in what seemed like minutes, they each called. I thanked them for their care of Bruce and our whole family. When Dr. Nerenstone told us she wished she could have done more for him, I assured her that there was nothing more she could have done, that we were at peace.

When it was clear that we'd had enough time for our goodbyes, Linda called the funeral home. A tastefully dressed-in-black man and woman from Carmon Funeral Home arrived in a hearse. After expressing their condolences, and asking if we wanted more time with Bruce, they went out to the hearse and returned with a gurney. We moved to the kitchen where we continued hugging and crying. Sasha and I openly bemoaned how unfair it was, something that Bruce had not allowed us to express in his presence. After covering Bruce's body in a beautiful quilt, they moved him to the gurney and wheeled him out the deck slider to the waiting hearse. They left the hospital bed with the linens straightened, a bookmark and an artificial red rose on top. It felt contrived but I'm sure it was soothing to many of the families they served. The respectful execution of their role in Bruce's passing was evident.

I accepted at some level that it was just the shell he had occupied, but it was still hard to let his body go, knowing I would never again see him in the flesh. I tried not to think about what would happen next. I was at peace with dying, and although the nature of his afterlife was still uncertain, I believed his energy, his soul, would survive in some form. I was not, however, comfortable with the step in between. Cremation was decidedly preferable to the other options, but thoughts about the actual process were unsettling. I focused instead on knowing that I would sprinkle him in waters that he loved, waters to which I knew I would return. Once he was in the ocean currents, I could be with him wherever there was salt water.

When John brought Mae back to the house, she went to the living room to see Pa, and was distressed to see the hospital bed without him in it. Sasha took her to another room while Justin and John quickly broke the bed down, moved it to the garage, and rearranged the living room furniture back to its previous state. More than a year later, Mae still talked about the "cancer bed."

At 4:30, I called Glenn to let him know of Bruce's passing and asked him to post a note for the Planning community.

On behalf of the Hoben family, and with my deepest sympathy for them, I pass along the following message from his wife, Sue. She writes:

"It is with great sadness that I tell you Bruce passed away on Monday, June 15. He wanted to personally and individually thank each of you for your emails, cards, letters, and attendance at the celebration of his life June 5th. He ran out of time and energy to do that himself, but asked that I write you a note of profound appreciation. Your kind and warm remembrances brightened the last days of his life and will be treasured by our family in the weeks and years to come.

"I knew he was very good at what he did, and that he was passionate about his participation in APA (the work and the fun), but I had no idea how admired he was by his colleagues. Our children, and especially our daughter Sasha, who was able to attend the celebration, now have a richer appreciation of this other dimension of the man they loved and admired as a father. He was, indeed, a good and courageous man."

I spent some time with Bruce last week and he told me how much it meant to him to have a chance to hear from many of you. He said he had fun at the June 5th celebration in his honor. He was also touched that the chapter leadership chose to name the CTAPA Distinguished Service Award after him. He joked with me later, "What did I do to deserve this!?"

Those of us who knew Bruce know exactly what he did to deserve this, and we are honored to have had the chance to know him. We will all miss him in ways we perhaps cannot yet appreciate.

Glenn Chalder, AICP

I sent what would be my final note to the distribution list I had created nine months earlier, informing them of Bruce's passing and thanking them for all their love and support.

True to form, having planned and prepared in advance, I had forged ahead with tasks, taking care of business. I knew what had to be done and I was well-prepared to execute. I'm sure subconsciously I was also keeping busy to prolong the time when I would be left alone with my thoughts, but I had been working my way through the stages of grief for months. I'd had the immeasurable benefit of grieving with my best friend. It was now time to help everyone else grieve, and most importantly, to celebrate who he was and how he had touched our lives. I was sure that they, too, would find his passing easier, having already had the chance to say goodbye.

Exhausted and numb, we had an early dinner delivered from the local pizzeria. In memory of Bruce, we washed it down with bottles of red wine and some chocolate for dessert. It had been a privilege being with him for this sacred rite of passage, and he had done it so well. His departure from this world had been exactly how he described it in his obituary. I would carry with me forever the image of him smiling at me, thumbs up, telling me without doubt, *love you forever*.

CHAPTER THIRTY-SIX

PREPARING A LIFE'S STORY

Tuesday, June 16, 2009

I took Justin to the airport, a day later than he had planned, and continued to Avon for my 11:30 AM meeting with John Carmon at the funeral home. At Mark's suggestion, I had interviewed him by phone the previous week. I had assumed we'd use the local funeral home that everyone in town used, the one that had handled my mother's and father's cremations, but Mark told me that Carmon offered more up-to-date options, including video tributes.

I found the funeral home easily, a sprawling, light-yellow, colonial-style building with a cupola, bordered by a white split-rail fence and nestled among woodlands and lawns in a suburban neighborhood. I had driven by it on occasion but was unaware it was a funeral home. Parking my car in a lot edged with flowers and shrubs, I walked past the proudly waving flag. John Carmon was waiting for me at the entrance, professionally polished in a well-tailored, subdued business suit. He looked to be close to Bruce's age, but his bald head made it tricky to ascertain for sure. He showed me to a conference room, its rich interior reminiscent of a law firm, though not as ostentatious, where we talked about Bruce, how he had lived, and the way he had died.

"When we talked last week, you told me Bruce was in the service."

"He was a First Lieutenant in the Eighty-Second Airborne from 1964 to 1966." John was aware of the storied history of the Eighty-Second Airborne.

"As an officer in Vietnam, he's eligible for inurnment at Arlington."

"But he didn't serve in Vietnam." I almost didn't want to reveal that, knowing what an honor it would be for Bruce, how proud he would have been if he'd known.

"That doesn't matter. He was an officer during a time that the government considers the Vietnam era, and as such, is eligible to be buried with full military honors." I doubted I would have learned about the Arlington option if I had gone to my local funeral home.

"I was planning to scatter his ashes in the ocean, at three of his favorite places: Hammonasset, Napa Tree, and the British Virgin Islands." Images of a military band leading his caisson, a twenty-one-gun salute and the presentation of a ceremoniously-folded American flag were stirring, but Bruce's request had been to scatter his ashes in the ocean.

"Arlington does require that all the ashes be inurned, but I can set aside a small amount for you in three separate pouches."

Swelling with pride, I signed the paperwork, and started looking forward to gathering the family once more, this time in September at Arlington.

"Would you like us to do the program for his memorial service?"

"Yes." I gave John a copy of the draft program schedule. "Mark told me you can do photos."

John showed me a variety of programs he'd done, many with photos, and gave me some great ideas for Bruce's program. Picking out the paper color and fonts reminded me of designing Sasha's wedding invitation.

Moving to one of their rooms used for calling hours, he showed me a sample video tribute, one of the things I had been most interested in. I'd never seen one, but apparently, they had become popular, at least for services where there were no religious restrictions, and I could see why.

We shook hands and I left with assignments to send him a photo for the obituary that he would reformat for publication and submit, to draft the memorial program and to select the photos for the video tribute. I had a good feeling about him and what he had to offer. The whole process had reminded me of working with the wedding professionals when we planned Sasha's reception.

I had already decided on the photo for the obituary. It was from a picture that is displayed prominently on a bookshelf in our living room. We are walking Sasha down the aisle to give her away. Bruce is handsome in his tux and ebullient in his smile. It had been taken nine years earlier, but he had aged very little until cancer claimed his hair, so it was a fair representation of him at this point in his life.

The cover photo for the program was also obvious, one of my all-time favorites that perfectly captured Bruce. He is standing in front of the Watch Hill Yacht Club with its weathered gray cedar shake shingles, in the background the small elegant harbor with a few sailboats at anchor. The muted colors of the late afternoon sky reflect the contentment and energy of another perfect day at the beach. Bruce is standing, shoulders raised and arms akimbo, wearing his summer khaki shorts and a tee-shirt, accessorized with his big goofy smile.

The inside cover would have his obituary. For the back of the program, I chose a picture of us that Marty had taken on one of our sailing trips. We are facing each other in a champagne toast, leaning in, with our lips just beginning to touch in a kiss. The only background visible is the sunset. Beneath the picture I'd put the poem "Bracelets," which Bruce had written for me on the occasion of our thirtieth anniversary.

Beneath that would be the invitation to continue the celebration of Bruce's life with a party at our home. Since I was experienced with creating presentations, I laid out the entire program. After showing it to Sasha, I emailed it to Glenn, Tom, and Bruce's brother John so they could see where they fit in the schedule, and to John Carmon. Finally, I emailed it to Justin, who'd had to go back to Maryland, still juggling coursework as the term was coming to an end.

Picking out the fifty to sixty photos for the video tribute proved much more difficult. It was a heavy responsibility to tell the story of Bruce's life on his behalf. In choosing the events and relationships to include, I wanted to not just put him in a time and place, but to capture who he was and what he was feeling, to transfer his presence to those who loved him. I wanted to show all his personas—the mentor, the negotiator, the grounded one, the soldier, the hands-on dad, the jokester, the crazy Pa, the love of my life, Charmaine.

I went upstairs where all the photos were stored and set up shop at the table and chairs at which we had sat together many times at his Planimetrics office. Some photos, from our early times together, were in albums. Most were in virtual or actual shoeboxes, with little or no organization. I was always going to get to it later. Now it was later. Without Bruce around to curate my life story, I would need to keep *organize photos* on my to-do list.

Sort and cull, sort and cull. There would have been fewer to go through if I were not pathologically unable to throw photos out, even when they aren't good or are duplicates. It always feels like I am throwing away the person, a piece of their life, a detail of their memory.

"Can I give you a hand?" Sasha offered.

"Thanks, sweetie. Maybe after I get the number reduced to something manageable." I felt that the responsibility for telling Bruce's story was mine, and that I needed to have sole veto power over every photo I deemed unworthy of depicting his life. Sasha would be the tiebreaker when I couldn't choose between several good options for one event or period.

I spent all afternoon and most of the next day on it, cloistered away, coming up only for bio breaks. As I went through the earlier photos, I relived being pulled into Bruce's orbit—this handsome, funny, literate young man—as though he had an energy field that I was powerless to resist, my senses remembering how passionately and generously he had loved me at all stages of our life together. It was a difficult, time-consuming task, but one that was ultimately extremely gratifying.

In the end, I chose exactly sixty photos, the maximum allowed: eight-year-old Bruce with a big toothy smile; the young adult sitting on a couch with his siblings; two very young lovers in the front seat of his MGB; the soldier standing in front of an Eighty-Second Airborne Battalion banner in the Dominican Republic, coffee in hand; walking down the aisle after our wedding; the handsome new husband posing in a photo shop in Manhattan; the insurance adjustor sitting in his office in Ithaca; bursting with pride as he held the newborn Sasha; on a camel at the Bronx zoo with Sasha and Justin; fishing with the kids off the jetty near our cottage in Westbrook; playing Kadima with Sasha at Watch Hill; dressed in Fifties' garb the night we won a twist contest; with Sasha at her college graduation; flanking Justin at his college graduation; on a barge in France with friends, glass of wine in hand; in Italy when we wrote the story of Ramona; sharing a laugh with Justin on the Grand Canal in Venice; walking Sasha down the aisle; toasting me with champagne at our first Celebration of Life party; the vivacious boa-clad Charmaine in dances, skits, and visiting with guests; sailing in the BVI with good food and friends; a joyous family at Aimée's wedding; walking the deserted beach with Ruby on Anegada; wearing hot pink heart-shaped sunglasses found in the sand; wearing paper birthday hats as we celebrated Ruby's third birthday on our boat; our fortieth wedding anniversary celebrated in Nashville with our growing family; at Justin and Kylie's wedding in Annapolis; bodysurfing with Justin on our last family trip in Florida.

With the task completed, I realized there couldn't have been a better way to spend my time. The tears of joy and gratitude threatened to stain all the stirring photos that had captured some of the best moments of our life together. This was one more thing I thought I was only doing for Bruce that turned out to be a huge benefit for me.

On a break, I finalized everything with Pastels. Suzanne wrote back.

I am so sorry that Bruce had to leave so soon, and I know so many will miss him. However, like you, I am glad his passing

was so peaceful. When I was there last week, I was so moved
at how lovely and calming your whole household was. With all
the gardens in bloom and especially all the beautiful children
and adults he had around him. It was truly an amazing sight
from an outsider's view. I have learned much from you both in
this last week.

Mark and the hospice staff had told us that it could take a few days for the soul to leave the body. A year ago, my response would have been a cynical, sarcastic "Yeah, sure," but having been part of Bruce's journey I was now certain that there was a soul, however it manifested itself, and that Bruce's soul had been preparing itself to leave. The night of June 17 was the day.

I had not been sleeping well. The painful void on the other side of the bed, the overstimulation of preparing for the memorial service, the unknown and unvoiced feelings churning around deep in my heart and spilling shock waves through my body all conspired to keep me tossing and turning.

I must have been lying on my left side, near the edge of the bed, because when I opened my eyes, there he was, standing next to me. Every part of his image was clear. I could feel the energy of his smile. I wasn't asleep, but I can't say I was awake either. It was not a dream. My dreams always shatter into pieces the instant I become aware of them. Bruce was peering out at me from what appeared to be a door, with a beautiful, transcendent smile and an impish gleam in his eyes. He didn't speak. I don't know if souls ever speak—but his message was unmistakable. He was at peace, smiling down on me and signaling that he was sure I would be OK. The warmth and love radiated through my body.

Months later, I struck up a conversation with a woman in a bar at JFK as I waited for my overnight flight to Paris. On hearing my story of Bruce's illness and death, she matter-of-factly asked if he had visited me yet. She told me that the Jewish faith believes the soul takes a while to leave and that it will sometimes visit as it begins to make its journey. I had never doubted that Bruce had come to me that night, but this confirmation was stunning.

By June 18, I had everything wrapped up for the memorial service. Carmon's had posted Bruce's obituary and video tribute online and I had sent the link to the distribution list of people who had been with Bruce on his journey. The responses confirmed I had accomplished exactly what I had set out to do and exactly what Bruce deserved. I felt confident I had done justice to curating my love's life story, the series of significant moments whose arc defined his narrative, and the people with whom he had shared them. I was ready to rest.

CELEBRATING A LIFE
WELL LIVED

Saturday, June 20, 2009

I wore a long, black, clingy dress we had bought together at a boutique
in New York. Originally purchased as a gift for Sasha, over the years it
had found its way to a home in my closet. It was a decidedly nontradi-
tional dress for this type of event, but one that Bruce loved to see me
in. He often proudly recounted the story of when I had worn it to a
Christmas gala at the Wadsworth Atheneum in Hartford. A couple, who
were complete strangers, came up to us and told me I was the most
striking woman there. I definitely wanted to be striking for Bruce's
sendoff. To accent the dress, I wore a favorite necklace and earring set
that we had bought in Chicago twenty years earlier. The earrings were
big silver disks with black and silver beads that reached my shoulder.
The necklace was black and silver beads ending in a silver disk with
more beads hanging from it. Strappy black heels finished the look. I felt
great, if somewhat unorthodox.

Justin, Kylie, Ruby, Sasha, John, and I met Mark in the pastor's
small utilitarian study. It was not Mark's office, in fact with an interim
minister it wasn't anyone's office, which explained why any warmth of
personal touch was absent. We stood in a circle holding hands as Mark
led us in prayer. Although I am not one to pray, I heartily

welcome anyone else's prayers, appreciative of the intent however it may manifest itself. Ruby, for whom this was a new experience, was doing great. Mae had stayed at home with her baby sisters. Too young to be part of the service, she was in the loving care of Susan Diters and her daughter Caitlin, the now-grown twin whose first babysitter was the teenaged Sasha.

We followed Mark through a side entrance at the front of the church. When the church was lovingly restored to its mid-nineteenth-century design, stained-glass windows had been replaced with tall-paned windows, letting light stream in and opening to the vista of woodlands that surrounded the church. I could almost hear the babbling brook that ran behind the church. The open two-story interior, with narrow balconies on three sides, invited reverence in its simplicity.

The video tribute, playing on a large screen at the front of the church, was stopped when it came to the last of the photos that had been depicting *A life of wonder and love/Forever missed/Forever loved*. The strains of Dave Brubeck and Miles Davis that were playing while people entered the church, gave way to Eva Cassidy's sweet rendition of "Fields of Gold." Her clear voice reverberated through the modest white Congregational church, to me a sound more spiritually moving than any hymn could have been.

The fruits of my labor of love were finally unfolding. Mark opened the service with a call to *celebrate a life well lived* and invited Tom to speak. Using vignettes from their thirty-four years of friendship, Tom described the many gifts Bruce had brought to Tom, as a planner and as a friend.

He was one of the most unselfish people I have ever met. As he came to life's ultimate test, that unselfishness and grace under fire allowed him to do what seemed almost impossible to the rest of us. He approached dying in that quiet, confident and understated manner. We will never forget how he attended the

Celebration of Bruce's Life just ten days before he passed away. And, once again, he was the calmest person in the room.

When I asked him how he could be so positive and constructive—he said when he first told Glenn and me of his impending demise he saw the horror in our faces and decided he had to change how he approached this because of the effect it would have on others.

I was lucky enough to be able to tell Bruce that one of the greatest gifts I have ever received was the gift of his friendship—the gift of Bruce Hoben.

I remembered this last visit near the end. I could feel the deep and abiding love that they'd shared. With a smile, I silently thanked Tom for his gift of friendship to Bruce—the gift of Tom Francoline.

Openly and unabashedly emotional, Glenn was next. For the first few minutes, I wondered if he would be able to speak at all. With a quavering voice he struggled before finding his footing. Glenn talked about the lessons he had learned from Bruce: to embrace family, to celebrate and cultivate friendships, to strive to do great things, and to inspire others to do great things.

Now, no story about Bruce would be complete without some reference to Charmaine. For those who know about Charmaine, no explanation is needed. For those who do not, I apologize, but no amount of explanation will suffice. You simply had to be there.

Now where do we go from here? I again found Bruce to be a source of more wisdom.

As you may know, Bruce was in the military and sometimes we would goof around in the office and I would salute Bruce. Bruce would salute back and smile at me and say, "At ease. Carry on." Then we would both start to laugh.

And so, I thank you for saluting Bruce today.

I think I can hear him now.
Be at ease.
Carry on.

I smiled at Glenn, at the confirmation that Bruce had passed on his wisdom and made contributions to Glenn and others beyond the purely professional ones. I trusted that when Bruce was alive, he knew of this, and I hoped the realization that his life had meaning had brought him great comfort at the end.

As Glenn cried, and many in the congregation joined him, Eva Cassidy's "Songbird" soared through the sacred space of this small New England church.

For you, there'll be no crying.
For you, the sun will be shining. . . .

'Cause I feel that when I'm with you,
It's alright, I know it's right.

And the songbirds are singing, like they know the score.
And I love you, I love you, I love you, like never before.

Like never before; like never before.

Bruce's brother John made his way to the podium, lowered his head, cleared his throat and after a short pause looked up.

I remember him as a Hammonasset lifeguard, which he was, really, all his life. Keeping people safe, being careful, watching out for the little kids.

    I remember a beery discussion with Bruce when we were young about all the things that young men talk about, and he said that men want to be heroes, and that he wanted to be a hero. Somebody said, "Any darn fool can be a hero for an instant, but that the real test of a man is in the long hard slog of every day, year after year," and Bruce made that long, long march, always ready to give you another chance, always ready to see the best in you, never to judge or condemn, to do the right thing.

I'll call him a hero. My brother, my hero.

The John I knew was thoughtful and pensive but had never been a big talker. His simply stated eloquence took my breath away as all those memories threatened to inundate me. My gut tensed, forcing my chest to rise, reminding my body to breathe.

Eva Cassidy's "I Know You by Heart" echoed my thought. I did know Bruce's sweet smile and warm laughter by heart, and he would be with me always.

Mark very slowly approached the lectern, giving us time to absorb and appreciate the powerful emotions filling every part of this sacred space.

Two weeks ago, Bruce, Sue, Justin, and Sasha met with me to discuss how to go about saying goodbye, both in the immediate reality and in memorial. This was a rich and rare thing to witness and be part of. In my experience when a person assists in their own memorial planning, it is a matter of a strong-willed patron or more often matron of a family who wishes to control the "whole thing." And even so, this is usually done in private and offered to either family member or pastor.

And more often than not, the requests are for certain psalms or hymns to be sung, speakers to speak, and such. This was not really that sort of gathering.

That morning we met, each person shared their sadness over the loss that was to be, their hopes for their remaining

*time together, and their desire to continue living fully as long
as life was present. The emphasis was clearly on continued experience one with another, engagement with one to another,
and loving kindness, one to another. We spoke about many
things.*

Mark then read what I had prepared, my eulogy to Bruce, the loving
husband, proud father, devoted friend, respected professional, jokester,
and dancer, ending with a tribute to how he chose to die.

*Bruce will be remembered for his courage—not for battling
cancer, but for knowing when to stop the battle, and focus on
enjoying life. He'll be remembered for his honesty and candor,
reaching out to friends and colleagues to give them the chance
to say goodbye. He'll be remembered for his generous spirit,
giving everyone the benefit of the doubt and criticizing no one.
Well, almost no one.*

*As Maya Angelou said, "People will forget what you said,
people will forget what you did, but people will never forget
how you made them feel." Bruce will be remembered by many
as a classy guy and a good man.*

I had clasped Sasha's hand when Mark started his remarks and held
on until the end, swept away by the words and emotions that seemed to
have nowhere to go but up to soaring heights. The stories touched me
anew, no less so because I was the author. I was struck by the power of
other people's words. All the remembrances had shown a part of Bruce,
like blindfolded people touching a part of an elephant, that now came
together in a glorious whole.

Justin, tasked with doing the impossible, rose and walked to the fold-
ing chair at the front of the church. I began crying as soon as he picked
up his guitar and sat down. He checked to make sure it was still in tune,
probably also giving himself time to prepare for this most important

performance of his life. Clearing his throat, he looked up. "My dad asked me to play this song in dedication to my mother." Before he even started, I felt a vise tightening around my eyes and forehead, and the base of my throat constricting. My senses turned inward as everything and everyone except Justin disappeared.

> *If not for you*
> *Babe, I couldn't find the door*
> *Couldn't even see the floor*
> *I'd be sad and blue*
> *If not for you*

Like the rest of the music, it had been carefully chosen for the lyrics, this time by Bruce, and Justin's performance was laced with love and respect. For months, years after, this performance was mentioned by many as one of the things that made Bruce's service so personal and special. Justin later told me that he had forgotten to sing the last verse, but no one noticed.

Following Justin's performance, and Sandra's reading of a Pablo Neruda poem, Eva Cassidy's rendition of "Autumn Leaves," a wistful lament of lost love, filled the air.

> *The falling leaves drift by my window*
> *The falling leaves of red and gold*
> *I see your lips the summer kisses*
> *The sunburned hands I used to hold*

Mark closed with a final prayer and benediction, and after the first few verses of the hauntingly beautiful "Somewhere Over the Rainbow," the family stood up and began a processional march down the aisle toward the exit.

We had been telling and reliving Bruce's life story ever since he entered Act III of his play called life—the scenes, the characters, the plot, the narrative arc, the crises, the resolutions. This day's celebration of a life well lived was only the latest of many, the denouement after months that included the walk down memory lane, the Irish wake, the week in Florida, his *Dear Colleagues* letter, the roast, his obituary, and now the eulogies. The ritual of this celebration, of the shared tears, made me feel that I was part of a team that had lovingly brought Bruce to his final destination. I could not have been prouder of this labor of love. It was exactly the celebration I had wanted for him.

Everyone came back for the party. The house was full. Mae ran out to give me a big hug as I swept her into my arms. My book club and Body Bar friends had heard about my children and grandchildren for years and I was delighted to finally introduce them in person. Pastels had done a wonderful job on the food, as always. I opened a couple of very, very large bottles of wine from our cellar that, over the years, Bruce had "won" at various charity auctions. This would have been, and indeed was, Bruce's kind of party. The party favor was a black-bordered glossy color photo of our F#CK CANCER statement.

Bruce had died in character, celebrating life, with boundless compassion and no regrets, his sense of humor intact. He had shared his stories and his wisdom, said meaningful goodbyes, and had known that his life had meaning, that he would not be forgotten. Since his diagnosis, we had been doing what we loved to do, with the people we loved most, being present and savoring every moment. The last months were some of the most celebratory, peaceful, and intimate we had shared during our forty-six years together. Bruce had lived and died by choice, not chance. He had not been able to finish writing his story, but I had filled in the blanks and written the last chapter.

In the end, we all want to see how the story works out as a whole. Endings matter.

ACKNOWLEDGMENTS

I never imagined myself a writer. But for Jody Dowling, it's unlikely I would have been. Her urging that I write a book about Bruce's death was the spark that got me started. Enthusiastically collecting emails, calendars, notes from medical appointments, and photos, I recorded the bones of the story. Then I found myself stalled, lacking the expertise and motivation to turn my outline into a book.

Five years later, a friend sent me an email about a memoir-writing workshop led by Judy Mandel and the time felt right to jump back in. Serving as my patient coach over the next months, Judy taught me about characters, settings, scenes, plot, and what it takes to be a writer.

As I completed my draft and was looking for someone to do the final edit, a friend led me to Denise Alfeld. Bruce and I had been friends with her in-laws for many years, but I hadn't known she was now an editor. Denise worked her magic, showing me that sometimes less is more, that precision matters when choosing words, and that a fine balance of character development and plot is required to keep the reader engaged.

My dear friend Beth van der Weerd was my most enthusiastic champion from start to finish. Her skilled editing went well beyond the specific changes she suggested. Yellow highlighting of the passages she loved, along with smiley, sad, and angry emoticons, showed me how a reader would react to my story. She always knew what I was trying to convey and tactfully pointed out areas where my words, and therefore my message, could be misinterpreted. To the extent that this is an inspiring story well told, it would not have been possible without her.

A book is only as good as its story and this story might have ended differently without Richard Abraham, M.D., our trusted family physician, hospice coordinator, and teacher. His honesty, forthrightness, knowledge, and compassion enabled us to make the well-informed decisions needed to achieve Bruce's goal of dying at home surrounded by his loving family.

Our children, Sasha Hoben Pickett and Justin Hoben, turned their lives upside down to give their father what he most wanted at the end of his life. I appreciate that it was never easy, and I am hopeful that they found our time together during those last months as exquisitely intimate, joyous, and celebratory as I did.

Lastly, I am profoundly indebted to Bruce who showed me how to live, how to love and how to die. He generously bestowed on me many gifts of a life well lived, but none more important than his final gift. He left me unafraid of death and with a role model for dying peacefully, with love and compassion for those who are left behind.

ABOUT THE AUTHOR

Susan Ducharme Hoben is an author and an advocate for making positive end-of-life decisions. She has appeared on top media outlets speaking about how we can all choose to "die well," including NBC and ABC, public radio affiliates, and has been published in newspapers across the country. Her memoir, *Dying Well: Our Journey of Love and Loss*, part love story, part "how to," is an inspirational retelling of her husband's nine-month journey from diagnosis through celebrations, sadness, and, ultimately, a peaceful death free of fear and regret. For more information visit www.susanducharmehoben.com.

78323068R00161

Made in the USA
Middletown, DE
01 July 2018